Windows® 2000 Administration For Dummies®

D1302703

Keyboard Shortcuts

Press	To	Press	To
CTRL+C	Copy.	F3	Search for a file or folder.
CTRL+X	Cut.	CTRL+O	Open an item.
CTRL+V	Paste.	ALT+ENTER	View properties for the selected item.
CTRL+Z	Undo.	ALT+F4	Close the active item, or quit the active program.
DELETE	Delete.		
SHIFT+DELETE	Delete selected item permanently without placing the item in the Recycle Bin.	CTRL+F4	Close the active document in programs that allow you to have multiple documents open simultaneously.
CTRL while dragging an item	Copy selected item.	ALT+TAB	Switch between open items.
CTRL+SHIFT while dragging item	Create shortcut to selected item.	ALT+ESC	Cycle through items in the order they were opened.
F2	Rename selected item.	F6	Cycle through screen elements in a window or on the desktop.
CTRL+RIGHT ARROW	Move the insertion point to the beginning of the next word.		
CTRL+LEFT ARROW	Move the insertion point to the beginning of the previous word.	SHIFT+F10	Display the shortcut menu for the selected item.
		ALT+SPACEBAR	Display the System menu for the active window.
CTRL+DOWN ARROW	Move the insertion point to the beginning of the next paragraph.	CTRL+ESC	Display the Start menu.
		F10	Activate menu bar in the active program.
CTRL+UP ARROW	Move the insertion point to the beginning of the previous paragraph.	RIGHT ARROW	Open the next menu to the right, or open a submenu.
CTRL+SHIFT with any arrow key	Highlight a block of text.	LEFT ARROW	Open the next menu to the left, or close a submenu.
SHIFT with any of the arrow keys	Select more than one item in a window or on the desktop, or select text within a document.	F5	Refresh the active window.
		BACKSPACE	View the folder one level up in My Computer or Windows Explorer.
CTRL+A	Select all.	ESC	Cancel the current task.

For Dummies®: Bestselling Book Series for Beginners

Windows® 2000 Administration For Dummies®

Cheat Sheet

Dialog Box Shortcuts

Press	To
CTRL+TAB	Move forward through tabs.
CTRL+SHIFT+TAB	Move backward through tabs.
TAB	Move forward through options.
SHIFT+TAB	Move backward through options.
ALT+Underlined letter	Carry out the corresponding command or select the corresponding option.
SPACEBAR	Select or clear the check box if the active option is a check box.
Arrow keys	Select a button if the active option is a group of option buttons.
F1	Display Help.
F4	Display the items in the active list.
BACKSPACE	Open a folder one level up if a folder is selected in the Save As or Open dialog box.

Windows Explorer Shortcuts

END	Display the bottom of the active window.
HOME	Display the top of the active window.
LEFT ARROW	Collapse current selection if it's expanded, or select parent folder.
RIGHT ARROW	Display current selection if it's collapsed, or select first subfolder.
NUM LOCK+ASTERISK on numeric keypad	Display all subfolders under the selected folder.
NUM LOCK+PLUS SIGN on numeric keypad	Display the contents of the selected folder.
NUM LOCK+MINUS SIGN on numeric keypad	Collapse the selected folder.

™

BESTSELLING BOOK SERIES

References for the Rest of Us! ®

Are you intimidated and confused by computers? Do you find that traditional manuals are overloaded with technical details you'll never use? Do your friends and family always call you to fix simple problems on their PCs? Then the ...*For Dummies*® computer book series from IDG Books Worldwide is for you.

...*For Dummies* books are written for those frustrated computer users who know they aren't really dumb but find that PC hardware, software, and indeed the unique vocabulary of computing make them feel helpless. ...*For Dummies* books use a lighthearted approach, a down-to-earth style, and even cartoons and humorous icons to dispel computer novices' fears and build their confidence. Lighthearted but not lightweight, these books are a perfect survival guide for anyone forced to use a computer.

> *"I like my copy so much I told friends; now they bought copies."*
> — Irene C., Orwell, Ohio

> *"Quick, concise, nontechnical, and humorous."*
> — Jay A., Elburn, Illinois

> *"Thanks, I needed this book. Now I can sleep at night."*
> — Robin F., British Columbia, Canada

Already, millions of satisfied readers agree. They have made ...*For Dummies* books the #1 introductory level computer book series and have written asking for more. So, if you're looking for the most fun and easy way to learn about computers, look to ...*For Dummies* books to give you a helping hand.

IDG BOOKS
WORLDWIDE ®

1/99

Windows® 2000 Administration

FOR DUMMIES®

Windows® 2000 Administration

FOR DUMMIES®

by Michael Bellomo

IDG Books Worldwide, Inc.
An International Data Group Company

Foster City, CA ◆ Chicago, IL ◆ Indianapolis, IN ◆ New York, NY

Windows® 2000 Administration For Dummies®

Published by
IDG Books Worldwide, Inc.
An International Data Group Company
919 E. Hillsdale Blvd.
Suite 400
Foster City, CA 94404
`www.idgbooks.com` (IDG Books Worldwide Web site)
`www.dummies.com` (Dummies Press Web site)

Library of Congress Catalog Card No.: 99-69371

ISBN: 0-7645-0682-X

Printed in the United States of America

10 9 8 7 6 5 4 3 2 1

1O/RR/QS/QQ/IN

Distributed in the United States by IDG Books Worldwide, Inc.

Distributed by CDG Books Canada Inc. for Canada; by Transworld Publishers Limited in the United Kingdom; by IDG Norge Books for Norway; by IDG Sweden Books for Sweden; by IDG Books Australia Publishing Corporation Pty. Ltd. for Australia and New Zealand; by TransQuest Publishers Pte Ltd. for Singapore, Malaysia, Thailand, Indonesia, and Hong Kong; by Gotop Information Inc. for Taiwan; by ICG Muse, Inc. for Japan; by Intersoft for South Africa; by Eyrolles for France; by International Thomson Publishing for Germany, Austria and Switzerland; by Distribuidora Cuspide for Argentina; by LR International for Brazil; by Galileo Libros for Chile; by Ediciones ZETA S.C.R. Ltda. for Peru; by WS Computer Publishing Corporation, Inc., for the Philippines; by Contemporanea de Ediciones for Venezuela; by Express Computer Distributors for the Caribbean and West Indies; by Micronesia Media Distributor, Inc. for Micronesia; by Chips Computadoras S.A. de C.V. for Mexico; by Editorial Norma de Panama S.A. for Panama; by American Bookshops for Finland.

For general information on IDG Books Worldwide's books in the U.S., please call our Consumer Customer Service department at 800-762-2974. For reseller information, including discounts and premium sales, please call our Reseller Customer Service department at 800-434-3422.

For information on where to purchase IDG Books Worldwide's books outside the U.S., please contact our International Sales department at 317-596-5530 or fax 317-572-4002.

For consumer information on foreign language translations, please contact our Customer Service department at 1-800-434-3422, fax 317-572-4002, or e-mail rights@idgbooks.com.

For information on licensing foreign or domestic rights, please phone +1-650-653-7098.

For sales inquiries and special prices for bulk quantities, please contact our Sales department at 800-762-2974 or write to the address above.

For information on using IDG Books Worldwide's books in the classroom or for ordering examination copies, please contact our Educational Sales department at 800-434-2086 or fax 317-572-4005.

For press review copies, author interviews, or other publicity information, please contact our Public Relations department at 650-653-7000 or fax 650-653-7500.

For authorization to photocopy items for corporate, personal, or educational use, please contact Copyright Clearance Center, 222 Rosewood Drive, Danvers, MA 01923, or fax 978-750-4470.

is a registered trademark under exclusive license to IDG Books Worldwide, Inc. from International Data Group, Inc.

About the Author

Michael Bellomo received a degree in law from the University of California, Hastings College of the Law, in San Francisco. Despite this awful start, he moved into the technical field and became certified in system administration at the University of California, Santa Cruz. (Go, Fighting Banana Slugs!) Michael's most recent book is *Linux Administration For Dummies*.

ABOUT IDG BOOKS WORLDWIDE

Welcome to the world of IDG Books Worldwide.

IDG Books Worldwide, Inc., is a subsidiary of International Data Group, the world's largest publisher of computer-related information and the leading global provider of information services on information technology. IDG was founded more than 30 years ago by Patrick J. McGovern and now employs more than 9,000 people worldwide. IDG publishes more than 290 computer publications in over 75 countries. More than 90 million people read one or more IDG publications each month.

Launched in 1990, IDG Books Worldwide is today the #1 publisher of best-selling computer books in the United States. We are proud to have received eight awards from the Computer Press Association in recognition of editorial excellence and three from Computer Currents' First Annual Readers' Choice Awards. Our best-selling ...*For Dummies*® series has more than 50 million copies in print with translations in 31 languages. IDG Books Worldwide, through a joint venture with IDG's Hi-Tech Beijing, became the first U.S. publisher to publish a computer book in the People's Republic of China. In record time, IDG Books Worldwide has become the first choice for millions of readers around the world who want to learn how to better manage their businesses.

Our mission is simple: Every one of our books is designed to bring extra value and skill-building instructions to the reader. Our books are written by experts who understand and care about our readers. The knowledge base of our editorial staff comes from years of experience in publishing, education, and journalism — experience we use to produce books to carry us into the new millennium. In short, we care about books, so we attract the best people. We devote special attention to details such as audience, interior design, use of icons, and illustrations. And because we use an efficient process of authoring, editing, and desktop publishing our books electronically, we can spend more time ensuring superior content and less time on the technicalities of making books.

You can count on our commitment to deliver high-quality books at competitive prices on topics you want to read about. At IDG Books Worldwide, we continue in the IDG tradition of delivering quality for more than 30 years. You'll find no better book on a subject than one from IDG Books Worldwide.

John J. Kilcullen

John Kilcullen
Chairman and CEO
IDG Books Worldwide, Inc.

Eighth Annual Computer Press Awards 1992

Ninth Annual Computer Press Awards 1993

Tenth Annual Computer Press Awards 1994

Eleventh Annual Computer Press Awards 1995

Dedication

To Carolyn, for being there on the highs, lows, and especially the wicked curves over the last year.

Author's Acknowledgments

I'd like to thank all the people at IDG Books Worldwide who have played a part in putting this together. Joyce, thanks for taking a chance on me back in *Linux Administration For Dummies*. Barry, Paula, Ted, Tonya, Pam, and Pat, here's to you for not wielding the red editorial pen like Darth Vader's lightsaber.

And thank you, Mr. William H. Gates III, for making this ride possible for *all* of us.

Publisher's Acknowledgments

We're proud of this book; please register your comments through our IDG Books Worldwide Online Registration Form located at `http://my2cents.dummies.com`.

Some of the people who helped bring this book to market include the following:

Acquisitions, Editorial, and Media Development

Project Editor: Pat O'Brien

Acquisitions Editor: Joyce Pepple

Copy Editors: Barry Childs-Helton, Ted Cains, Paula Lowell, Tonya Maddox, Pam Wilson-Wykes

Technical Editors: Mike Moulliet, Sally Neuman

Editorial Manager: Rev Mengle

Media Development Manager: Heather Heath Dismore

Production

Project Coordinator: Maridee V. Ennis

Layout and Graphics: Barry Offringa, Tracy K. Oliver, Jill Piscitelli, Brent Savage, Michael A. Sullivan, Brian Torwelle, Dan Whetstine, Erin Zeltner

Proofreaders: Vickie Broyles, Corey Bowen, John Greenough, Paula Lowell, Marianne Santy, Charles Spencer

Indexer: Lori Lathrop

Special Help
Teresa Artman, Proof Editor; Dwight Ramsey, Proof Editor; Kim Darosett, Amanda Foxworth

---

General and Administrative

IDG Books Worldwide, Inc.: John Kilcullen, CEO

IDG Books Technology Publishing Group: Richard Swadley, Senior Vice President and Publisher; Walter Bruce III, Vice President and Associate Publisher; Joseph Wikert, Associate Publisher; Mary Bednarek, Branded Product Development Director; Mary Corder, Editorial Director; Barry Pruett, Publishing Manager; Michelle Baxter, Publishing Manager

IDG Books Consumer Publishing Group: Roland Elgey, Senior Vice President and Publisher; Kathleen A. Welton, Vice President and Publisher; Kevin Thornton, Acquisitions Manager; Kristin A. Cocks, Editorial Director

IDG Books Internet Publishing Group: Brenda McLaughlin, Senior Vice President and Publisher; Diane Graves Steele, Vice President and Associate Publisher; Sofia Marchant, Online Marketing Manager

IDG Books Production for Dummies Press: Debbie Stailey, Associate Director of Production; Cindy L. Phipps, Manager of Project Coordination, Production Proofreading, and Indexing; Tony Augsburger, Manager of Prepress, Reprints, and Systems; Laura Carpenter, Production Control Manager; Shelley Lea, Supervisor of Graphics and Design; Debbie J. Gates, Production Systems Specialist; Robert Springer, Supervisor of Proofreading; Kathie Schutte, Production Supervisor

Dummies Packaging and Book Design: Patty Page, Manager, Promotions Marketing

◆

The publisher would like to give special thanks to Patrick J. McGovern, without whom this book would not have been possible.

◆

Contents at a Glance

Cartoons at a Glance

By Rich Tennant

"Oh sure, it's nice working at home, except my boss drives by every morning and blasts his horn to make sure I'm awake."

page 181

Maintenance is chagrined to find out the squeak in Clark's disk drive is really a whistle in Clark's nose.

page 297

"Remember—I want the bleeding file server surrounded by flaming workstations with the word 'Motherboard' scrolling underneath."

page 215

"We're not sure what it is. Rob cobbled it together from paper clips and stuff in the mail room, but MAN wait till you see how scalable it is."

page 259

"Okay, here's your problem. You've got warts on your motherboard."

page 325

"I'm sure there will be a good job market when I graduate. I created a virus that will go off that year."

page 345

"This part of the test tells us whether you're personally suited to the job of network administrator."

page 53

"You the guy having trouble staying connected to the network?"

page 7

Fax: 978-546-7747
E-mail: richtennant@the5thwave.com
World Wide Web: www.the5thwave.com

Table of Contents

Introduction

• •

*W*elcome to the third millennium! We're entering a time when electric automobiles, travel to Mars, and hot pizza delivery are right around the corner or already here. If you've picked this book up, you also know that you're about to begin work with Windows 2000, the culmination (according to the folks in Seattle) of three millennia of software development.

Maybe that's a slight overstatement, but not by much. Windows 2000 indeed is the pinnacle of the best that Microsoft has to offer.

Networked computers are the result of decades of computer research. Mostly, they're incredibly efficient. The client-server and other network models are driving today's information-based economy. However, the network model has been known to cause disasters, such as file servers crashing, e-mail being misdelivered, and the price of stamps going up.

This book is designed to steer you clear of these pitfalls.

You Don't Need Geek Credentials

Many books on administering Windows systems assume that you've already gotten your Microsoft Developer's certification, earned by programming an Etch-a-Sketch to play chess with Garry Kasparov. If that describes you, congratulations — you should do well writing treatises on Windows 2000's social impact at Cal Tech.

More commonly, a Windows administrator is (like the main character in a grade-B action flick) someone unfortunate enough to have been in the wrong place at the wrong time. Suddenly, you're the new person in charge of the network. Your user community has problems — and you need to know what to do, right now.

If you fall into this category, welcome. You're among friends here.

About This Book

Windows 2000 Administration For Dummies is a reference book to guide you through problems you'll face. The topics you'll find in this book include:

- ✔ Windows utilities an administrator should know how to use
- ✔ Networking concepts under Windows 2000
- ✔ Managing users and user accounts
- ✔ Setting up networked devices such as printers
- ✔ Troubleshooting your systems

Who Should Read This Book?

Whether you've been kidnapped and put in the position of Windows 2000 administrator or not, this book is for you. You'll find that you get the most out of this book if

- ✔ You're familiar with the basic components of a computer system. That is, you know your way around a keyboard, you know how to turn the CPU on and off, and you can figure out when your screen is off and when it's just running a screen saver.
- ✔ You have a copy of the Windows 2000 system on CD-ROM or floppy disks. You can also be the proud inheritor of a running Windows 2000 system. Or a limping system, anyway.
- ✔ You have access to a copy of Windows 2000 Server, as well as Professional. If you have the Server but not Professional, that's all right as well. If you only have Professional, you can still use this book, but some of the administrative functions discussed may not be directly available to you.

How This Book Is Organized

If you expect this book to be organized along the same lines as the other *For Dummies* books you've encountered, you're right.

If you're among the vast majority of Windows administrators who have been press-ganged into supporting a networked environment against your will, you'll probably be best off with reading the first three parts. You'll have the basic Windows issues firmly in your grasp.

Breathe deep. Don't panic. Figure it out. And if the answer doesn't pop up, remember, you have your handy *Windows 2000 Administration For Dummies* book to turn to.

Part I: Starting Out with Windows 2000

Here's the overview of what's new in the world of Windows 2000, why you should be using it, and what you can do with it.

Part II: Administering Users and Disks

Part II shows what it's like being the alpha geek on the block. In other words, you start using your administrative super-powers as the local Windows 2000 guru.

After reading this part, you'll be convinced that you possess administrative powers far beyond those any mortal on your system. So lay off the Kryptonite and salami sandwiches!

Part III: Configuring Hardware and Software

This part shows how to handle your client base with something besides e-mail announcements and promises of future upgrades.

Part IV: Administering Windows 2000 Server

This part moves into areas that are the exclusive territory of the Windows 2000 Server. Although some of these functions can be executed from the Professional version or via remote access, they are designed to be used primarily (and sometimes exclusively) on the Server.

Part V: Securing the Environment

Up nights worrying about hackers, crackers, and phreaks? Oh my! Take a deep breath. Relax. Here's what you need to protect your system.

Part VI: Troubleshooting

Here are the basic techniques to prepare for system crashes. If I were optimistic, I could tell you that Windows 2000 never crashes, but I think that this feature is reserved for Windows 3000.

Part VII: The Part of Tens

Here are fantastically useful chunks of information, diced into decimally defined delights. Enjoy!

Part VIII: Appendixes

The Appendixes include a special glossary for Windows 2000 administrators and the steps you need to make your own recovery disks for emergencies.

Icons and Conventions in This Book

Multiple-keystroke commands in the text are shown with a plus sign (+) between the keys. For example, Ctrl+Alt+Delete means you need to press the Control, Alt, and Delete keys all at the same time. You don't have to use one hand to do this unless you're convinced you're immune to carpal tunnel syndrome.

As you read the book, you'll notice these little pictures to mark paragraphs.

Tie a string to your finger so you won't forget this information — it's important.

Nerd stuff. You'll enjoy this stuff if you like to participate in debates over who's a better *Star Trek* character — James T. Kirk or Jean-Luc Picard.

Think of me as the Microsoft-conversant equivalent of Martha Stewart. These are timesavers and generally useful information that I've uncovered from working with Windows machines.

Beware! This is a strong warning that you'd better pay attention to the information that's coming up. Not to do so may invite the unwelcome attention of the fates.

Where to Go from Here

Unless you have a horde of angry users outside your office with pitchforks and torches, start with Chapter 1's overview on the new features in Windows 2000. They haven't been put in to pad Microsoft's bottom line, they're in the program because they'll make your life better. Get familiar with what the new Windows 2000 can do, and the rest will fall into place.

Ready? E Pluribus Microsoft!

"From Many, to Microsoft!"

Part I
Starting Out with Windows 2000

The 5th Wave   By Rich Tennant

"You the guy having trouble staying connected to the network?"

In this part . . .

You may be a Windows system administrator by accident. Of course, not all Windows administrators are impressed into service like surprised draftees. You may be a Microsoft enthusiast who has volunteered to run the entire network. Or you may be someone who really, really admires Bill Gates. (Try getting his autograph — it's easier.)

This part covers the basic capabilities of Windows, where Windows is going, and some of the new, improved features that Windows 2000 has tucked away in its code. The changes (unlike beauty) are much more than skin deep.

Chapter 1

Let 2000 Windows Blossom

In This Chapter
▶ Pondering the past
▶ Comparing the versions
▶ Filtering the hype
▶ Getting at the truth

*W*indows 2000 didn't just appear out of the ether and land on your desktop. As with the climactic chapter of any long, epic saga (is there any other kind?), a beginning is mandatory — a tale of origins.

Windows 2000 Administration For Dummies doesn't buck this trend. In this chapter, you find out where Windows 2000 came from, where it appears to be heading, and why this operating system probably has a healthy future.

Thus Spake Bill Gates: What Windows 2000 Is All About

You have to hunt around a bit, but (barring a mass software extinction in the wake of Y2K) you can still find older computers running the first big entry on the Microsoft hit parade: Windows 3.1. Legions of technically astute critics claimed that it was little more than a shell of a program that ran atop DOS. But all the criticism in the world couldn't alter a single, important fact: Windows 3.1 sold like hotcakes.

Compared to today's operating systems — and even some of its contemporaries — Windows 3.1 had some real disadvantages. For starters, it was a real memory hog. Second, it took up a huge chunk of disk space at a time when hard drive space was at a premium. Those arguments can still be made today — but you could also say that technology has caught up with Windows rather than the other way around.

If Windows is so good, why hasn't it crushed all opposition?

Say what you want about the Justice Department, our antitrust laws aren't the only reason that Windows still isn't our only choice for an operating system. The simple fact of the matter is that operating systems, like all software, are merely sophisticated tools. And some tools are better at certain jobs than others.

As GUI-based systems, all forms of Windows are more than competent. However, until Windows 95, the clear advantage in ease of use (and simple attractiveness) was the Macintosh operating system. In other areas, the story is similar:

✔ To this day, the Macintosh OS has the rep for performing certain graphic-design tasks better than Windows. The Mac also has an inherent speed advantage: Mac software is designed from the ground up to work with a single kind of hardware. Perhaps the only thing holding back the Mac OS is a smaller number of available platforms in the business world. (If you are a Mac faithful, please don't send me angry letters explaining that

the Mac OS is akin to the second coming. However, you may send me large checks to persuade me to write a *For Dummies* book on the new Mac OS!

✔ UNIX: The UNIX OS and its derivatives (such as Solaris, IRIX, HPUX, and Linux) have attracted a lot of press lately, but they've been around for a while, holding key positions at the extreme high — and low — ends of the OS market. On the lower end, UNIX/Linux is extremely popular because no matter how cheap Windows gets, it can't beat *free*. On the high end, UNIX is still the primary choice for production-level servers due to the claims of better stability and scalability than Windows can offer.

By the way, if you're a member of the UNIX/Linux faithful, don't send me angry letters. Instead, take your revenge symbolically: Buy multiple copies of *Linux Administration For Dummies* (also by Michael Bellomo), and pass 'em around. That should do the trick.

The Windows of today is still a resource hog in the truest sense of the word. The difference is that the price of RAM and the price of hard drive space — dropping so fast that whole *gigabytes* of memory are available for the price of a fancy dinner — are no longer a barrier to computer manufacturers.

Even the early Windows offered a user interface that beat all other operating systems hands down, which catapulted Microsoft into the leading position. Today, you can still find other graphically based operating systems out in the field. But in the main office and home-user markets, they're as much out of their element as a third-string linebacker at a *Star Trek* convention.

Just so you know . . .

We're throwing around a couple terms here that you may not be completely familiar with if you're new to the technical world. While they're not purely technical, you'll be hearing these terms a lot so you should be aware of them.

GUI: *Graphic User Interface* — an operating system like Windows or the Mac OS is *GUI-based* because it uses pictures and objects for the user to interact with the computer. In simplest terms, your *desktop* and *icons* are GUI-based ways of doing things.

E-commerce: *Electronic commerce* is a general term for companies who do the bulk of their sales over the Internet. Some companies such as Amazon.com or eBay do 100 percent of their sales this way.

Bill (also known as The Big Kahuna): William H. Gates, Chairman and Chief Executive Officer, Microsoft Corporation. Although we kid around about Bill in this book a lot, we have his vision to thank for making Windows so abundantly available. All of the jokes about him or his company being out to take over the world are just that, jokes. . . um, right Bill?

Ready or Not, Here Comes Bill

If you want to be a player in the field of network administration, then now — more than ever — you have to know something about Windows (at least how your systems will interact with Windows). Sales of Microsoft Windows, in all its current forms, still grow at an astounding rate. IDC reported that the Windows server market grew over 73 percent in 1998 alone.

Still skeptical? *PC Magazine* estimates that the Windows workstation market will triple in size by 2003. This is especially notable, given that in early 1999, more than *28 million* Windows NT 4.0 user licenses were purchased from Microsoft.

On the Internet side of doing business, more than 1 million Web servers now use some form of Microsoft product. Most recently, the *Wall Street Journal* reports that Microsoft has made it an official company goal to nearly double the existing installations of their network servers in the e-commerce business world.

The Microsoft focus will be particularly aimed at the finance and Web-based *dot-com* start-up companies. The reason? Such companies need extensive networking hardware and software the way a vintage New England cottage needs a dozen coats of waterproof wood stain.

Version Vision

From the start, Windows 2000 was not designed to be a *one-shot* product solution for both workstations and servers. Windows 2000, much like the UNIX or Linux world, comes in distinct versions designed for different market segments. In *Windows 2000 Administration For Dummies*, I provide detailed coverage on the two primary versions of the Windows 2000 operating system:

- ✔ Windows 2000 Professional
- ✔ Windows 2000 Server

What you need to run Windows 2000

Don't be fooled into thinking that if you're able to run Windows 95 or 98 on your network, that you'll be able to run Windows 2000 freely. In fact, the requirements and restrictions on what will run this new operating system have increased and intensified.

As a bare minimum, you need the following hardware to run Windows 2000 Professional or Server:

- ✔ Pentium chip, of 166MHz or better
- ✔ 64MB RAM
- ✔ 2GB Hard Drive
- ✔ 12X CD-ROM drive
- ✔ SVGA monitor capable of displaying 800 × 600 resolution
- ✔ Microsoft or comparable mouse/pointing device

By the way, keep in mind that these specifications are absolute minimums — that is, the equivalent of giving your computer just enough air, food, and water to stagger about in a daze and collapse on the couch after a day's work. On even a small network, running Windows 2000 Server on anything less than a 300MHz Pentium means that a reboot can take up to ten minutes.

On the plus side of things, once Windows 2000 gets moving, it stays moving. The speed problem is less noticeable after boot-up and login is completed.

Microsoft calls its specifications list the *Microsoft HCL*. In this case, *HCL* doesn't stand for hydrochloric acid (regardless of what your high-school chemistry class taught you) — it means *Hardware Compatibility List*. You can find the HCL by going to Microsoft's Web site (www.microsoft.com) and using its handy site-search engine to locate those pesky requirements.

So what if my system doesn't the HCL requirements?

If you use hardware that doesn't fit the HCL's expectations, you'll be marooned in the middle of a long and tortuous installation process. Right about the time that Windows 2000 copies all the needed files onto your disk (assuming you didn't wimp out on the 2GB requirement) the Setup program will complain.

The Setup program will tell you, in rather smug language, that you just don't have what it takes

to finish the installation (Setup was probably a butler in a previous life). Setup also makes reference to possible ways to get around the problem, but take my advice: Trying to cheat the requirements is a hassle just below pulling teeth. Bite the bullet and get new hardware.

Requirements don't mean *specifications*. Windows 2000 can be a little fussier than some operating systems when it comes to the machines it will work on. Listing hardware specifications can get more than a little complex, because new machines are always being manufactured. However, rest assured that with the market dominance of Microsoft, the newer the machine is, the more likely it will be compatible.

Although it won't be quite as current, if you have the Windows 2000 installation CD-ROM, you can access the HCL more conveniently. If you have this installation media, use the following steps:

1. **Insert the CD into your CD-ROM drive.**
2. **Double-click the drive's icon on your desktop (usually D: or E:).**
3. **When the contents of the CD-ROM are displayed in a separate window, look for the folder labeled** Support.
4. **To open the file, double-click Support. Locate the file** HCL.TXT. **This file is accessible in Microsoft Word and WordPad. This gives you the entire list at a glance.**

The HCL.TXT file is not available with any other installation media aside from the CD-ROM. If you have Windows 2000 on floppies, you're best off going to the Microsoft Web site and locating the information you need there. (Why on earth you'd *have* Windows 2000 on floppies in the first place is one of those inscrutable cosmic mysteries. But just in case you do, be kind to yourself and snag that HCL online.)

Amateurs not allowed: Windows 2000 Professional

The Windows 2000 Professional version is designed to replace and extend the user base that works with Windows 95 and 98. Microsoft's goal is to include the client interface advantages first seen in Windows NT 4.0 Workstation with this version. As of late 1999, Microsoft has stated that it plans to make 2000 Professional the new desktop standard through the coming decade.

To protect and serve: Windows 2000 Server

Windows 2000 Server is the *networked* version of Windows 2000. This flavor of Windows is slated to replace the Windows NT 4.0 Server. In a nutshell, the Server version of the Windows 2000 suite is to provide the main administrative core of a Windows network. The product's target market is small- to medium-size application deployments, such as

- ✔ Corporate e-mail
- ✔ Shared printers
- ✔ Web development

Microsoft plans to release two other versions of Windows 2000 — *Windows 2000 Advanced Server* and *Windows 2000 Datacenter Server*. Both of these products are designed specifically for production-level server environments and will most likely challenge installations using high-end UNIX environments. This includes corporate data warehousing and large-scale computing projects in the scientific or financial fields. These products are aimed at a very high-end corporate and academic market — not the vast majority of Windows 2000 administrators.

What about Microsoft Windows NT 5.0?

To steal a line from the old Palmolive commercials, "You're soaking in it!" Windows NT 5.0 *is* Windows 2000. The *5.0* moniker was a casualty of the extremely astute Microsoft Marketing Department.

Earlier in 1999, Microsoft simply decided to rename the upcoming release of Windows NT 5.0

as Windows 2000. (Windows 5.0 just didn't sound, well, *apocalyptic* enough for the new millennium.) And before you scoff at the name change, ask yourself whether you think first of a new *x586-based chip* or a new *Pentium*?

When Zero Really Has Value

Microsoft's main goals in creating the suite of Windows 2000 products has been to improve upon the following aspects of operating system software:

- ✔ User friendliness
- ✔ Networking
- ✔ Scalability (a million machines on your network work as well as 100)
- ✔ Stability (the system crashes less)

Give credit to Microsoft, though: Not satisfied with improving existing standards, they are trying to forge all new ones. One of the big ideas that has given a big push in Windows 2000 is the idea of *Zero Administration*.

Zero Administration means exactly what it says: Reduce administration overhead and the reasons for it (such as lost time due to server crashes) to zero. Some wonder whether this idea means that the administrator is to be cut out of the loop entirely. This is one interpretation, but I see it as similar to the idea of the *paperless office* that took the world by storm in the 1980s. Great idea, but do you know of any company that actually went out and buried its copy machines?

What's impressive here is that like the paperless office, the Zero Administration idea may come halfway to its goal. Just as offices today use less paper per communication (thanks to e-mail), Windows 2000 may put us on the road to less administration per machine.

TCO as an accountant's TLC

The Zero Administration idea focuses on reducing the TCO of a business or other operation using a Windows 2000 network. TCO stands for *total cost outlay*, which as calculated includes the price of all the hardware, software, labor, and administrative costs of running Windows 2000.

According to Microsoft Press, when a study of TCO was finally broken down, technical support, hardware/software costs, and administration weren't the main portion of TCO!

Over half the TCO came from lost user productivity. There were several reasons that users lost productive time from the network, some benign, some not.

- ✔ Time spent training or otherwise learning how a system worked
- ✔ System *down time* from fixing a broken network cable, rebooting a server, or general administrative tasks

✔ *Unproductive* applications not approved by the network administrator. This could be a database or e-mail program that failed to work with Windows properly, though the user liked the application enough to try it.

IntelliMirror — taking the seven years' bad luck out of breaking it

One of the more hotly anticipated and yet mysterious features of Windows 2000, IntelliMirror is a completely new idea for the Windows world. It's hotly anticipated because IntelliMirror is touted as a way to reduce the risk of problems with the most important — and vulnerable part — of a computer network — the *network*. It's also mysterious; as of this writing, Microsoft's plans for this feature are still less than clear. Otherwise, you'd have to slog through a whole chapter of jokes about the IntelliMirror!

To get an idea for how interesting IntelliMirror is as a concept, think of the well-known saying that a chain is only as strong as its weakest link. IntelliMirror doesn't strengthen the links — it makes the chain less relevant!

The computer network is both the salvation and bane of people dependent on modern computers. The network is the backbone of a system due to the growth of the *client-server* model, which has become the dominant way of doing things in the computer world. The client-server model is the electronic equivalent to *outsourcing* tasks from a given company. In this model, the server (or servers) provides their resources to multiple client machines.

Think of the client-server model as a really efficient restaurant. Suppose that the restaurant has fifty diners who are served from one central kitchen. If this restaurant was operated like a bunch of standalone computers, then each of the fifty people would have to have a separate kitchen, gas stove, microwave, pots to cook with, and plates to serve their own food.

With the client-server model, the clients — in this example, the customers — don't need to have their own setups. They're only here to consume! The server side, in this case, is the restaurant. The restaurant shares its resources on demand as each diner orders food and is served as the resource (the piping hot food, or data), becomes available.

The *downside* of this model is that it's all centralized. Imagine that we're back to where each diner has his or her own stove. If one stove breaks, it's too bad for that diner, but the rest of the people in the restaurant can continue to enjoy their data fondue and data etoufee without problems. On the other hand, if you're running the client-server model, if the kitchen breaks down, everyone's left nibbling the toothpicks and munching their cocktail doilies.

Everyone has become dependent to a degree on the server. For example, in most cases, you may run Microsoft Word *locally*, meaning that the program resides on the machine sitting on your desktop. However, you are most likely storing the memo or report you're creating on the network file server, which sits downstairs in the computer lab or in a locked closet behind the toilet paper and cleaning supplies.

The file may look like it's local, but that's because most networked applications try for what's called *user transparency* — so it looks like everything's the same to you, the user. While this can be very efficient, if the server goes down, it's the same as if you ran an electromagnet over your desktop — the file is gone! In some companies this can be even worse, as even the Word application itself can be stored on a network server, leaving you with a *dumb* terminal which is, as its name says, about as smart as a leftover brick in a network outage.

IntelliMirror is designed to keep users productive and working even when a server outage occurs. IntelliMirror — much as its name suggests — does this by mirroring data between clients and servers. Data that is normally stored on the client, such as a client's desktop preferences, are saved on the server. Data that is normally kept on the server side, such as user documents, are mirrored to the client machine.

This two-way mirroring is very convenient. On the client side, Windows 2000 emulates the UNIX strength of being able to access all aspects of a user's account, no matter where the user is logging in from. The user's preferences, like in UNIX, *follow* the user from machine to machine. While this feature was available to a limited degree in Windows NT 4.0, Windows 2000 expands it to user applications as well.

On the server end of things, having a stored copy of a centrally located document prevents down time when the server is on the mat for a count of ten. The client machine allows the user to open and work on a cached copy of the document during the server's self-imposed vacation. When the server comes back on-line, the new version of the document is synchronized with the old.

The Remote Installation Service — have operating system, will travel

A second application devoted to the TOC reduction plan of Zero Administration is the RIS, or *Remote Installation Service*. Again, following the literal name of the feature, Microsoft allows an administrator to boot up a machine on the network, even if the machine doesn't have an operating system installed.

The main advantage of having this feature is that an administrator can boot and install Windows 2000 on any machine, completely off the network. This is another convenient feature that's been around on various platforms such as UNIX, but it's the most sophisticated form of the idea to date. As shown in Table 1-1, you need the following components of the Windows system to implement this feature:

Table 1-1	Windows 2000 Components Needed for Running RIS
Component	*What It Does*
DHCP Server	Provides the client an Internet Protocol Address as it boots up
DNS Server	Locates the Active Directory Servers on the network
Active Directory Server	Contains the RIS information
RIS Server	Stores the information about the operating system required for the client to boot up

Also, according to Microsoft, this feature is not compatible with all forms of network cards. Luckily, the network cards that Microsoft Windows 2000 can work with are the mainstream ones (see Table 1-2).

Table 1-2	Acceptable Network Cards
Company	*Models*
3Com	3c900, 3c900B, 3c905, 3c905B
AMD	PC Net and PC Fast Net
Intel	Intel Pro 10+, 100+, 100B, and the E100B series
Compaq	Netflex II and III
Hewlett-Packard	Deskdirect 10/100 TX
SMC	8432, 9332, and 9432

Pulling yourself up by your reboot-straps

A final aspect of the Zero Administration paradigm is to reduce down time by simply reducing the number of times you need to reboot the server. This stunningly simple, yet useful direction taken by Microsoft is a welcome breath of fresh air. While there are no statistics in yet to back up the claim that Windows 2000 will need to be rebooted less often than any preceding Microsoft system, this advance makes it a safe bet.

Some of the processes you no longer need to reboot your server for are listed in Table 1-3.

Table 1-3	Items No Longer Requiring Rebooting
Process	*Why You Don't Have to Reboot*
Changing IP addresses	A more dynamic IP addressing is now supported by the OS
Adding & Removing Network Protocols	Improved Plug and Play standards
Changing Audio Drivers	Improved and expanded Plug and Play
Changing Video Drivers	Expanded DVD and other video Plug and Play standards

So Why Bother?

Windows 2000 is a fascinating product in the evolution of the Microsoft line of operating systems in that it is both *evolutionary* and *revolutionary*. That is, Windows 2000 contains many small, but distinctive improvements, and a couple really large changes to challenge the most dedicated Microsoft administrator.

Getting caught in the Internet: A more Weblike interface

The most obvious change in the Microsoft world is on the surface. When you open windows and start clicking through the Windows file directories, you'll see some small, but noticeable differences.

In what used to be (back in the late twentieth century) the most recent incarnation of Windows (Windows 98), the idea of blending the operating-system interface with the Internet really began in earnest. Return with us to those thrilling days of yesteryear: In Figure 1-1, Windows 98 rides again!

When a user opened windows, the toolbar at the top began to resemble the earlier forms of Internet Explorer, Microsoft's Web browser. As a rule, this interface was more than just a gimmick — the Back and Forward buttons, for example, greatly simplified movement through multiple directory levels.

With Windows 2000, you can see the continued growth in this direction. The new icons on the window toolbar give whole new realms of functionality to the windowing interface. For example, the Folders icon now allows you to browse file systems with greater ease, much like the Windows Explorer view. For an amazing live-action view of all this muscular capability, see Figure 1-2.

Figure 1-1: That good ol' My Computer screen in Windows 98. Ah, nostalgia. Notice anything familiar about the toolbar along the top?

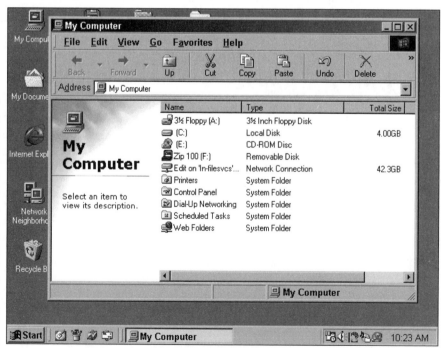

Figure 1-2:
Plowing
through file
systems
with
Windows
Explorer.

Curing your insecurity complex

The Windows 2000 authentication process, which I cover in more detail in
Part VI, provides extra layers of security for your network. Users are authenticated before they can gain access to networked system resources or sensitive data.

Network security and system auditing is also provided for your Windows
resources, including files, folders, and printers.

Going upscale: Multiple-processor scalability

The Professional version of Windows 2000 has the ability to support up to
two microprocessors (such as a dual-Pentium II machine). The Server version
is the equivalent to the industrial-strength version of a product and can
handle up to four processors.

Networking and communication without smoke signals

Windows 2000 provides improved connectivity with Novell NetWare, all flavors of UNIX (including Linux), and Macintosh's AppleTalk. On the scalability side of things, Windows 2000 Server really shines, supporting up to 256 simultaneous inbound dial-up sessions!

Supporting the Universe-al

Windows 2000 continues with the Microsoft tradition of supporting as much Plug-and-Play hardware as possible, automatically detecting and configuring hardware drivers. Windows 2000 now supports an ambitious standard known as USB (for *Universal Serial Bus*), which increases the number of computer peripherals on which Windows 2000 will work.

Directory services you won't find in your Yellow Pages

Windows 2000 stores information about network resources, such as user accounts, system resources, and security information. The directory service in Windows 2000 resides on the Server version of the software, and is called the *Active Directory*.

This directory serves as a kind of database of information on printers, computers, and services that make the system resources available to remote users. One major advantage of the new Active Directory is that it allows administrators more fine-tuned control over how (and to whom) resources are allocated.

For more about Active Directory, take a gander at Chapter 19.

Chapter 2

Managing Workgroups and Domains

In This Chapter

▶ Organizing workgroups

▶ Mastering domains

▶ Topping trees

*W*hen you log in to Windows 2000, more than likely you're not just activating an account on a standalone computer. Unless you've set up your system to work completely off a network, then you're going to be linking your machine up with a Windows 2000 *workgroup* or a Windows 2000 *domain*.

In this chapter, I explain how the tricky terms *Windows workstation* and *Windows workgroup* — even though people use them to pinch-hit for each other — are not the same. You also separate Windows *domains* from their *domain trees* — and nail down which does what. Finally, you see examples of how each system works, so you know how the Windows network is actually divvied up among its network lines.

Windows 2000 Workstations

Although the distinction between these two terms may seem simple, many people inaccurately use *Windows workstations* and *Window workgroups* interchangeably. These terms are *not* equivalent — you have been warned! All a *workstation* really can claim to be is a single Windows machine, whether attached to or unattached to a network of any kind.

A workstation not networked is called a *standalone* machine. Of course, the typical machine that you find being used by someone strictly for home use is the most common standalone you find. Even though this machine is *networked* in the sense that this person might use a modem to connect to

America Online and download the latest Britney Spears album photos, it's not hooked up to a dedicated network connection, interacting with multiple machines on a private *intranet*.

As you move courageously into the jungle of Windows terms, be on the lookout for the following behaviors that can help you identify the wild Windows 2000 server in its natural habitat:

✔ A workstation hooked up to a network full-time is (ready for this?) a *networked* workstation. Hook a bunch of workstations together and you get either a workgroup or a domain (depending on how it's organized), but you definitely have a different creature.

You can get the definitions that untangle the whole workstation-workgroup-domain brouhaha by turning calmly to "Windows 2000 Groups," later in this chapter. Meanwhile, here's a trick question: How many times does the word *work* occur in this chapter? (No, don't count 'em — it's too much work.)

✔ Another handy clue: What version of Windows 2000 is the machine running? Although a workstation usually runs Windows 2000 Professional, it can still run Windows 2000 Server and be *called* a workstation — although if it's networked, you should call it a *server* (to avoid confusion if nothing else).

✔ As a rule of thumb, you can determine whether a machine is networked by running your fingers down the back of the machine until you find a cord (or pair of cords) that terminate in what look like phone jacks.

The ties that bind: Intranet versus Internet

You may have heard all you care to about *the Internet*, but what is an *intra*net? Well, the Internet is the big-league realm of worldwide computer connections — known, in its most familiar form, as the *World Wide Web*. An *intranet* is normally smaller in scale, privately operated, and what you're most likely to work with directly — a collection of computers (designated as either a workgroup or domain) within an organization or company.

So if yours is one of the 20 machines that runs World Wide Widgets, Inc., then you're on

Widget's intranet. (Of course, to make things a little more confusing, you can usually use Netscape Navigator or Windows Internet Explorer to access the Internet from your intranet.) In case this is becoming clear as mud, here's how to tell which is which: If you've been on your network for at least fifteen minutes and there's nothing on your screen inviting you to buy something, you're on your intranet, not the Internet.

If you're not sure whether you're actually dealing with a phone-jack-like extension, examine those pesky cords plugged into the back of the machine and observe what you have to do in order to pull them out gently. If you have to use your thumb to depress a stud on one side of the cord, you've got the correct extensions in hand. But don't do it while the machine is turned on and connected or the results could get really . . . um . . . *annoying*. Worse, if the machine in question *is* the server, then you could suddenly acquire a following that ranges from *annoyed users* to *homicidally perturbed users*.

Windows 2000 Groups

A bunch of Windows 2000 workstations hooked together can form one of two configurations: a *workgroup* or a *domain*. You can start to tell those two creatures apart by gauging the size of their stomping grounds:

- ✔ Workgroups are relatively simple and compact, so you find them more commonly in a small working environment.
- ✔ Domains show the greater administrative load needed to handle the complexity of a large working environment.

Size isn't the only thing that matters here. Workgroups are organized differently, so they behave differently from domains. Stay tuned for details.

System resources: Central or decentralized?

Workgroups and domains are both logical groupings of machines — but they use system resources quite differently. The workstations that make up a workgroup are few enough that they enjoy equal access to those resources (sort of a cheerful anarchy). When the group gets too big for its decentralized britches, restrictions start to appear; a domain has a stricter network hierarchy (and you hear the word *prioritize* a lot).

One telltale difference between a Windows 2000 *workgroup* and a *domain* is that a workgroup's system resources are *decentralized* — spread around in several locations — instead of clumped on a primary server that controls who gets what, and how much (resource allocation).

This cyberdemocracy makes a *workgroup* an appropriate synonym for *peer-to-peer network*. (Nobody but peers here, it appears.)

No server is an island — unless it's in a workgroup!

Keep in mind that you can have Windows 2000 Professional and Server both running in a workgroup. The proportions of the software are irrelevant — you could have ten machines, seven running Professional and three running Server, five running each version, or even ten machines each running Windows 2000 Server.

Time to throw one more bit of terminology at you to see whether it sticks. In a workgroup, if a machine is running Windows 2000 Server, it's called a *standalone server*, even if it's networked. This is because in a workgroup environment, a server isn't pushed to the logical end of its function. Because each machine operates independently, no machine is dependent on the functioning of the server to hand out resources. And because no machine needs to lean on the server in this manner, the server sort of *stands alone*.

The second key difference between a workgroup and a domain is that, as with resource allocation, security is also decentralized. Each machine in the workgroup has its own local security database. This database is each machine's own list of user accounts and system-resource security information.

As a user in a workgroup, you're in a situation that's a bit like owning five different houses. Although you're happy to be a minor real-estate mogul, you probably won't have duplicate locks (all opening to the same key) at every house. Instead, you have to carry around separate keys for entering each house. In time, your key ring might start to clank enough to attract the attention of the local scrap-metal dealer.

As a workgroup administrator, this situation means you get lots of legwork: Every time the list of user accounts changes — say, adds a new user or changes an existing user's password — you have to make the change available on every system. It's like being the landlord of a large apartment building — every time a new resident moves in, you have to get new keys. If you're a Windows 2000 kind of landlord, you may have to make new keys for existing tenants every few months, not to mention making separate keys so that each tenant can get into everyone else's apartment . . . (ah, the pitfalls of utopia).

So, how much work does a workgroup work, if a workgroup in fact works?

The advantages to using the workgroup model — and yes, advantages, despite the bleak picture I've painted for dramatic purposes — relate to cost, speed, and simplicity.

✔ On the cost side of things, you actually don't need to have even a single copy of Windows 2000 Server in a workgroup. Windows 2000 Server does cost more — in fact, a good deal more — so this is an ideal strategy to reduce what Microsoft calls your TCO (Total Cost of Ownership) right off the bat.

✔ Starting up and maintaining a workgroup is simple. Due to its decentralized nature, a workgroup simply doesn't need a lot of administration. The compartmentalized way of doing things is a pain in the neck to keep synchronized, but it also limits damage — one crazy user on a delete-hungry rampage will find it difficult to delete files across the network.

✔ Running Windows 2000 Server on anything but a seriously muscular machine will get you into long boot times. Because Windows 2000 Professional is moderately more *lightweight*, then you have less of a problem here. Of course, if you try to run 2000 Professional on an old 486 machine, you're on your own!

Cozy as it is, a Windows 2000 workgroup gets bogged down in serious inefficiency on networks of more than ten machines; those decentralized resources become just too hard to ride herd on. It's a sign that the workgroup would really rather be a domain.

Mastering your Windows 2000 domain

Like the Windows workstation, a Windows domain is a logical grouping of machines on a network. The network is also usually an intranet with connections to the Internet. A domain differs; it is actually *centralized.* The user preference settings, security information, and resource allocation is controlled by at least one server, running (what else?) the Windows 2000 Server software.

Instead of multiple, local security databases, the domain system holds all information in a central directory database. This database is called the *Directory* — otherwise known as the *database* portion of the Active Directory feature.

There are no such things as standalone servers on a Windows domain grouping. This is because in a domain, all the servers are actually *doing* something, even if they're just backup!

The main repository of the domain information (that is, uses the Active Directory) is called the *domain controller.* You can have more than one machine running Windows 2000 Server in the domain group, but the *subservient servers* — try saying that ten times fast — are called *member servers.*

A domain's defining characteristic is that it has a central server that controls the functions of user access and resource allocation. Although all domains are networked, no specific network architecture defines a domain.

- ✓ A domain can be a grouping of Windows machines stacked in a single cabinet, hooked up in a series-circuit configuration like a string of Christmas lights.
- ✓ A domain can be purely logical and have no physical connections whatsoever.

In either case, the domain is not defined by its physical connectivity. In fact; a domain can stretch over vast distances (at least as far as you can stretch phone cable); one of domain's chief advantages is its immense scalability.

In a domain, the administration is centralized and not limited by physical access, so you're better off running a Windows domain when you have

- ✓ A large network
- ✓ A small network separated by large distances.

It's pretty inefficient if you were running the earlier example of a domain as a workgroup. Do you really want to fly out to Sydney or New York to add a new user? Unless you want to rack up those frequent-flyer miles . . .

The domain tree — Arbor Day in cyberspace

The next step up in size, as far as our logical grouping is concerned, is the *domain tree*. A domain tree is a logical grouping of a bunch of logical groupings. in effect, it's a network architecture concept where two or more domains are grouped together in a hierarchy.

In a domain tree, all domains are not (apologies to Thomas Jefferson) created equal. The main controlling domain is called the *parent domain* and the lesser ones are called *child domains*. I've also heard of the child domains being called *client domains* but that's a but inaccurate. Take care of your kids properly and call them *child* domains.

Domain trees have a couple unique characteristics that separate them from the run-of-the-mill local domain.

First off, Windows 2000 combines all the Directory information from each domain's main server, or master controller. Combining all this information into a single Active Directory location makes the information globally available and enables you to synchronize information across the network.

You won't have to wonder whether a change you make in Frankfurt, Germany will show up in Franklin, Missouri — it will. Each child domain provides the parent with an index of its unique domain information. Users automatically search this index to locate the resources they need, regardless of whether the resource exists on their local domain or elsewhere.

Users can also enter the network from any point in any domain; the indexes provided to the parent domain controller synchronizes user information across all the domains. For ease of user and ironclad network security, this is extremely convenient. This type of universal access is also called *transitive trust*.

Finally, a unique aspect to the domain tree structure is the *contiguous namespace*. The *namespace* is the set of naming rules set up by the network to define the domain tree. *Contiguous* means that the name of the child domain must somehow incorporate the name of the parent. To go back to our World Wide Widgets example, a contiguous namespace scheme might be divided by domains that correspond to physical location

Machine	*Location*
wwwidgets.com	Parent domain controller (Seattle)
sdiego.wwwidgets.com	Child domain in San Diego, California
tempe.wwwidgets.com	Child domain in Tempe, Arizona
dangitscold.wwwidgets.com	Child domain in Barrow, Alaska

Or, the groupings might be where domains are divided by department, as shown in Table 2-1:

Table 2-1	Domain Tree by Department
Domain Name	*Domain Purpose*
wwwidgets.com	Parent domain
sales.wwwidgets.com	Sales Department domain
scribbleforms.wwwidgets.com	HR department domain
imanerd.wwwidgets.com	Engineering Department domain
snnnnore.wwwidgets.com	Accounting Department domain

Seeing the forest for the trees

After that introduction to the idea of a domain tree, you might wonder: Is that all there is? A silly question to ask when Microsoft is involved. You can actually group domain trees together into *domain forests* — and no, I am not making this up.

You see domain forests rarely, unless your company becomes the size of one of the smaller NATO member nations. Or if it becomes one of the smaller regional offices of Microsoft. Take your pick.

A key point to keep in mind is that the domain trees in a domain forest are not grouped in a hierarchical manner, so No forest controller. So, your domain trees in the forest do not share a contiguous namespace.

In either case, here's the short list of key points:

- Domains have to be arranged in a logical grouping if they're going to work right.
- The grouping must incorporate the parent name. (The kids get their own first names.)

Regardless of whether you use a domain tree, forest, or plain-vanilla domain, you still need to know how to boot up the machine in it. And if you run into any problems, you may need to boot the machine into a different mode to deal with the problem.

Chapter 3

These Boots Are Made for Windows

*T*he boot process is so fundamental to the operation of a computer that it's actually hard to give a full definition of it. I could give you a rather Zen-like answer and say, "It is the beginning of all that is."

I could also give you the old technical definition, which is that the boot process is *the start-up process the computer uses to get ready for users to log in and make use of the system resources.* This is rather like your early morning ritual when you rise groggily from bed, shower, shave your beard, brush your teeth, put on your mascara, and grab a bagel before you head out the door (the sequence of events may vary depending on your gender or inclination).

But even this definition doesn't quite cut it anymore. Today's boot processes are much more sophisticated, for starters, due to the fact that they're completely self-contained on the computer.

No joke! Those of you with fond memories of the DOS era may recall having to stick a *boot disk* into the machine at startup. Even further back — in the TRS-80 days — early man used an ancient device called a *tape recorder* for this purpose.

The More Things Remain the Same, the More They Change

Back in the idyllic, innocent days of the early PC era, the boot process simply copied a few files to a computer's memory. But those days are past — and your computer still needs to wake up before it can do useful work. The boot processes of today now check your hard drive, scan for corrupt segments, detect and install new hardware drivers on the fly, and do everything else except serve coffee.

The two styles of boot process you're likely to see are based on two different hardware platforms:

- **Alpha:** The new kid on the block (relatively speaking), the Alpha-based machine is one that uses a special *Alpha* chip. These are relatively rare, unless you happen to be working on a large server machine. Alphas differ from the Intel-style machines in that more of the functionality on an Alpha is actually embedded in the chip. This is known as *firmware*, and it increases reliability and speed.

- **Intel:** Famous for the first TV commercials to feature dancing spacesuits in designer colors, Intel (and the style of chip it makes) has quickly come to dominate the PC market. Even if you don't have an *Intel Inside* sticker on your machine, there's a 99 percent chance that your machine has less of a firmware orientation than an Alpha. Unlike an Alpha, you're sacrificing a bit of speed for greater flexibility, such as using many different kinds of programs, sounds, files, and graphics.

What of it? Glad you asked. Stay tuned.

Alpha-boots

The booting sequence on an Alpha-based machine is markedly simpler than on an Intel machine. Alpha-based machines go through only two general stages:

- The *Pre-boot* sequence
- The *Boot* sequence proper

Alpha- and Intel-based machines have enough differences in hardware and functionality that they need different files to run properly. Much of the functionality Intel put in the Ntldr and Ntdetect.com files is embedded in the Alpha hardware, which means the chip doesn't have to go looking for it.

The Intel Ntldr and Ntdetect.com files do exactly what their names say (even if they say it with a mouthful of cornflakes). *Ntldr* — the Windows NT loader — searches for and confirms whether you have the basic files to begin loading the NT operating system. *Ntdetect.com* detects new hardware to run under the operating system.

Nope, Ntdetect.com isn't a private eye's Web site. The *.com* stands for *command*, as it did in the DOS era. Rule of thumb: If it's outside your machine on the Internet, it's probably a Web site; if it's inside your machine, it's probably a command.

The booting steps of an Alpha-based system look like this:

1. In the *pre-boot* sequence, the read-only memory (ROM) selects the location of the default boot device from the random-access memory.

   Of course, the needed boot device *should* be on the hard drive where you (or the system installer) thoughtfully placed it. If ROM turns up blank or invalid data, then it issues a query to the CD-ROM and floppy drive, asking *Where the #&!! is the boot medium?*

2. The Alpha hardware and its henchman, an executable file called Osloader.exe, detect and load the functions of Ntldr and assorted files.

   An Alpha machine doesn't mess with Ntldr and Ntdetect.com, so it can also dispense with the standard Intel-style boot.ini file. This makes for a simpler process and fewer software failures, but it's also more difficult to get in there and customize the boot sequence. Oh well. No pain, no gain.

3. Another executable file, Ntoskrnl.exe, takes control over the rest of the boot process. When all system checks have completed with no serious errors (okay, call me an optimist), the machine displays the login screen.

If your Alpha system doesn't boot, check the hard drive to make sure it has the files listed in Table 3-1 (which also tells you where they hang out). Any Alpha-based system has to have 'em or it won't boot.

Table 3-1	Files Used in the Alpha Boot Process
Filename	*File Location*
Osloader.exe	os\\<winnt>
Ntoskrnl.exe	Systemroot\System32
Hal.dll	os\\<winnt>
*.pal	os\\<winnt>
System	Systemroot\System32\Config
Device Drivers (files end in .sys)	Systemroot\System32\Drivers

Systemroot refers to the location where you installed Windows 2000. By default, this is usually C:\winnt. As the ancient sages say, life is simpler if you follow the system defaults!

Intel-igence

The Intel way of booting has been around longer than the Alpha way. It's also more complex. The booting requirements — and the entire sequence of boot-and-load commands — are more complex for an Intel-based machine. And until Alphas become more generally available, you're most likely to be using an Intel-based machine (cue the scary theme music and zoom in on an innocent user's expression of terror).

Not to worry; you're off the hook: You don't actually have to hunt down and wrestle with any of the files listed in Table 3-2. The Windows 2000 installation process installs them automatically in the right locations; but knowing what they are and where they are can help you if (heaven forbid) you run into booting difficulties. And here's more good news: Although Intel-based machines need slightly different files (and more of them) to start booting, some are actually optional. To keep life blissfully simple, this chapter sticks to only those files that install automatically.

Table 3-2	Files Used in the Intel Boot Process
Filename	*File Location*
Ntldr (hidden)	System Partition root (usually C:\)
Boot.ini	System Partition root
Bootsec.dos (optional)	System Partition root
Ntdetect.com (hidden)	System Partition root
Ntbootdd.sys (optional)	System Partition root
Ntoskrnl.exe	Systemroot\System32
Hal.dll	Systemroot\System32
System	Systemroot\System32\Config
Device Drivers (files end in .sys)	Systemroot\System32\Drivers

Once again, Systemroot refers to the location where you installed Windows 2000 (by default, that's usually C:\winnt).

When a file is *hidden* (not shown on-screen, either for security reasons or to make the system easier to work with), you can view it if you know the mystic secret: In Windows Explorer, select <u>V</u>iew⇨<u>O</u>ptions, select the View tab in the Options dialog box, and make sure the *Show all files* radio button is selected. (If only finding lost car keys could be that easy.)

An Intel machine boots up in five stages:

1. The pre-boot sequence for an Intel machine is much like that on an Alpha machine. The big difference here is that the major portion of the work is done by the self-test routines and, if available, the basic input/output system (BIOS).

2. The BIOS locates the boot device and then runs the MBR (*master boot record*) to make sure it's booting up strictly by the book.

3. The machine loads and initializes the Ntldr file, which begins to load the operating system, kicking off the main boot sequence. (A cheer goes up.)

4. Ntldr switches the microprocessor in your computer from real mode to 32-bit flat-memory mode. (The crowd gasps in admiration.)

5. The Ntdetect.com file starts a hardware-detection scan so Windows 2000 can identify (and, if necessary, load) any needed Plug-and-Play drivers.

   According to Microsoft, the Windows 2000 Ntdetect.com file can locate and handle drivers for the following hardware components:

   • Busses or adapters of specific types

   • Communications ports

   • Floating-point coprocessors

   • Floppy disk drives

   • Standard and non-standard keyboards

   • Mice and/or pointing devices, including optical mice and trackballs

   • Parallel ports (traditionally used for printers)

   • SCSI ("scuzzy") adapters

   • Video adapters

Selecting an Operating System

Probably the most useful portion of the boot process is when the system takes a break, pausing to give you time to select an operating system (if you have more than one listed in your boot.ini file). Whether you run an Alpha or Intel-based computer, your system will take this short "lunch break" immediately after it completes its pre-boot sequence. If you do have multiple operating systems on your computer, Windows 2000 stops the boot process at this point and offers a menu from which you can choose your OS du jour.

A boot by any other name . . . if you have two operating systems available on your computer, you have (technically speaking, of course) a *dual-boot* machine that'll get you off on the right foot on either platform. Yet another difference between human beings (who can use two boots at the same time) and computers (which can't).

You can select the operating system you want by using the up- and down-pointing arrow keys, and then pressing Enter when the selection you want is highlighted. The Operating System Selection Menu gives you either five or thirty whole seconds to choose, depending on what software you have installed. If you're caught with a sandwich halfway to your mouth, no problem: If you don't choose an OS in the time provided, the computer takes the default road and completes the boot process with nary a snort.

You can alter both the selection of the operating systems and the time allotted for your choice by boldly opening the boot.ini file. You can find instructions for doing so (without triggering any rolling boulders) at the end of this chapter!

Finally, the boot process loads and initializes of the kernel (the core of the operating system), which kicks off the login process. (The spectators immediately do The Wave and recall their passwords.) If the login goes well, you find yourself back at your familiar login screen, ready for action.

While the kernel is busy loading and getting initialized, two files are loaded and/or created under the HKEY_LOCAL_MACHINE heading. Both these files may come in handy for you if you ever need to (heaven help you!) start poking around in the Windows 2000 Registry:

- ✔ You can find the Registry key loaded under HKEY_LOCAL_MACHINE\ SYSTEM, — and you can find *that* puppy under Systemroot\System32\Config\System.

- ✔ Similarly, the Hardware key is tucked neatly away in the directory HKEY_LOCAL_MACHINE\HARDWARE, under the same file-system path as the Registry key.

Advanced Boot Options

Okay, suppose you've mastered the basics of your boot process and you're ready to do some techno-swashbuckling. You can access the Windows 2000 *advanced boot options* (Last Known Good Configuration and Directory Services Restoration) by using these methods, respectively:

✔ Press the spacebar while the OS Loader is running.

✔ Press F8 when the Operating System Selection screen appears.

Directory Services Restoration is available only for Windows 2000 Server, but both of these lifesavers can help get you out of a jam if you encounter problems with bootup or login. Neither option is exclusive to Server. Both Server and Professional can use these boot methods.

Last Known Good Configuration

Suppose you discover that (not to name names) *somebody* made a royal hash of your system's configuration, and you have *one last chance* to fix a problem in the boot profile. Hey, it's not an emergency — it's an adventure! Time to break out the boot option known as the Last Known Good Configuration:

1. **Make sure the OS Loader is running.**

   You can spot the OS Loader by its name, and by the dots that move from left to right across the top of your screen when it's running.

   (Rumor has it that this awesome special effect was inspired by the *Mission Impossible* opening sequence of a fuse burning across the screen. Sorry, theme music not included.)

2. **Press the spacebar and waft away to the Hardware Profile/Configuration Recovery menu.**

   The Configuration Recovery menu shows a list of the hardware profiles you've set up on your machine.

3. **Use the up and down arrow keys to highlight a profile; press Enter to select the one you want.**

   You can make life simpler for yourself by pressing L, which allows your machine to pick the Last Known Good Configuration automatically.

Directory Services Restoration

The second of the two *recovery*-oriented advanced boot options — Directory Services Restoration — is available only on Windows 2000 Server. This option is designed to handle some complexity, so it's only available when the Windows 2000 Server machine is running in a domain — which normally means a larger network — specifically as the domain controller.

This seemingly overbearing restriction is necessary because the recovery services affect *all users' machines in the domain grouping*. Directory Services restoration mode enables you (as administrator) to recover the settings in your Active Directory.

Enable VGA

The Enable VGA mode can be found on many variations of Windows operating system. Essentially, it's a way for you to select a mode that affects only the display variables. Enabling VGA takes some load off the system by letting Windows 2000 start with a simpler video driver — basic VGA.

Debug mode

Debugging mode turns on the logging function under Windows 2000 and creates what is known as *verbose* logs with information particularly useful to developers and coders.

Debug mode is only available on Windows 2000 Server, although the 2000 server doesn't have to be the domain controller or even part of a domain.

Enable Boot Logging

You can use the Enable Boot Logging mode when you're starting to run into certain difficulties — say, trouble with logging in or a hardware device that fails repeatedly on startup. Enabling this option keeps track of the loading and initialization of drivers and services, which can help you pinpoint problems. This mode is so useful that it's automatically switched on in the Safe and Debug modes.

The boot log is written to a file called ntbtlog.txt, a special text file created in a default Systemroot directory. If you need to find exactly where this file lives on your main drive, use the Windows Explorer's Find function to locate it.

When you use Last Known Good Configuration, boot logging isn't activated.

Booting in Safe Mode

Safe mode is a tool to use when you're truly in dire straits. Not that Safe mode is inherently dangerous, but you'll only really find this useful if your machine simply refuses to boot. While in Safe mode, your Windows 2000 operating system does no more than load and use the most basic files and drivers. Because no network connections start, you can view and edit the connections if they are causing problems. You'll also be able to save valuable files to disk or an attached tape drive before you begin to fix the system so you can minimize losses due to the outage.

Running in Safe mode also allows you to determine the root cause of your system's problems. For example, if a file or driver was the source of the problem, your system might not boot, even when in Safe mode. This tells you that a core function has been damaged and you'll have to reinstall Windows 2000.

Note that I said *refuses to boot*, not *refuses to power up*. If your machine does its best imitation of a boulder when you power it on, check the power cord. If *that's* working, you have much larger problems than the operating system. Get a new box and start the Windows 2000 installation procedure!

You can activate Safe mode by performing the following steps:

1. **Press F8 during the OS loading procedure.**

2. **Select Safe Mode by using your keyboard's arrow keys and pressing Enter.**

   When the machine comes up in Safe mode, it displays the wording *Safe Mode* in the four corners of the screen. The background appears in an appropriately somber shade of black.

In Safe mode, the machine boots up with the absolute minimum of software — basic VGA and hardware drivers — and no networking capability.

If you're from the UNIX side of the universe, Safe mode is the equivalent of booting your machine in Single User mode.

Of course, if you want to start Safe mode with networking turned on, that option is available. You'll want to do so only if you're trying to locate a bug in the network itself.

Editing the Boot.ini File

The boot.ini file is the file that contains the information used by the Ntldr when starting up your machine. The information here directly affects what you see on the Operating System Selection screen.

You can view and edit your boot.ini file by locating it with Windows Explorer. Normally, you can find the file right in the C:\ area. Open it by double-clicking the file. It opens in WordPad. An example boot.ini file might look something like the following:

```
[Boot Loader]
Timeout=30
Default=C:\="Microsoft Windows"
[Operating Systems]
signature(f7cf)disk(0)rdisk(0)partition(1)\WINNT="Microsoft
        Windows 2000 Server" /fastdetect
C:\="Microsoft Windows"
```

In this example, you should look for a couple key pieces of information. The Timeout setting, in the second line from the top, is what controls the amount of time you have to select one of multiple operating systems. Normally it's set for either 5 or 30 seconds.

The Default in the next line signifies what operating system will be chosen and loaded at the end of the timeout. The final lines in this example show that both Windows and Windows 2000 Server are available for loading on this machine.

As a precautionary measure, before you edit the boot.ini file, copy and save the file in the same location as a backup. Name it something you'll remember, such as *boot1.txt* or *boot-that-works.txt*. Next, edit the file as you would a Word document. If you want to change the Timeout setting from 30 seconds to 15, delete the 30 and type in **15**. To change the default operating system selection, cut out one named operating system and paste in the other . . .

. . . but don't bet on it happening every time. In certain cases, deleting Windows 2000 from the boot.ini file *won't* remove it from your list of choices on rebooting.

Chapter 4

Logging Roads

*P*recious little is simple these days. Take running a Windows 2000 network, for example: Ya can't just flick the power switch to *On* and let 'er rip, pilgrim. Instead, you interact with the Windows Authentication program, a security feature designed to screen out people who don't have user accounts on the network.

This chapter unveils the mysterious process called *the login*, otherwise known as *logging in*. As you might expect, logging in to a machine that's part of a network is considerably more arcane than logging in to a local machine. Same goes for *logging out* of a machine. Proper procedure is absolutely necessary to placate the monster.

The absolute *wrong* method is just hitting the power button to turn the machine off. The only worse fate is a network full of users who log out that way. Only two consolations here:

✔ Yours won't be a network like that. (Will it? Of course not.)

✔ Such a network wouldn't be functional very long anyway.

Throw Another Log in the Computer (Say What?)

Whoa, put down that tree trunk — wrong log! (But you knew that.) Those among you who might have daydreamed of running away to sea may know *log* as the written record of a ship's voyage, or data describing the operation of a machine. So when you *log in,* your actions become part of the system's account of its own operations; when you *log out,* you've officially stopped participating, which the system duly notes.

In a way, this is similar to what happens on your PC. When you log in, you are officially connected to your computer. You're able to make use of your computer's connection to the Internet, write documents, or create code for programs. While you're logged in, your computer dutifully notes all the actions you take from the moment you came on board. When you *log out,* you've officially stopped participating, which the system also duly notes. Therefore you can think of the login process as both your personal auditor and your gateway to get onto the machine.

But operating systems that are specifically designed for networks, such as UNIX, Linux, Windows NT, and Windows 2000, will ask for a specific login name before you get to the desktop. This is because computers are always grouped into a network for a specific reason or task. This task could be as trivial as holding a company's budget for the next year, or as crucial as hosting the annual Shoot 'Em and Boot 'Em turbo-monster video-game rally. In either case, the task that you've grouped these machines for would quickly degenerate into chaos if an unauthorized user began changing budget numbers or deleting game files. On an *open network,* such as UNIX, (in theory, at least) anyone with the right know-how could log in to any machine and wreak havoc on the other users.

The point is that access needs be restricted to a networked machine. This is so the task can be completed in a timely fashion, and to prevent meddling by unwanted third parties. The Login procedure is the first line — and in many cases, the last line — of defense for a computer system.

Normally, a login process looks fairly straightforward: After you boot up your system, you come to a prompt that calls for your user account name and a password. This prompt could be in an open graphics field (as it is in Windows) or a simple line of text (as it is in UNIX or Linux). The all-important point here is how you answer the prompt.

Logging In: Taking the Local

Logging in *locally* doesn't mean running down to the neighborhood drugstore every time you want to use a computer; the term refers to working on a machine that isn't part of the larger network. . If you're from the UNIX or Linux world, a *local login* is an attempt to get up and running on the computer that's actually attached to the keyboard you're pounding away at. In the Windows world, however, the process is not so blissfully simple; you can only log in locally in one of these situations:

✔ Your machine is a standalone computer, not on a network.

✔ Your computer is a member of a Windows workgroup, not a domain.

✔ Your computer is a member of a Windows domain, but it isn't the domain controller. (You have to alter your login procedure to do this, as explained in detail shortly.)

When you log in locally, the system responds with two (relatively) friendly gestures:

✔ It checks your user account name and password against a local security database, but not a centralized one.

✔ It grants you a local access token.

An *access token* won't get you onto a New York subway. It's an electronic version of the pass you had to have if the teacher stopped you in the hall during class time. A computer creates access tokens to identify users for all the computers in the granting machine's domain — in this case, for the single machine or for every machine in a workgroup. To create this token, the computer uses information it gets from the user's account. If the account's security settings indicate that the user is allowed to see certain files but not others, he or she has the system's permission to act accordingly.

To log in to a machine at either a local or domain level, do the following:

1. **If the machine you're logging in to isn't already on, turn on the power.**

2. **Wait for the machine to finish booting up.**

   After the machine boots up, Windows 2000 displays a splash screen inviting you to attempt a login by pressing Ctrl+Alt+Delete.

3. **Press Ctrl+Alt+Delete to start the login.**

   Windows 2000 displays a Log In screen, containing a graphics box with two empty fields for you to fill in: the User name and Password.

4. **Type your user name and password in the boxes; then press Enter or click OK.**

   If you don't know these or forget them, see your Windows administrator. (Of course, if you *are* the administrator and you can't remember the password that opens your administration account, you already know you're in serious trouble.)

   Use Tab to go between the fields, or use the mouse to click each field to enter the information.

When you're logging in locally a grouping of Windows machines such as a workgroup, you may only have access to the one machine you logged in to. If you're recently made a change to your account of any kind and the change hasn't been placed on each other individual machine in the workgroup, you could find that the old account that used to get you into all the workgroup machines now has *very* local access indeed!

Locally mastering your domain

When you log in locally to a domain grouping of computers, you're essentially telling the computer that you want to be able to access your permissions locally, not on the domain. If you've made a change to your account on this machine, and it hasn't been propagated to the server yet, then you'll be referenced *only* against the machine's local security database, not the domain controller's.

This is why you can't locally log in to a domain if you're on the domain controller. A domain controller by its very nature doesn't have a local security database, because it's the keeper of the database that affects the entire system.

To log in locally on a domain,

1. **Go to the Log In screen.**
2. **Select the computer name in the Enter Password field.**

A login by any other domain would smell as sweet. . . .

When you log in to a machine on a domain, you'll be checked out and authenticated by the domain's Big Kahuna, also known as the domain controller. You'll be matched up to the central security database in the Active Directory function. In return, you'll be granted a domain-specific access token. This token allows you to go to any machine within the domain and, depending on your permissioning, to different domains on the network.

The login procedure for the domain is slightly different than one for a stand-alone machine or a workgroup. When you get to the Log In screen, you'll have a couple more options available to you in a new graphics field underneath the Login Name and Password areas.

Fifty ways to leave your lover, but only one (good) way to leave your computer

Rule Number One when you're logging out of your computer: Unless you're in desperate straits, never hit the *BRB* (Big Red Button, or *power switch*) to shut down your machine!

Rule Number Two: If you think you're in desperate straits, see Rule Number One.

Always, always leave your computer by logging out or shutting down your machine. When you exit your machine via the Big Red Button, you run the serious risk of losing data from programs you've been working with, or the corruption of the files that make up your user profile. A mangled user profile isn't good for much, aside

from presenting you with an *interesting* challenge when you try to log back in.

These problems are only about ten times more intense if you're working on a server. Shutting down prematurely can result in corruption of your entire operating system — and if that happens on a domain controller, you've effectively *lost* much of your user profile data, and perhaps documents and applications as well.

Basically, you shouldn't be hitting the BRB unless the computer is frozen, out of control, spitting sparks, or playing the *Brady Bunch* theme at high volume.

The new field is a pull-down menu; use it to select the domain name that contains your user account. All domains within the domain tree (if your network has multiple domains) show up on-screen in a list. Also, you have to select the name of the computer you want to log in to. Entering a correct user name and password probably won't get you access if you've specified the wrong domain!

Keep in mind that the password field in Windows 2000 is *case-sensitive*. If you're having trouble logging in and you're sure your typing skills haven't mysteriously degenerated, check the Caps Lock key. Leaving this key depressed is a major source of login woes.

Turned on and tuned in? Log out and shut down

Shutting down and logging out both get you out of the computer system. Logging out takes you out of the network and any networked applications; shutting down closes the applications and the operating system; the only remaining step in the process is to turn off the computer itself.

> ✔ A *shutdown* command actually takes a computer out of the operating system mode and back to a state right above power-down. (Some machines, especially laptops, let the operating system shut the power off for you.)

> ✔ By comparison, a *logout* command tells the computer that you want off the system. But you won't be deactivating the operating system — you'll be leaving it up and running, ready to accept a new login from another user. This saves system resources — and a good deal of time if you're running Windows 2000 on a slightly older machine.

There are two ways you can go about logging out or shutting down. To get to the command (or the button that allows you to access this command), you have two main options:

> ✔ The Windows 2000 Security Box (that's actually what it's called)
>
> ✔ The Shut Down menu that takes you all the way out of the applications and operating system

Thinking outside the Security Box

The most commonly used way of getting to this fateful choice is to click the Start button at the lower-left corner of the screen and select the bottom choice from the pop-up menu, Shut Down. The Shut Down menu box displays immediately.

A second pop-up menu is displayed in the Shut Down menu, accessible through clicking the arrow to the right of the choices (as shown in Figure 4-1). By default, the selection available to you is *Log off* (simply an older way of saying *log out*), which is less taxing for the machine. If this is what you want, then click the OK button.

Figure 4-1: Choose Log Off Administrator if that's what you want to do.

On the other hand, if you want to select the Shut Down or Restart options, take the appropriate selection from the pop-up menu and click OK.

The Spock touch

By the way, the triple-key combination Ctrl+Alt+Delete has become something of a standard in the computer world for shutting down or rebooting. On some systems, simply pressing this combo reboots the system, no questions asked.

For this reason, Ctrl+Alt+Delete has become immortalized by the pocket-protector set as the *Three-Finger Salute* (or, for the *Star Trek* fans in the audience, the *Vulcan Nerve Pinch*).

Thinking "inside" the Security Box

The second method of getting to the logout-or-shutdown choice is to go through the Windows Security Box. You get there by pressing Ctrl+Alt+Delete. A screen labeled Windows Security comes up and gives you a fishy look (just kidding).

From the Security Box, you have two separate buttons for Logging Off and Shutting Down your machine. Select whichever option you want simply by clicking its button. The Security Box gives you the same choice between logging out and shutting down that you get when you use the Shut Down utility under the Start button.

Now How Much Would You Pay? Don't Answer Yet . . .

Here's a quick peek at the other options available to the hardworking administrator (that's you!) courtesy of the Windows Security Box. Although the various options on the box don't all pertain to security matters, two buttons at the left in the box do have a clear connection to network security: Lock Computer and Change Password.

✔ **Change Password** does exactly what it says — it gives you the means to change your user-account password.

As a safety feature, you'll need to input your old password one final time — which is handy, in case anyone tries to change your password while you leave your screen unattended.

✔ **Lock Computer** is also designed to thwart a mischievous fellow user who happens upon your logged-in account while you're out getting a Quadruple Bypass Cheeseburger at the local eatery.

Pressing this button takes you to the Lock screen, where you can use the computer equivalent of the Vulcan Nerve Pinch to get to a password screen — from which you have to enter your password before you can return to your own desktop! This rigmarole may sound pretty cheesy to some people, but it's actually proven effective as a deterrent to casual snoops and pass-by hackers who just can't leave *anything* alone.

On the right side of the screen, you'll see the Cancel button. In case you're wondering, the Cancel is there to get you out of the Windows Security Box without selecting Log off, Lock Screen, or any of the other security/logging options. This feature is especially useful if you're always hitting that pesky Ctrl+Alt+Del as you type, at all the same time! (If so, don't write to me, write to Ripley's Believe It Or Not. And you might want to take those mittens off. . . .)

The final option available to you is the Task Manager button in the lower center of the screen. Clicking this button takes you to back to the desktop, with the Task Manager screen activated.

The Task Manager is a wellspring of excellent information for the administrator. By default, the Task Manager comes up with the Applications tab on top, as shown in Figure 4-2.

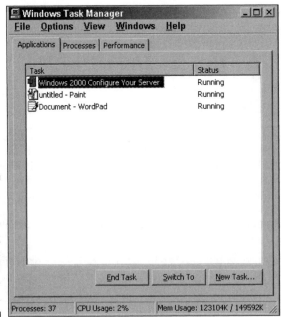

Figure 4-2:
The
Windows
Task
Manager is
a useful tool
for adminis-
trators.

Task Master . . . uh, Task *Manager* . . . lists the actual applications running on the machine, each one complete with its own little icon on the left. This window is useful for a basic administration test — is that program sitting there actually frozen, or is it just taking its own sweet time to finish?

If a program is still working, Task Manager lists its status as Running. If the program is frozen, on strike, or in a snit, its status reads Not Responding.

The third tab on the Task Manager window, labeled Performance, is also moderately useful to an administrator. Not only does it give the actual configuration of the system (in Physical and Kernel Memory), but it also helps track system performance. The CPU and Memory Usage charts are not only handy, they're pretty cool to look at, as Figure 4-3 demonstrates.

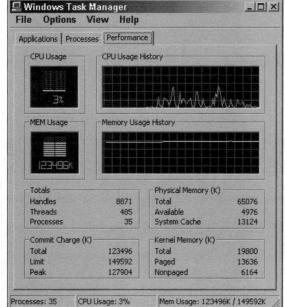

Figure 4-3:
The Performance tab helps track system performance.

By and large, I've found this tab most useful when I'm trying to replicate a problem. (Yep, that's right, as in *make that glitch happen again so I can clobber it.*) Activate the Task Manager and move to this tab if you think a specific application is causing problems.

Start up the troublesome application and watch the CPU and Memory usage. If these start to grow out of control, you've found your culprit.

You may also notice that if you're watching the Task Manager while running other programs, the Task Manager will always stay on top. This is to help you use the Manager as a system monitor. If it starts to get in your way, you can minimize it.

The middle tab of the Task Manager, Processes, might be the least exciting to look at (have a look at Figure 4-4 and decide for yourself), but it's probably the most useful to the administrator.

Figure 4-4:
The information on the Processes tab can help you track problems.

Image Name	PID	CPU	CPU Time	Mem Usage
System Idle Process	0	97	42:01:35	16 K
System	8	00	0:01:08	120 K
smss.exe	152	00	0:00:01	44 K
csrss.exe	180	00	0:00:31	916 K
winlogon.exe	204	00	0:01:08	1,488 K
services.exe	232	00	0:00:45	1,752 K
lsass.exe	244	00	0:02:45	5,272 K
svchost.exe	420	00	0:00:01	1,596 K
SPOOLSV.EXE	448	00	0:00:01	1,128 K
msdtc.exe	624	00	0:00:00	1,056 K
dfssvc.exe	720	00	0:00:00	584 K
tcpsvcs.exe	740	00	0:00:05	1,068 K
svchost.exe	772	00	0:00:05	2,128 K
ismserv.exe	796	00	0:00:00	988 K
llssrv.exe	816	00	0:00:08	1,712 K
sfmsvc.exe	876	00	0:00:00	216 K
mshta.exe	920	00	0:00:01	2,428 K
sfmprint.exe	928	00	0:00:00	312 K
ntfrs.exe	996	00	0:00:20	672 K

☐ Show processes from all users   End Process

Processes: 35   CPU Usage: 4%   Mem Usage: 120180K / 149592K

This tab gives you more useful information, especially when you're tracking a problem. While it lacks the gee-whiz factor of the Performance window, you can still refer to the CPU column of the window to determine how much computer power a specific process is soaking up.

The other nice thing about this tab is that it shows *processes* (what's actually going on), not just *applications* (the pretty packages that processes come in). An application is a software product such as Word or Internet Explorer. A process, on the other hand, can often run behind the scenes, handling system resources or juggling memory. Processes are usually more stable than applications (maybe because they don't talk much to people); the Processes tab allows you to check to see whether one of these hidden daemons has gone a little bonkers and slowed down the system.

Idle CPUs aren't the Devil's workshop

If you see the first entry on the Processes tab taking up 95 to 98 percent of the CPU cycles, don't panic just yet. Check to see whether all those resources are being taken up by the System idle process. If they are, relax — you've just seen an indicator that your machine isn't being worked too hard. The idle process cleans up after closed processes, dusts off those freed-up system resources, and makes them readily available for whatever demands might be coming up.

Part II
Administering Users and Disks

The 5th Wave   By Rich Tennant

"This part of the test tells us whether you're personally suited to the job of network administrator."

In this part . . .

*N*ow you're ready to go beyond your initial administration machine and begin to branch out onto the network. Your efforts will affect remote users. But managing a Windows network isn't all nuts, bolts, and disk drives. So pick up these special techniques to keep your user community in tall clover instead of up in arms.

Chapter 5

Accounting 101

● ●

In This Chapter

▶ Defining a user account

▶ Determining differences between local accounts and domain accounts

▶ Identifying Windows 2000 default accounts

▶ Developing conventions

▶ Assigning accounts

● ●

*T*here are many mysteries in this world. So many secrets to reveal: where Elvis currently resides (it ain't at Graceland), how they get that filling into the Twinkie (it ain't easy), and there's more than just one kind of user account. Windows 2000 actually gives you *three* kinds of user account — ain't it grand?

The first kind is rather like the pictures that come inside a picture frame when you purchase it; whether you like it or not, it's already there. You shouldn't have to edit them, which is a good thing because you can't do much to affect the account's properties anyway. (So there!) These default accounts exist to help you run your machine.

The second and third kinds of accounts are those you can edit and change to your heart's content. Hopefully, your heart's content doesn't extend to daily changes — if that's the case, your users will definitely be put out. These accounts are divided along network architecture lines — local versus domain. The following sections of this chapter show you the differences between the two and how to set up all of them.

User Accounts and Their Purpose in Life

A *user account*'s most basic function is allowing users to log in to your Windows 2000 network. However, that's not the user account's only raison d'être (reason for being, if you're not a Francophone). You should be aware of the multiple reasons for using the user account system on the Windows 2000 — or any other — network.

Now and then, someone — usually a person new to technology administration — asks why a computer network can't be completely *open*. Why can't anyone can log in from anywhere, with a press of a button, without having to remember a password, type in a user name, or kowtow to any of the typical system rigmarole? It would be so easy, so efficient, and so free of administrative duties that anyone would jump at the chance to install a network that followed that model.

Only a couple of network models have come close to implementing a system like that. UNIX, for example, is considered an *open* system, but most die-hard administrators from that side of the silicon pond would blanch at the thought of giving up the use of all user accounts — particularly the account used to administer the network, called the *root* account.

Another attempt at making the pure open network a reality came from Larry Ellison, the CEO of the Oracle database company. Ellison's idea was to create a sort of *network computer* — all you'd have would be a monitor and keyboard at your desk (well, okay, maybe a mouse). A server machine would allow you to download a copy of any program you wanted use, such as a word processor. However, even this system needed user accounts for it to operate successfully.

Finally, you could argue that the Guest account in Windows 2000 (and earlier incarnations of Windows NT) is close to being an open account. You can always log in to a Guest account, you never have to remember more than one password, and so on and so forth. You can read more about the Guest account in "Guest towels, guest rooms, Guest accounts" later in this chapter, but let's stay in the moment for now. I invite you to suggest an open account to your user community. (Go ahead, I'll wait. Go on.) Did they give you a look you've seen before on the faces of Tokyo crowds as they run from Godzilla? I thought so.

Operating your user community from the Guest account is a lot like suggesting to apartment building residents that they'd all be happier living together in one large room. You could argue that they'll save money on heat, air conditioning, and electricity, and that they'd never have to remember that pesky apartment number when ordering a pizza, but to no avail.

User accounts give user information logical definition. Like the walls of an apartment building provide privacy and security for all of the residents, user accounts

✔ Give users a separate piece of disk space to store their own files

✔ Allow the network to retrieve files for editing and use

✔ Prevent others from playing with — and possibly breaking — personal files and programs

When a user ain't a user . . . or something

Make sure that you always distinguish *user accounts* from *users* in your mind. They're not always the same thing! For example, say that you find a rude e-mail in your mailbox from someone called joebob. Do you stomp around the office trying to locate Joseph Robert, the user assigned to this account, and proceed to thrash him with a handful of wet noodles?

Not necessarily! Who's to say that poor Joe didn't leave for a Snickers break while some

nefarious character sent the e-mail to you? This is an example of a user who is making use of someone else's computer identity (the user account) to send you a false message. You'll be more effective in combating system security problems if you keep in mind that just because problems came from a given user's account, it means that the user — or anyone else using that account — could have caused the problem.

From an administrative standpoint, the ability to provide additional service to your users makes up for the additional burden of having individual user accounts. As an administrator, your goals are also to provide system security and system stability. User accounts aid you in both these areas.

- ✔ By establishing an effective password scheme, you provide a good front-line defense against the casual cracker. (Those Saltines are persistent!)

- ✔ By establishing an administrative account to oversee and give sole permission to edit system files, you increase system stability. Your system is placed in the most trustworthy hands — yours.

Who's That Account in the Window?

Microsoft 2000 provides an administrator three kinds of accounts:

- ✔ Built-in (system) accounts
- ✔ Local user accounts
- ✔ Domain accounts

The built-in accounts effectively run your systems; therefore, you won't edit them very much, if at all. On the other hand, you'll spend a lot of time working with the local and domain user accounts forms. Your Windows 2000 network structure determines which type of account you work with.

One of the locals: The local user account

If you run a Windows 2000 workgroup or a standalone terminal, you'll create local user accounts to run on your network. A *local user account* has permissions and resources that are only available locally to the user: She probably will either be unable to log in to the network or to make full use of other Windows 2000 machines on the network. So much lost potential; a network is a terrible thing to waste.

More administrative hassles exist for you upon local user account creation. When you whip up or edit a local user account, you're not entering information into a centralized repository, which is what the Active Directory in Windows 2000 Server is designed to be. Instead, you're editing the local security database, as described in Chapter 2.

You can't edit or shut down the user account unless you're at that local machine. Because of this flaw, the local user account model isn't the best Windows user solution. (The exception is if you run a very small network. If you're using such a small network, this may work just fine for you — don't let me unnecessarily discourage you. You'll get no peer pressure here.)

You shouldn't create a local user account on any machine that's part of a Windows 2000 domain. Windows 2000 *domains* (like snooty, gated communities) won't recognize rogue local accounts. Therefore, a local account is unable to access domain resources or public files gathered under the domain.

Going cosmopolitan: The domain user account

Domain user accounts provide more user functionality because they allow a user access to resources from a bigger world. What does this world consist of? The rest of the resources you have hooked up into your network. By the time you cultivate your network to such a size that you have multiple remote printers, user groups, and more than a 20-foot slog to the espresso machine, you'll use the domain model. With a domain model, you'll use domain accounts.

When you create and edit domain user accounts, you're making changes in the central repository for all this information: the Active Directory subsection that takes care of users and computers on your network.

The ripple effect

Windows texts call the phenomenon *replication*. UNIX books call it *propagation*. Administrators who have a more poetic frame of mind call it the *ripple* effect. Regardless of what you call it (a rose by any other name, you know), it's something to always take into account when you're creating or editing user accounts on your Windows 2000 network.

So, how does a change made on the Active Directory make its way to the local domain controller? (It's that whole filling-in-the-Twinkie quandary again. . . .) Windows 2000 Server, by default, performs an Active Directory replication every five minutes. With this replication process, all Active Directories on local domain controllers are kept in proper synchronization with the main domain tree controller (see Chapter 3). Because this change radiates outward from the central control area like a wave in a pool of water, people have taken to calling it the *ripple effect*.

Administration

From an administrator's point of view, the ripple effect is more than a pretty expression — it's a reminder. Tying a string around their fingers didn't help them remember that the larger the network, the longer it takes for a user account change to *wash* from one end of the network to the other.

Assume you add a new user account to the network. When you use the Windows 2000 domain network model, that user has to wait for up to five minutes before logging on. In reality, it seems that you have to add a couple more minutes for every layer of network you have between your server and your destination.

This is most likely the result of network traffic or routers misbehaving when you have a far-flung network of machines, but it's something to keep in mind when you're promising to make an important change for a user who has had little sleep and three double cappuccinos to keep him going! Best to play it cool and add a couple more minutes before he tries to log in and comes after you in a caffeine-induced rage.

Editing

You need Active Directory on a Windows 2000 server to create and edit domain user accounts. Because of this, you shouldn't have both local and domain accounts together on the same network. The local account can't use the domain resources; as the administrator, you have no remote power over anything the user with the local account does on that account's machine.

Although this won't necessarily torch your network, even one broken machine will take valuable time out of your day, time that could be better spent upgrading the network, fiddling with routers, or checking out Internet auction sites for that sound system you want for your car. . . .

He Just Followed Me Home; Can I Keep Him?

When you installed Windows 2000, the installation processes automatically created several *default* accounts that are used primarily for system maintenance, administration, or limited user accessibility. If you're from the UNIX side of the operating system universe, you probably know of the standard system account *nobody*. The nobody account performs a lot of the dirty work for the root administrative account (you know, pouring the concrete shoes, polishing the brass knuckles, that sort of thing).

Windows works things out similarly. To take care of the system administration, Microsoft has the default *root* account called Administrator. The Guest account is also created; it provides limited user access when needed. You aren't allowed to delete either of these accounts, but you shouldn't do that, anyway — the Microsoft programmers worked hard to bring you these accounts, the least you can do is use them, right?

Administrator — the big root Kahuna

The Administrative account is responsible for all the system-changing work and maintenance you will perform on your system. You can change file permissions so that other accounts can also edit your Windows world, but it's best not to do so — all it takes is one misinformed user to knock out the right file at the wrong time. It's kind of like the *Titanic* disaster; everything would have been fine if it weren't for that itty-bitty iceberg thing.

Why Superman was Clark Kent most of the time

You don't need any other accounts for yourself if you're the Windows administrator, right? Wrong! Too many administrators make the critical mistake of doing all of their work (system administration and sending e-mail to their significant others, for instance) on the Administrator account.

That's a bad idea all around:

✔ You increase the chance of making an error that whacks the system. Say you're deleting personal files and . . . oops, that Domain Controller directory wasn't critical, was it?

✔ You increase the potential for a security hazard if you leave your terminal unattended when making a run for the local Taco Bell.

Your best bet is to create your own user account and to log in as a typical user most of the time. When trouble strikes, you can dash off into the nearest phone booth (hopefully empty), switch to red underwear and cape, and log in again as Administrator to save the day!

The administrator fake-out move

One clever thing you can do as an administrator is *hide* the administrative account. If someone with criminal intent looks up a list of system users, she's going to look for the account labeled Administrator. It's like leaving out on your desk sensitive documents labeled TOP SECRET NUCLEAR INFORMATION.

Solution? Change the name of the Administrator account to something like *Fred* or any other name that won't stick out of the list of user names. Hint: Don't pick something that's a dead giveaway, like *bossdude, big_kahuna,* or *da_wonderful_wizardofoz.*

Guest towels, guest rooms, Guest accounts

Across from Administrator, at the other end of the user power spectrum, is the Guest account. Being the guest on the system is kind of like being the off-season tourist at a cheap motel. You're here, you have the basics, and you'd better not expect any service. Forget the mint on the pillow — checkout is at 8:00 a.m. sharp.

Truth be told, this is exactly what the Guest account should be (minus the missing lampshades and the broken ice machine). A Guest account is designed to offer a short-term user extremely limited access to your network. The account is not designed to encourage the user to stay.

Security through creative use of frustration

If the guest frequents your system, one of two things happen. If the user is there illegally, he won't be able to save or edit files on your server, so he'll get frustrated and leave. If the user is there legally, she won't be able to save or edit files on your server, so she'll get frustrated and come to you for a brand-spanking new Domain user account. It's a nice device, that Guest account.

Typically, the only people who use a guest account are temporary employees or employees visiting from another office branch. Employees in both cases probably need very limited services. By giving these folks Guest accounts, you save yourself the hassle of setting up a new user account.

My guest is lazy — it won't work

Your Guest account comes disabled by default. It comes that way for the same reason your computer came in a box filled with Styrofoam peanuts — to make an absolute mess on your floor. Just kidding. In actuality, it prevents system damage by not giving anyone access to your system until you're ready for them. Figure 5-1 is what you see if you look at the Active Directory's Users and Computers screen.

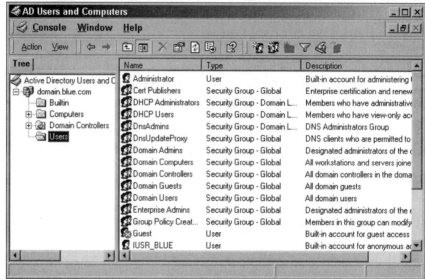

Figure 5-1:
The AD User and Computers screen, also known as Directory Management Snap-In, a profoundly ambiguous name.

The Guest account, second from the bottom, is listed with a red X over the face of the user icon. Things have definitely passed the expiration date in Denmark here. (Translation for the non-Danish: The account is disabled.)

Enable the account by right-clicking the account. A window comes up; it should bear an uncanny resemblance to Figure 5-2. Select Enable (third from the top) to remove the X from the account listing and to activate your Guest account facilities.

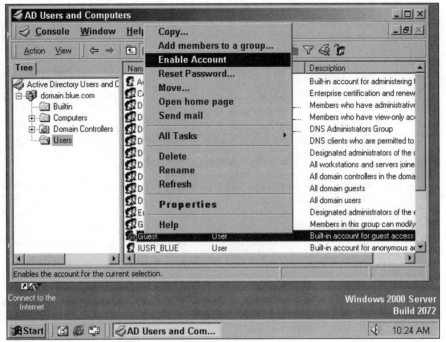

Figure 5-2:
The Enable
User
Command in
action!

User Account Architecture

Administrators have their own boatload of quirks. Although most will draw diagrams for network architecture on a user dinner napkin at the drop of a hat, comparatively few will sit still long enough to figure out what conventions they plan to follow when creating user accounts. Setting user *conventions,* also known as creating user *architecture,* gives predictable structure to this aspect of the network.

Before you ever create a user account, you should consider what you need to enter on your Windows network; tailor the requirements so that you can easily understand, follow, and duplicate them. Those things you set up now determine what you'll do each time you add someone to your system.

The most important thing is to select a unique name for each user account. For example, if you have two people with the same name (say Edward Johnson), then you can't both allow them to be called *ejohn*. The account information has to be unique to each user. A large user community will probably have two guys named Edward Johnson. You're going to have problems if you assign them the same account name.

Depending on the naming scheme you set up, you could set up the two Edward Johnsons as *ed1* and *ed2, ejohnson* and *edj,* or *ted-ward* and *teddybear.*

The names don't even have to match the user's real name. Edward Johnson doesn't need to be ejohnson or ed1; he could just as easily be ted, ted-ward, or teddybear.

The administrator decides on the user naming conventions. It doesn't have to be complex or precise; it doesn't even have to make sense. It does, however, have to be used consistently.

Most network naming schemes follow the *first initial, last name* rule. User Jonathan Smith becomes *jsmith* and Samuel Olsen Terry McRosen becomes *smcrosen.* Another popular method is *first name, last name initial.* Sherlock Holmes becomes *sherlockh* and Ted Stravinsky-Korenson becomes *teds.* You can even assign people numbers, so that Rico Mayberry Alexrod De Blanco becomes *1user.*

You may also assign a functional prefix or suffix to a user account name. For example, any user account from a temporary employee may start with a *T* or an engineering department employee may start with an *E.* Again, what matters here is consistency.

Consistency must be paired with some other rules. Here are the other factors you should take into account when putting your conventions together:

- ✔ **User names must be unique.** If I've told you once, I've told you a thousand times. Make that 1001.

- ✔ **User names are *not* case-sensitive.** This is important to remember in light of the first requirement: You're not doing yourself any favors by creating accounts davidr and DavidR.

- ✔ **User names are up to 20 characters long.** I have heard of people being baffled when they invariably interpret this as *20 letters* or *20 numbers.* A character is something you get by banging away the keyboard, and if you think otherwise, *you* are the character.

There are several characters that are not valid for a user name. Table 5-1 lists the invalid characters.

Table 5-1	Invalid User Name Characters
Characters	*Description*
" "	Quotation marks, forward and backward.
/ \	Forward and backward slash.

Characters	Description
[ ]	Beginning and ending bracket.
,	Comma.
: ;	Colon and semicolon. (Although they are useful for making smiley faces, don't put them in your user names if you expect to see smiling users.)
< >	Greater-than and less-than symbols.
*	Asterisk.
|	Pipe symbol (Note to all non-UNIX users: This is a *pipe,* even though it looks like a letter l on an all-protein diet.)
=	Equal symbol equals what? An invalid character!
+	Plus, this one is invalid.
?	Question? Yes, this is also invalid.

Adding New User Accounts

When creating a new user account in your domain, you'll use Active Directory, a new tool for managing accounts and objects in Windows 2000. We'll be going into its full capabilities more thoroughly in Chapter 19, but for now you just need to use it for this one task. To create a new user account, complete the following steps:

1. **Click the Start button.**

2. **On the menu that pops up, move your mouse pointer to point to the Programs setting.**

3. **When a second set of menus appears, move your mouse pointer to Administrative Tools, and then to Active Directory Users and Computers. Click Active Directory Users and Computers.**

4. **When the Active Directory screen appears, click the directory labeled Users (it's in the left pane of the window, as shown in Figure 5-3).**

5. **When you get a list of the user accounts currently on your system, right-click Users. A new pop-up menu appears. Move your mouse pointer over New.**

6. **When a new submenu appears, select User by clicking it. The New Object — User screen appears, as shown in Figure 5-4.**

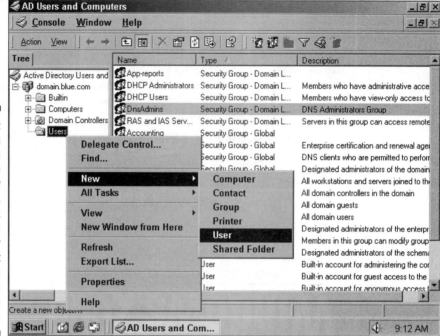

Figure 5-3:
After you
open the
Active
Directory
screen,
right-click
the Users
directory
and select
New, then
Users from
the pop-up
menus.

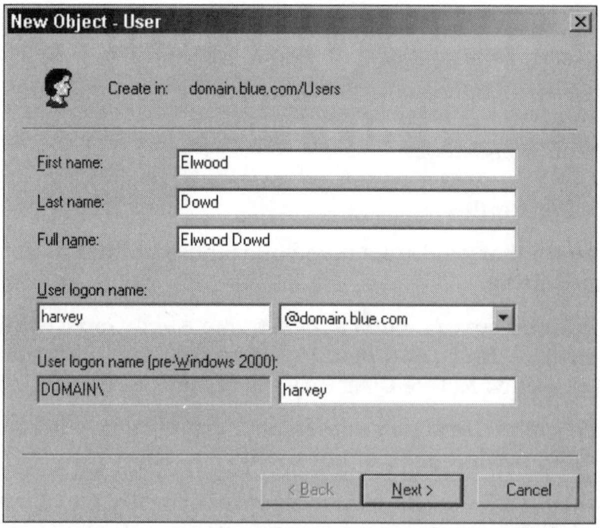

Figure 5-4:
The New
Object —
User
screen,
after our
example
account has
been added.
To continue,
click the
Next button.

7. **Click the empty fields to type in the user information. For the example, we've added user *Elwood Dowd* and granted him the user name *harvey*.**

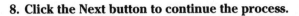

8. Click the Next button to continue the process.

Instead of clicking each field, you can use the Tab key to move between fields in Windows 2000. The Enter key, sensibly enough, is strictly for entering data. By default, pressing Enter cancels whatever you're doing and puts you back at square one. This prevents unfortunate accidents from occurring. Wish they had one of those defaults on my commuter plane . . . .

9. You are asked to put in the user's password. Type a password in the Password field and then re-type it in the Confirm Password field below it.

Note: Two things — the password is not displayed as what you type, and your effort is not duplicated in the Confirm Password field. The former is to prevent someone from reading the password over your shoulder. The latter is a safety check to prevent typos from slipping into your password-creation cycle.

Want to be popular with your users? (Who doesn't want to be popular? Nobody popular, that's fer sure.) Check the box to the left of the User Must Change Password at Next Login setting.

10. Press Next to move to the final User Account creation screen.

You won't actually enter anything here — it's a sort of a preview to ensure that you've entered everything to your satisfaction. If you want to change anything, click the Back button. If you've made a complete hash of things, click Cancel to start again.

11. Click Finish when you're satisfied.

Wizard creep

(Who you calling a wizard? Never mind that — who you calling a creep?) Those of you who are used to the environments in Windows 3.1, 95, and 98 may be unfamiliar with this — since when were you channeled into completely predetermined steps for this task? This is another concept that has expanded in Windows 2000 — what I call the "Wizard interface." Using this type of interface results in fewer oddball results — or so goes the theory. Fortunately, it's probably true.

Chapter 6

Management 101

In This Chapter

▶ Assigning personal properties

▶ Setting General Organizational properties

▶ Seeing the bigger picture

*Y*ou have more control over each aspect of the user's account privileges than ever before. The long and short of it is that Windows 2000 lets you fine-tune your user's privileges, from the user name she is given to the dial-in properties that control how she logs in to the network. Sound dictatorial? Possibly. But then, you could argue that administering a network was never a job for a democracy.

Why Bother Setting User Account Properties?

User properties control all aspects of an account's functionality, from the user's group membership to the hours the user can actually log in to the system. Areas that relate to dial-up connectivity and general user account information are those you should read about first. (Some of the aspects you see in this chapter are covered in other chapters more thoroughly. See Chapter 17 for more information about connecting to the network.)

Ever try to find Waldo? If so, you may have a leg up from the start. The bigger the page, the more you could use some kind of help finding the inconspicuous, striped character. Insert general user account information — the very reason you fill out all the blank fields in the user account's properties. Each bit of information is useful when you're in the middle of a directory search. If you have a Cisco-, Intel-, or Oracle-sized directory to go through, you'll appreciate reference markers when locating a specific user account.

Setting General Organizational Properties

If you need to look for a user's account, you can search for it via basic account property information, such as the user's name. However, you can also search for a user by the following properties, so be sure to enter them when you create a user account:

- ✔ General
- ✔ Address
- ✔ Telephones
- ✔ Organization

Perform the following steps to enter information in these areas:

1. **Click the Start button.**

2. **Click Programs.**

   The Administrative Tools menu comes up.

3. **Select Directory Management.**

   The Users and Computers screen comes up.

4. **Click the Users icon (in the left frame).**

   The contents of the directory are displayed in the right frame.

5. **Right-click the icon of the user account you want to edit.**

   The Properties window appears.

   Note the large number of tabs that are available for you to edit. Although editing any of these tabs is purely optional, you can edit the ones you're interested in by clicking them. For example, to view and edit the Organization information, click the Organization tab, as shown in Figure 6-1.

Of all the general information fields, Organization is the most useful in the majority of situations. The majority of Windows workgroups and domains are located in the corporate world. In these environments, often the most *search-worthy* data is the information that specifically follows the organization of a given department.

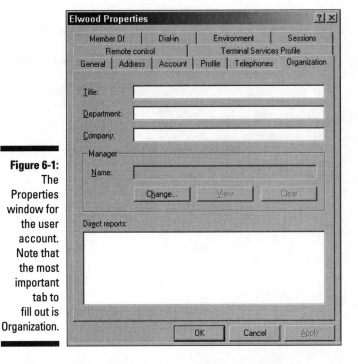

Figure 6-1:
The
Properties
window for
the user
account.
Note that
the most
important
tab to
fill out is
Organization.

Setting Dial-In Properties

Dial-in settings are the second of the user account properties you should know about at the start. To get to the Properties screen, follow Steps 1 through 5 in this chapter's preceding "Setting General Organizational Properties" section. From there, click the Dial-in tab.

The Dial-in settings determine how easy it's going to be for a user to log in to your Windows network from a remote location — or if he can do it at all. When a user tries to log in to the network remotely, he uses his modem to dial in to a computer running *RAS,* which is how the technonerds refer to the Windows 2000 Remote Access Service.

When you check the Verify Caller-ID box, you add an extra layer of security to your system. If you decide to use this, you have to add the telephone number with which the user dials in. Overall, this is an excellent way to funnel the calls to your system into a single connection, which improves security if you've purchased a program to monitor incoming user calls for unauthorized entries.

You should set the Callback options after setting the user account and dial-in properties. The system is set to No Callback by default (as shown in Figure 6-2). This means that the RAS server won't call the user back — and that the lucky user gets to pay the telephone charges! (That serves her right for not calling you on Christmas!)

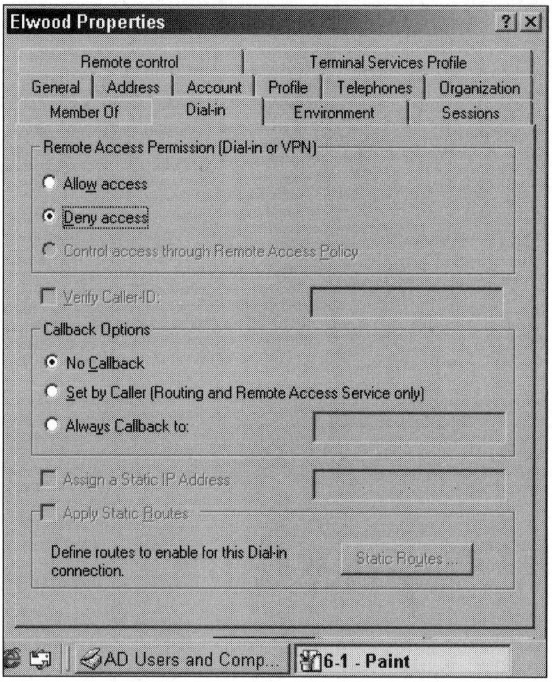

Figure 6-2:
The No
Callback
setting
appears in
the Callback
Options
area.

You can switch this setting to Set by Caller, whereby the caller provides the callback number for the RAS to use. In this environment, the company pays for the callback. (You don't see too many of these settings gaining popularity, do you?)

You can increase network security by setting the Always Callback To option. The RAS server uses the number entered in the Always Callback To field when calling back the user. The user must be at that specific telephone number in order for the connection to be made. This feature reduces the risk of an unauthorized person dialing in a preconfigured number and gaining access to your system.

Don't forget to write . . .

Just because a machine is classified as remote doesn't necessarily mean that it's physically far away. A networked machine a continent away from you can be local and a laptop that's plugged into the phone line next to you can be remote.

The most basic requirement for the remote user is being allowed to access the RAS. This service is set to Deny by default. This is called a *default high security* setting. I call it "default paranoia." Always make sure to allow your users access if they ever conceivably plan to log in to your network remotely.

User Management Principles to Live By

If you're not a people person, it's worth your time to make sure your human interactions go as smoothly as your technical ones. Although you do hold administrative power over all systems, it's better to be a kind and gentle dictator. You'll find your subjects (users) more receptive when you have an emergency or are changing the system.

If you don't have time to sign up for charm school, the following principles can help you get your job done *and* keep you looking good to the world at large (what a concept).

The Simplicity Principle

When explaining a process to a user, don't assume that he knows what you do. Very often, users are only pressing keys, sending e-mail, and reading newsgroups dedicated to their favorite rock stars. Instead of giving him a full technical explanation, just say, "You tried to save the file to an area that didn't have enough space," or, "I'll need to make sure your machine can talk to mine."

The Fair Warning Principle

If you're going to take the system down for repair or maintenance, be kind and let people know ahead of time. Send an e-mail or use whatever other system your company uses. You're best bet is to warn people three or four days in advance. Too late, and people complain. Too early, and people forget. Don't expect people to notice large, brightly colored signs posted in a public location. Most folks just assume that it's another charity drive or company press release.

The Principle of Reason

If someone demands that you perform the impossible (something other than the *routine* impossible), don't just refuse. Make it clear to her that you're not saying that you *won't* do something, but that you *can't*. Give a clear reason. That reason can be as simple as "This would seriously inconvenience everyone else."

The Microsoft Principle

People seem to accept downtime or a major, inconvenient system change if you say that that's "the way Microsoft does it." Perhaps this is because Microsoft has the reputation (right or wrong) of being somewhat monolithic in its approach. On the other hand, it could be that it's one of the most successful corporations around. Surely they know what they're doing. They couldn't possibly be wrong about this, right?

The Scotty Principle

Use the time principle founded by Montgomery "I Canna Do It!" Scott, chief engineer of the starship *Enterprise*. No matter how long you estimate a job will take, multiply that time needed by 4. Not only does this give you some crush space if you run into problems, but you'll be branded a bona fide Miracle Worker if you finish early.

Chapter 7

Playing Well with Groups

● ●

In This Chapter

▶ Choosing group types

▶ Creating special groups

▶ Fine-tuning groups

▶ Customizing built-in groups

● ●

Managing user groups includes operations such as adding groups, deleting groups, editing, feeding, disciplining, and generally lording your administrative superiority over the user groups that make up your Windows 2000 community.

Who said being an administrator isn't fun?

What You Should Know

One school of thought says you should treat your users as if you were a *business owner* and they were your *customer base*. This reasoning follows the Golden Rule that you learned in third grade: You depend on users for your livelihood and you should therefore treat them well.

Yeah, right!

I'm not telling you to treat people rudely, but that just doesn't work in the harsh world of administration. If someone claims she lost a file she swears she saved to a directory that simply doesn't exist, you can pretty well bet she's wrong. (If she's right, then you have some serious supernatural problems with your network that go beyond the scope of this book!)

Instead of a store owner/customer idea, think of your user community like a small town. You're Sheriff Andy, the smartest person in town. Your users are important, but they're not customers. If you can't agree to their request, you'll have to say no and give a reasonable explanation why. It's also up to you to discipline and protect your user community (you're the police and fire chief, too) so you can ensure everyone's right to privacy, clean streets, and working printers.

Good group administration is one of your chief tools in ensuring safety and privacy, and good administration begins with knowing what options you have available and taking advantage of the organizational structure of your company, university, think-tank, or home network.

All Right, Pair Up in Groups of Three . . .

Webster's dictionary describes a *group* as ". . . a number of persons or things ranged or considered together as being related in some way." Far be it for me to argue with Mr. Webster. Of course, in Windows 2000, a group is more than a simple cluster of things — user accounts, in this case.

Groups are a landmark around which you can plot the divisions of your user accounts for easier access and control. Using groups also can improve security and channel information, and generally move your life away from the stress area known as *the hair-pulling point*.

At first glance, it may appear that using multiple user groups makes your life more complicated, forcing you to learn more information. There is some logic to this thought — after all, you wouldn't have to read this chapter if you didn't use groups.

However, it's usually a case of short-term work in exchange for handsome long-term payoffs. You know about the value of investing your time learning something. If you didn't, you wouldn't be the enviable, highly sought-after Windows 2000 administrator, you are, right?

TECHNICAL STUFF

Oh Magoo, you've done it again!

Windows administrators have their own jargon. You'll be bumping into bits and pieces of that slang as you make your way through this book.

A couple of useful (though uncomplimentary) words in basic adminese (akin to legalese) are *ostrich* and *magoo* — terms for a Windows user (particularly an administrator) who ignores pertinent information. *Ostrich* is, of course, a

reference to the bird that in folk tales sticks its head into the sand. A *magoo* is a reference to *Mr. Magoo,* an animated series starring a short-sighted gentleman voiced by Jim Backus.

These terms aren't exactly kudos, so using them isn't exactly polite. Understand them, but you might want to think twice before you use them.

Sure, I've heard of a Windows 2000 administrator successfully working without user groups — but those times were on a home system or in a company whose employee payroll is so small, the entire staff could squeeze into a phone booth. Just because you're in such a situation (the small payroll, not in a phone booth) doesn't mean you can skip this chapter and come back to it before bedtime rolls around. There are default system settings and system groups that you need to be aware of, and believe you me, it's in your best interest to learn about them. The default system groups, for example, allow you to allocate system resources and permissions for all kinds of objects on your system.

Working with user groups actually simplifies your tasks as an administrator; it allows you to apply changes to a large number of users all at once. For example, assume you want to grant access permissions to 40 of 50 users on your network. Without a grouping system, you'd have to change *each and every one* of those 40 accounts — and you may even have to edit the remaining 10 accounts to ensure that they don't have access to the same permissioned files as the original 40!

Say that the task would take you three minutes per user account. (I assume that your typing speed is a little above the *hunt and peck* variety, and that your mousing skills are also above average.) Multiplying the effort by 40, you've just burned a good three hours of your day on a relatively mundane task, and acquired a nice case of carpal tunnel syndrome to boot.

You can spare the hassle by using the groups that come with your system or those you create. Instead of three hours working on a task, you'll spend closer to ten minutes. If you're convinced that easier is better in the long run, start with the basic terminology you need to know when planning, implementing, and administering user groups in Windows 2000.

Group Concepts You Need to Know

You can plot the divisions of your user accounts around *groups*. The words listed here involve group administration. Read them, breathe them, sleep them; they are your friends.

- ✔ Permissions
- ✔ File resources
- ✔ Hardware resources
- ✔ Nesting

Which permissions permit peering, perchance?

Remember when you got that awesome Hot Wheels car you wanted and your kid brother immediately wanted to "see it?" You told him that you see with your eyes not with your hands — and rightly so. That maxim remains true in the Windows world, as well: *Seeing* is not touching. Just because a user is allowed to access a file, doesn't mean that he has complete permission to do whatever he wants with it.

There is a distinct difference in the Windows world between being able to *see* a file (open it, read it, and copy it) versus being able to *touch* a file (edit it, re-save it, and delete it). Keep this in mind: Your multiple users should be able to view a file, but you probably don't want all of them making changes to your master copy.

Permissions

These things are just what their name implies. Depending on what *permissions* are assigned to a given user, the user is allowed to access, edit, or copy files. The user is also permitted to use — or barred from using — commonly accessed pieces of hardware, such as specific servers or printers.

The capabilities each user is a given is subject to your whim; try not to be corrupted by your vast administrator power. I'd be lying if I said wielding such power weren't fun at least some of the time, but rumor has it that abusing that power is how Darth Maul got hooked up with the Dark Side of the Force in the *Star Wars* saga. . . .

File resources

People have a tendency to toss the terms *system resource* and *network resource* around as carelessly as defective hand grenades. Guess who's fault it is if you misinterpret a request for a resource as access to a folder instead of permission to print on the color laser printer?

File resources are, for lack of a better definition, any resource that exists on a computer and cannot be touched, picked up, sat on, or used as a tobacco spittoon. Why such a specific designation? Because someone could ask you for the file server resource, which is an actual PC. Because it's a material object, it flunks the touch test — it can be touched, picked up, and sat on, although it doesn't make a very handy spittoon.

TECHNICAL STUFF

To permit or not to permit, that is the question. . .

What happens if a user's permissions allow him access to a file, but his group permissions deny him access to that file? Does he have access or not?

Such a situation is called *overlapping permissions*. This can easily happen to any administrator who is working on an extremely large or complex system with user accounts that span multiple groups. My experience has been that specific user permissions override group permissions.

At base, Windows wants to grant you maximum flexibility when choosing who gets to do what. In the technical world, this is called *granularity of control*. Use it if you want to sound erudite at your next cocktail party.

Here is a related question: What if user A belongs to multiple groups group X and group Y? If I permit group X for one thing and restrict group Y from another, which permission does the user have?

The party line on this issue is that Windows 2000 is designed to follow the most conservative path. That is, given a choice between a *permit* and a *restrict* order, Windows chooses to restrict — that way, in the event of a glitch, the less damage is likely. On the other hand, there are administrators who swear by all the silicon in the Valley that Windows instead follows chronological order and grants the last permissions set that applies to the user.

If you get into a situation you're unsure of, follow this golden rule: When in doubt, test it out!

Whether someone refers to a resource as *system* or *network* is irrelevant. Those who toss around these terms want to appear more technically knowledgeable than they are. Instead of saying "I want system resource X," they should probably be saying, "I want to be able to see and edit the accounting reports for the Underhill division."

The most common file resource? Documents that at least a sizable division of the company find valuable enough to want access to on 24-7 (24 hours a day, 7 days a week). File resources are also commonly other kinds of files that you can find stored on a server, such as graphics, Excel spreadsheets, or a directory's entire contents, which may include PowerPoint files, MP3 sound bites, and Java applets. These are the kind of file resources you'll use whenever you edit a group's permissions.

Hardware resources

Hardware resources are, by definition, any resource that exists on a computer and can be touched, petted, spray-painted, or taken for a quick drag down the corridor. Common hardware resources include printers (color or black and white, inkjet or laser), file servers, and zip drives.

Keep in mind that a hardware resource *doesn't* have to be external. Say there's a CD-ROM that holds thousands of images and graphics; your company uses them for creating those annoying paper inserts that fall out of magazines as you stand in line at the grocery store reading. The CD-ROM could be kept spinning at all times in an internal CD-ROM drive on the main file server.

Just because you can't pull the CD-ROM drive out of the machine without some quick work with a Phillips screwdriver doesn't mean it can't be a hardware resource — it's just a less accessible one. Similarly, permissioning or denying a group is a little more work, but it can be done.

Nesting

If you're an administrator who performs nesting functions, there's no need to scout around the lawn for twigs, bark, and string for your young. Nesting is actually one of the more misused and abused organizational systems out there.

Nesting occurs when you add one group under another group. For instance, say you have 90 salespeople with user accounts; they're divided into three groups of 30 each. The groups are called Salty_Sales, Sour_Sales, and Soupy_Sales. For one reason or another, you want to grant all 90 salespeople access to a new group of files. Instead of granting the permissions three times, you create one mega-group, called Universal_Sales and place the three groups (Salty, Sour, and Soupy) into the one big Universal group.

You've just created a single level of nesting. The *nested groups* are the aforementioned Salty, Sour, and Soupy, which are also known as *subgroups* or *child groups,* depending on which computer tradition you come from. Any permissioning change you make to Universal_Sales affects all the groups below it — all the nested groups.

Don't abuse this system of simplification. The simple can transmogrify in no time into something much more complex and difficult to handle. Nesting groups multiple times increases the worry that the permissions you apply at one level may not filter down to the lower levels — or worse, may mix things up by granting permissions to inappropriate groups.

If you want to know the true technical way to express this, it's as follows: For every step you take toward simplicity, you sacrifice granularity of control. (*Granularity* is a nice, executive way of saying *flexibility.*)

As a rule of thumb, try to resist the siren song of *nesting simplicity.* Keep your nesting to one level.

Types of Groups

In the Windows 2000 world, there are two types of groups that you can create, edit, and assign users to. The groups are called *distribution groups* or *security groups.* Naturally, the security groups deal with system security, and the distribution group controls the distribution of information to applications. The only real difference between the two groups turns on the role each plays in your Windows network's security.

Distribution groups

Distribution groups do not play any role in providing or enhancing security on your Windows system. Applications use *distribution groups* to provide lists for their internal databases. You cannot use distribution groups for security-related purposes, such as assigning or revoking permissions for either file- or hardware-related resources.

On the other hand, these groups are handy for tasks other than permissioning. You can use a distribution group to, oddly enough, distribute information, such as sending an important e-mail to all the user accounts for members included in the selected distribution group.

Security groups

System security is a security group's primary purpose. (Say that five times really fast.) This security is not at the *networking* level, such as setting up firewalls and bastion hosts. Instead, this is the more basic — but just as important — security related to file and hardware permissioning.

News flash: Microsoft announces impending software changes!

At this point in time, Windows 2000 doesn't take full advantage of the use of distribution groups. According to the big cheeses in Seattle, this capability is due to reach the market in the near future. Only applications designed to work with the Active Directory will use this kind of distribution group.

On the drawing board right now is the latest version of Microsoft Exchange Server — the primary method by which Windows 2000 utilizes distribution groups to send out mass e-mails by group.

Security groups also allow you to assign and control resources across the entire system. Because of this, plain-vanilla security just ain't their thing. Instead, the security groups also enable you to more fairly allocate system resources like disk space or printers.

Clever and well-planned resources allocation will save you user complaints about disk space. More importantly, allocating resources in an intelligent manner can prevent waiting queues at printers or can prevent a network from getting log-jammed with requests for files from a particular server. Woohoo!

A security group has all the capabilities that a distribution group has. Again, that demonstrates that despite the name, a security group actually has a broader role to play in the system as a whole. Like distribution groups, you can use the groupings to send out targeted mass e-mails.

Various other groups are described later in this chapter. Unfortunately, things can get very confusing because of the way Microsoft has divided types of groups. There are really only two types of groups — distribution and security — which you select when you create or edit the group.

There are different kinds of groups. *Kinds* relate to the *scope* of the group. Distribution and security groups, the two *types,* relate to the *function* of the group.

A group can be *local* or *domain* in its *scope* (the logical network placement of the group, among other things), and yet it also has to be either a security or distribution group.

You can set the kind or type of group in the Active Directory database, but the type of group is more apparent at first glance. The type of group is listed at the top of the middle column in the right pane on the opening screen of the Active Directory, which you can see in Figure 7-1.

If this causes any confusion, don't worry about it. You're not alone! I hope that Microsoft comes out with some new vocabulary words for *type* and *kind* in the next upgrade for 2010. Perhaps Mr. Gates can collaborate with Mr. Webster.

Up Scope, Down Scope — Group Scopes

Groups have to be one of three kinds of groups set acccording to what Microsoft calls *scope*.

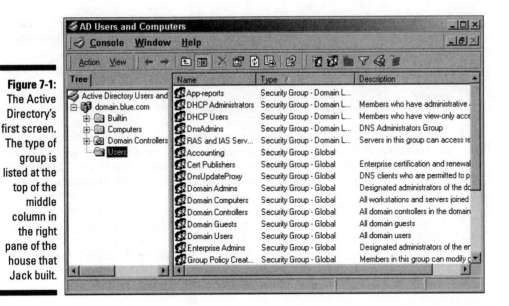

Figure 7-1:
The Active
Directory's
first screen.
The type of
group is
listed at the
top of the
middle
column in
the right
pane of the
house that
Jack built.

A group's *scope* relates directly to the network groupings available for your machines in a Windows 2000 network. (For review on the kinds of logical machines groupings, such as workgroups and domains, see Chapter 2.) Specifically, scope allows you to more easily make use of the security group functions in terms of file and other resource permissioning.

The type and scale of a group's scope determine where on the network you can assign the group's permissions. There are three types of group scopes:

- Global
- Domain local
- Universal

These grandiose names conjure up images of great scale, but are not much use in helping you remember what each one does. Fortunately, these following sections guide you through this land of darkness. Look at each to see what these group scope divisions are about.

The global group

The global group has probably the worst misnomer. *Global* makes it sound like an all-encompassing group. A *global group* is, in fact, usually a subgroup whose purpose is to organize users who share the same, or similar, network access requirements.

Global group members can come only from the local domain. However, members of a global group can use resources from any domain. The domain can be local, but is doesn't have to be.

The domain local group

Members of a *domain local group* come from a broader spectrum of locations than do global groups, but they are more limited in what they can access. A domain local group is also known as an *open membership* group. This means that you can add members to this group from any domain on your network.

Conversely, the *domain local group* does not allow its members free reign to whatever resources they choose. Instead, members of a domain local group may use only resources in the local domain. You can only assign access permissions to resources located in the local domain for these members to use. This is the case primarily because domain local groups are designed for assigning permissions to access hardware and file resources.

The universal group

The universal group has a grandiose name that it can live up to. The *universal group* really does encompass the widest scope of all the groups. To help you remember which is more inclusive, think of something global as a planet that resides inside a universe. However, you're on your own figuring out how to remember that a domain local group is somewhere in between the two!

Universal groups assign access permissions to file and hardware resources across multiple domains. Like the domain local groups, a major distinguishing feature of any universal group is that it is *open membership*. You can add members from any domain to a universal group. Unlike the domain local group designation, a universal group member can be permissioned to have all resources available to her, regardless of the domain.

Windows à lá mode

Universal groups are not available in mixed mode. By default, Windows 2000 installs in *mixed mode,* meaning it is set to work with multiple versions of Microsoft Windows, such as 98 or NT 4.0.

However, you can take advantage of the universal group designation's greater flexibility after you decide to move to a pure Windows 2000 environment. If that happy event takes place, you can switch Windows 2000 to *native mode* and successfully implement universal grouping.

For more information on how to switch modes, flip to Chapter 25.

Welcome to the Club: Rules for Membership in Group Types

Table 7-1 reveals the basic rules of each group type. When in doubt, it's best to review the table. Doing so will enable you to assign members to the right groups and understand how which scope of group can be properly nested into another.

Table 7-1	Group Membership Rules	
Group	*May Contain*	*Can Be Member Of*
Global	User accounts and other global groups in the same domain	Universal and domain local groups in any domain
Domain local	User accounts, global and universal groups from any domain, plus domain local groups from the same domain	Domain local groups in the same domain
Universal	User accounts, universal and global groups from any domain	Domain local or universal groups in any domain

Zoning out: What to keep in mind when planning your groups

Here's a chance to play *Zoning Commission*. (Don't all jump out of your seat at once; you'll get your chance.) Planning your group structure and how you will place every one of your user accounts is crucial in a large Windows network.

Some administrators feel that they need groups only to organize the target mass e-mails they send when an upgrade has come due. You know that there's more to group administration than that. It's all about resource allocation, resource allocation, resource allocation!

This level of emphasis on allocation is probably new to you if you're from the Linux or UNIX side of the world. The UNIX world is a purely *open* environment, with little or no way to channel users into particular servers or printers. (However, a knowledgeable user can do mostly as he or she pleases on a Linux or UNIX network.)

That kind of anarchic thinking doesn't quite cut it in the Windows world. System resources are a big topic; in addition, the ease of administration is much more dependent on successful group administration. Nuzzle up to the following sections and read about methods for organizing and dividing your vast numbers (hordes, gaggles, even?) of users.

To conquer, divide

Location is the old method of creating groups. With today's more complex roles, group resource allocation is much more important. You have to divide accordingly.

Dividing user accounts into groups according to job function is a much better method. I didn't say *job title,* I said *function.* When you allocate resources, you should be able to make the most efficient (that is, minimal) numbers of changes.

Accountants won't care too much about R&D specs. Engineers probably won't care about ad copy. Upper management is probably more interested about when the local golf course is going to open. Plan accordingly.

With a functional outlook in your group setup, you'll probably end up with job class titles as groups. For example, you may have the groups Accounting, Administration, Public_Relations, HR, and Dilbertme (for the engineers). After you've determined the group divisions, create a global group (for example, Accounting) and place all the user accounts that belong to your office's accountants in it.

Can't decide whether a person fits into your group designations? No worries. Assume that you have an accountant who also does a lot of human resources work. Unless there's a compelling reason not to, simply make sure that he has access to both groups — and cross your fingers that there aren't any jokes about HR going around the Accounting group.

1. **Identify which resources (file and otherwise) that you plan to assign each group.**

   Most of the time, these decisions are obvious. Files that contain records of company expenditures will probably be of more interest to HR and Accounting than to Engineering or Facilities. On the hardware side, it's probably best to allot a greater share of the color laser printers to the Marketing divisions than to the folks in Administration.

2. **Create a second group.**

   Create a domain local group for the resource(s) that go together. (Refer to "Up Scope, Down Scope — Group Scopes" in this chapter for pertinent info.) For instance, color printers may go into the Rainbow group, and legal documents may go into a Boremesilly group.

Give Misc. a miss

You're a go-getter, a hard worker, a day tripper (wait . . .), which is exactly why you will probably not make this mistake — but I have seen it before. Never, never call a group *Misc*. It (or any other form, abbreviation, or mangling of the word *miscellaneous*) may seem like a good catch-all group, but it's an insidious crutch for the lazy administrator.

After you have a group that lets you throw in anything you're not sure about, you'll find yourself straying from a clean, orderly set of user groups administered properly. Trust me on this one — place someone in the right group the first time and you'll never have to do it again.

3. **Add the appropriate global groups (which contain user accounts) to the domain local groups (which contain the needed resources).**

   Add the legal and administrative global groups to the Boremesilly domain local group to complete this example of resource allocation.

REMEMBER

Don't forget to assign the proper permissions to the global groups: that way they can access the resources in the domain local groups. Simply adding the global to the domain local groups will not grant access. It simply creates structure, not the open permissions your users need to complete their work.

When global isn't enough for your globetrotters

If it comes time to shift Windows 2000 into its native mode on a pure 2000 network, using universal groups is an option. Never thought you'd be able to do the splits? Think again. Universal groups — because they allow you to grant access to resources from outside the local domain — give you unparalleled flexibility.

Case in point: Does it matter whether your Los Angeles user can access and print documents to the laser printer in Anchorage, Alaska? Universal groups are a major asset only if your company has a reasonable number of people who move from office to office (even if only temporarily).

Say, for instance, that your company employs a group of consultants who routinely make a circuit between your offices in Seattle, Dallas, and Chicago. These folks should indeed be part of a universal group scope. They need to bounce from one domain to another, using printers and other necessary hardware in any place they touch earth while on the move.

Trial and error beats trial by fire

Never stress your nerves over allocating resources perfectly, particularly right out of the gate. Unless you're a blood relative of Nostradamus, you won't be able to get everything right. Be flexible and listen to your user complaints. If Marketing says that they have a six-person line at the color printers, you need to allocate more printers to that department.

If you don't have direct control over the company purse strings, you'll have to do some walking and talking. Mill around, snoop a bit; you may discover (for purely hypothetical example) that the programmers are using a dozen spare color printers to make their own calendar art. You have to be a fast talker to get those resources channeled to where they need to be — seldom does any group freely give up a resource, no matter how little it is needed. The whole brouhaha may remind you of a playground squabble; the administrator sometimes has to be the designated grownup.

The touch of life, the touch of death: Creating and deleting groups

Ever fantasized about being Napoleon, Orville Wright, or one of those crazy Egyptians who built the pyramids? Ever dreamed of being something more along the lines of Godzilla, Mrs. O'Leary's cow, or a killer tomato? Whether your inclinations are more toward creation or destruction, you do a little bit of both when you're a Windows administrator. A little yin, a little yang — it's good for the soul.

First things first: Make sure you're actually on the machine as the Administrative account before creating a group. I know it sounds odd, but there's always a difference between you (the user) and how your computer knows you (the user account).

Group administration is usually the first complicated thing that new Windows administrators tackle. It is also one that is a lot less frustrating if you make sure you have the authority to enforce your will upon the machine. (Domination is key here.) If you're not in as the Administrator account, log off and then come back in. Dog-ear this page if you need to; I'll wait for you to come back.

Creating your very own groups

After you have the Administrative moxie to handle the job, follow these steps to make groups:

1. **Open the Directory Management snap-in.**

2. **Choose Users and click the Action menu.**

   A pull-down menu appears.

3. **Select New from the pull-down menu.**

   A submenu appears, with choices such as Computer, Contact, Group, Printer, and so on.

4. **Select Group.**

   A new dialog box appears: New Object - Group (see Figure 7-2). By default, any group you create is global in scope and security in type. That is true because global and security are the two most actively used settings when creating a group.

5. **Fill out both the Group Name and Group Name (pre-Windows 2000) open fields.**

   In this example you create a group called **Accounting**. As a rule of thumb, try to limit your creative fancy and select intuitive names for your groups.

   All group names should be unique. If you have to create similar groups, do so with similar intuitive names that are distinguished by specific job tasks or geographic location. It is a lot easier to locate a group like Accounting or Accounting-West versus nonsensical names like Ay-of-Tranquillity or Jade-Flower.

6. **Click OK to complete the task.**

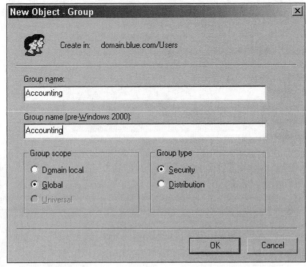

Figure 7-2: Global security: Sounds like a New Wave band.

Minimize the minimization

Minimizing and then *maximizing* a window does not have the same effect as opening and closing it. Opening and closing a window allows the Windows operating system to get on with its business behind the scenes. Minimizing and maximizing simply resize the window.

There is a funky new alternative to closing and reopening. The Refresh function is yet another Web-interface-based tool that Microsoft has imported into Windows 2000. Refresh acts just like Reload does when you're looking at a Web page.

The accompanying figure shows you some steps. Activate the Refresh function by choosing Action⇨Refresh:

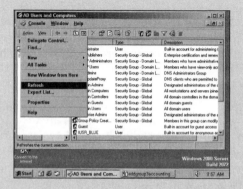

After the window refreshes, you'll see the new group (or groups, if you made multiple changes) you created. Unless you choose otherwise, the list of users and groups is in alphabetical order.

If Xena - Warrior Users doesn't appear after a refresh, scroll down to the bottom of the list before grabbing your sword and jumping to conclusions. Accounting is your example name, and it (hold onto your hats; a breakthrough bit of info here for you) begins with an *A*. You can see Accounting at the top row in the following figure.

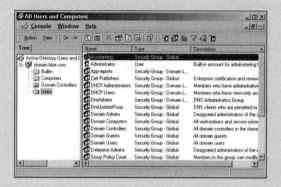

A refreshing look at windows

Take a gander at the Active Directory groups and users display immediately after you create the new group. The new group you created hasn't appeared. Figure 7-3 (doesn't) show you the (non)results.

Never fear! In an odd way, you could say that Windows 2000 prefers to operate behind the scenes. Instead of changing things in front of you, it normally performs only when not in view; it's a shy program. This is called *user transparency.*

As a matter of fact, making the changes *transparent,* or *out of sight, out of mind* is very useful. Above all else, users are concerned with the operating system's stability and performance. To display things as they work would unnerve them. This would result in a lot of telephone calls and e-mails directed to you. You don't want to spend all day reassuring users that the sky is not falling.

Adding a domain local group

The procedure for creating a domain local group is similar to creating a global group:

1. **Choose Users and click the Action menu.**

   You get a pull-down menu.

2. **Select New from the pull-down menu.**

   A submenu appears, with choices such as Computer, Contact, Group, Printer, and so on.

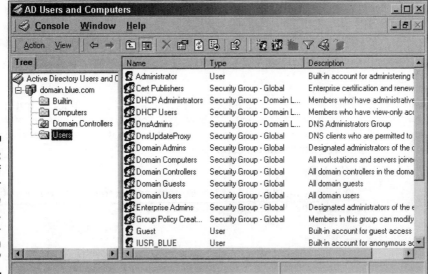

Figure 7-3: None of your changes are displayed. How anticli-mactic can you get?

3. Select Group.

The Create Object - Group dialog box appears. The default settings to any group you create in this dialog box are global in scope and security in type.

4. Click the Domain Local button.

The button is located above the Global setting in the Group Scope portion of the window.

5. Type the name App-reports **into the Group Name field.**

This is for the domain local group example.

6. Click OK when you're satisfied with your changes.

You can see how this should look in Figure 7-4.

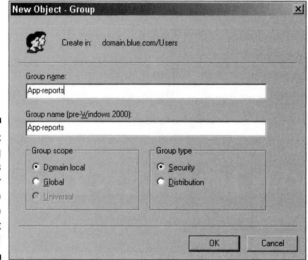

Figure 7-4:
Creating
App-reports
has never
been so
quick or so
easy. And it
dices, too!

The scope settings have been switched to domain local, but the default group type is security. This may change in future releases of Windows if Microsoft begins shipping applications that make more active use of setting distribution group types.

7. Click OK.

You may need to select the Refresh action to see the results of your work. Check out Figure 7-5 for a look.

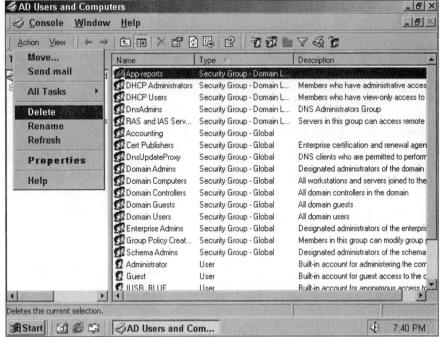

Figure 7-5:
Clicking
Refresh may
be manda-
tory. Black
tie optional.

The key to staying in Ctrl

Are you moused out? You can make your selections another way in Microsoft Windows.

Windows 2000 (and other recent Windows products like Windows 95, 98, and NT) applications always come with Ctrl keys allocated to special commands. Most selections in application panels (such as the Create Object - Group) have an underlined letter in their name.

The underlined letter is the key that you can press to activate the command. This key must be pressed at the same time as you press the Ctrl key to take effect.

It's important to know how to select the commands by key for only one reason: Should your mouse connection break or be disabled when you're in the middle of administrative tasks, things could get very messy if you exit. You can do one of two things if this occurs: Use the command keys to get to a place where you can finish the task or exit the application without crashing the system or rebooting the machine.

These Ctrl keys are not the default or even the recommended way to select commands in Windows; doing so can get very confusing. Because there are only 26 letters in the alphabet (at least the last time I checked), command letters are repeatedly reused. (Is that redundant?) Ctrl+S may mean Security here, but in a Word application it could mean Save.

And now, it's time to say goodbye

You worked, planning and executing a Windows 2000 group system that is nothing short of Michaelangelo's David. Why would you want to delete anything? Unfortunately, Windows 2000 is not like a storage attic, where you throw anything that's not immediately useful. There are many instances when you should delete user groups to keep your environment clean and easy to administer.

You should always promptly delete any groups that you no longer need. Aside from keeping your job simpler, it also increases the base level of system security. Removing defunct groups prevents you from accidentally assigning access privileges to unnecessary groups and eliminates a possible security hole.

To delete a group, follow these steps:

1. **Select the group object you want to delete.**

2. **Click the group object. Click the Action command (above the window's left pane).**

3. **Select Delete from the pull-down menu.**

   As a safeguard, Windows 2000 won't delete the selected group without asking if you're sure that you want to take this great administrative step into the unknown. Figure 7-6 shows the persistent little box.

4. **Click OK if you're sure.**

   If you click Cancel, none of the changes will be applied. You can see how this would look in Figure 7-6.

Assuming that you selected OK, the domain local group App-reports vanishes into the ether.

You can get to the Delete command another way: Right-click the group object. A pop-up menu appears; the Delete option is there. The remainder of the delete process is exactly the same, including a dialog box that ensures that your decision is final.

One for you, two for me

Editing group properties and group memberships are really one and the same thing. In the Windows world, the size and composition of the group's user account membership is also treated as a property of the group itself. You have two methods of editing group properties:

- ✔ Action menu
- ✔ Properties screen

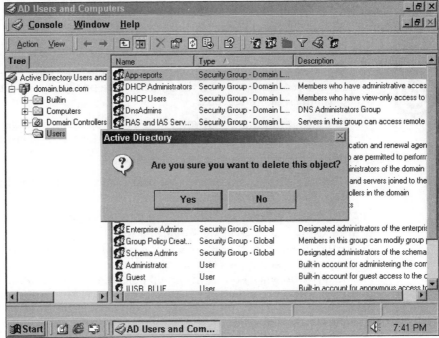

Figure 7-6:
Decisions,
decisions.

Lights, camera, Action menu

The Action menu is limited but can save you a few mouse clicks on certain basic tasks. The Action menu serves two final important functions:

- ✔ It is one method of activating the Properties screen that allows more fine-tuned control over the group's various properties.

- ✔ Use the menu for the last of the big changes to a group. The biggest change you can make to a group (aside from adding or deleting a group) is renaming it.

  This may not seem like a big deal, but reconsider: Would the masses have loved Marilyn as much if her name had remained Norma Jean? A group name change completely alters the landscape of the user account groupings (from the computer's point of view). Accordingly, you should avoid doing many group name changes unless your company's organization is going through major growth or restructure.

Here's how to use the Action menu:

1. **Click the group object you'd like to rename.**

   The group is highlighted after it is successfully selected.

2. **Select the Action menu.**

A pull-down menu appears.

3. **Choose the Rename command, as shown in Figure 7-7.**

If you want to avoid all the rigmarole, right-click the group object you want to rename and select Rename from the pop-up menu. Figure 7-8 displays the rigmarole bypass.

Regardless of the method you use, a cursor appears in the group object's Name field. The field is shaded and the cursor is inside the field.

4. **Delete the old name and type in the new.**

5. **Click anywhere on the screen or press Enter when you're finished.**

The Properties screen — Fine-tuning your changes

Who knew there were so many options for renaming groups? A group's Properties menu is another route you can take when renaming. When using the Properties menu versus the Action menu, however, you have much more fine-tuning to do when editing the group object. Action deals with fundamental changes, such as adding or deleting its existence; Properties allows you to make changes inside the group itself, without changing the overall structure on your Windows machine.

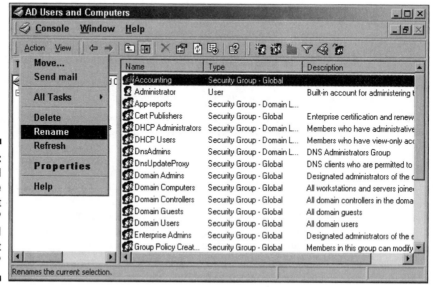

Figure 7-7:
If you could rename one group, what would it be? Kiss? Toad the Wet Sprocket?

Want to get to the Properties screen?

✔ Choose Action⇨Properties. Don't forget to select the group you want to edit by clicking it. Otherwise, you may end up editing the properties of a completely different group than you intended. See Figure 7-9 for some lights and some camera.

✔ Right-click the group you want to edit.

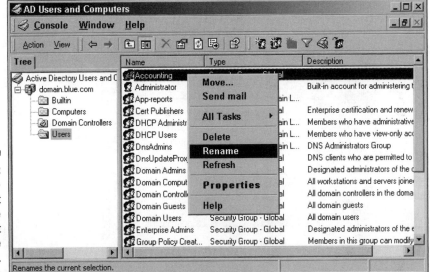

Figure 7-8: This short-cut doesn't turn into the longest route possible.

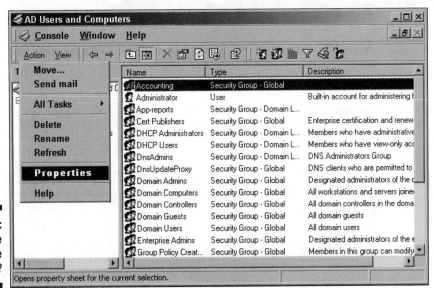

Figure 7-9: Wanna see some action?

Whichever way you access it, the Properties screen comes up to the General information pane. The pane, which comes up by default, is shown in Figure 7-10.

The General panel allows you to add several bits of information, such as a description of the group. That's very useful if you've called groups names like THX-1148, Bad Hair Day Users, or Major Mojo.

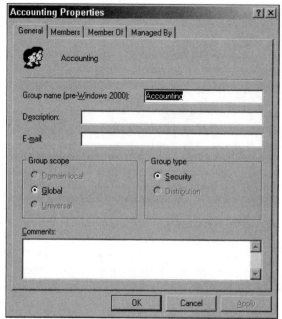

Figure 7-10: It's not an inspiring sight, but it helps you get your work done.

Not bucking the system: Working with built-in system groups

Groups are built into your Windows 2000 system during the installation process. When you create a Windows 2000 domain grouping of machines, built-in global groups such as the following are created:

- Domain users
- Domain guests
- Enterprise administrators

These built-in groups offer a baseline when you start using your Windows 2000 network — particularly if you add new user accounts before completing the design and implementation of the group structure you want. By default, an added new guest user account is placed in the domain guest group. Similarly, an added new user is placed in the domain user group until you assign it elsewhere.

The default domain local groups are a second built-in system. The default domain local groups are automatically set up for allocating system permissions and administrative rights. You can view these groups by clicking the Builtin folder in the Active Directory's Users and Computers screen. Sneak a peek at Figure 7-11.

Membership in any of these groups determines the rights and privileges of the user account.

✔ General users are placed in the Users group.

✔ Accounts with the privileges of setting up and managing networked printers on the domain controllers are located in the Print Operators group.

✔ Accounts with administrative rights reside in the Administrators group.

Don't give out too many of these administrative rights — even ones that seem less consequential, such as printing setup. Too many people with the ability to go around the administrator will stunt your ability to allocate network resources (and maybe even your growth, but those results aren't confirmed). Besides, controlling permissions and access increases your power and makes the job more fun.

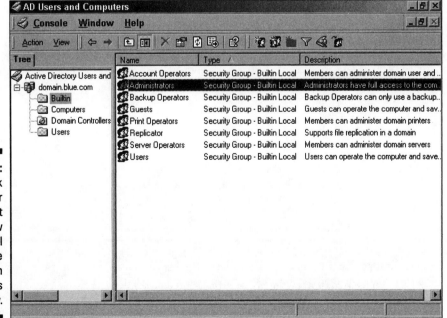

Figure 7-11:
Take a look out your right window pane; you'll see the domain local groups below.

Don't let picking up the tab become a pane in the neck

Panels, panes, and tabs (oh, my!) are terms that everyone likes to apply to anything that can have a label slapped on it. *Panes* are subdivisions of a window, as in the Microsoft Windows system. You can have a left pane and a right pane, like the Active Directory window does.

You can also have panes that are *stacked* behind one another, like the Properties screen has. These panes (in the neck) can only be brought to the foreground one at a time. Because they're not all visible at once like the panes in a window (the regular kind, not the Microsoft kind), they're called *panels*.

To access each in turn, you need to click the name of the pane, which is displayed at the top of the panel. (The name of the pain when it rains in Spain is normally something like General or Members.) This part of the panel is what's called a *tab* because it resembles the divider tab you find to label a manila folder in a filing cabinet.

The Group Properties screen has an additional three panels; more substantive changes can be made there. For example, clicking the Members tab shown in the accompanying figure takes you to the screen that allows you to add group members. The newly created group is empty by default, so the screen is blank.

Accounting Properties   ? | ×

General | Members | Member Of | Managed By

Members:

Name	Active Directory Folder

[Add...]   [Remove]

[OK]   [Cancel]   [Apply]

Clicking the Add button lets you add users, groups, or resources: It stands to reason, no? The only restriction that Windows 2000 places on you at this point is preventing the nesting of a higher-level group, such as Universal under Global. Obviously, the reverse is okay and is even expected.

Chapter 8

Dealing with Disks

· ·

In This Chapter

▶ Reviewing the Disk Management utility

▶ Viewing disks and volumes graphically

▶ Finding your disk properties

▶ Understanding basic and dynamic disks

▶ Locating, moving, adding, and remotely managing disks

▶ Upgrading disks from basic to dynamic

▶ Re-scanning disks

▶ Restoring previous disk configurations

· ·

*T*o any experienced administrator, the art of disk management is always a case of feast or famine, because your data production and data storage needs will never, ever truly be in synch with each other. Like a reluctant bottle of ketchup fresh out of the refrigerator, you're either going to get nothing, or you'll get a Niagara Falls–size torrent pouring down when you least expect it.

First, you need to understand that your system, even if 99 percent of the users are on vacations in Tahiti celebrating the cashing of their dot-com company stock options, is still producing data. The system creates data in the same way that we humans burn off calories — when at rest, the burn rate is much lower, but it never stops. For your system, the data production comes mostly from logs and other monitoring processes. So unless you're especially rigorous about going through the system with your cybernetic weed whackers, you're always going to suffer some *space erosion*, even when activity is at a minimum.

Second, in a normal business week, you're going to have *spikes* of data coming in that impact your space allotments. Users download files off the Internet or upload files they've been working on at home, and nothing irks a user more than running out of space. Always try to build as large a *buffer zone* between your space limit and what typically resides on the system.

Finally, understand that just as data can come in sharp increments, so will your storage capacity. To my knowledge, nobody installs a 500MB hard drive 1MB at a time over a month. Instead, you'll go from famine to feast in no time. But beware! Users in the know always want a slice of the new space, and given enough time, the amount of data in any system will expand to fill the space available.

So remember the old saying about disk space, told to me by a very wise administrator: "There are those who need more disk space, and there are those who don't use computer systems."

To help you make the most efficient use of the disk space that you do have, Microsoft's latest advance in disk-administration technology is unearthed here. You also dig up how to monitor space usage and even change disks from basic to dynamic. Best of all, you shake off the dirt and see that with Windows 2000 you can perform these changes without having to shut down or even halt the system.

Introducing the New Disk Management Utility

In a nutshell, you must be able to monitor the health of your hard drives and the space available on your equipment, as well as be able to format or install new hard drives as you fill up the old ones. If anyone tells you, "Oh, don't worry about installing or formatting drives, you'll never need to do that *here*," you have my permission to smack them with a copy of this book. In hardcover, if necessary.

What happened to my Disk Administrator?

If you're from the Windows NT world, you may be wondering what happened to the Disk Administrator utility. (If Windows 2000 is your first exposure to Windows network product, don't worry about it — you *are* the Disk Administrator, okay?) The Disk Management utility was designed to replace the Disk Administrator utility used in Windows NT 4.0.

Whether you're new to the Windows world or not, Windows 2000 comes with a couple of new features you need to know how to use effectively. To Wild Bill's credit, most of these new features are ones that make Windows administration even more powerful.

Luckily, the kind folks at Gates Gulch in Seattle have provided you with an all-new Disk Management utility — a built-in solution for managing hard disks and the partitions that reside on the drives. You can use Disk Management in creating or formatting volumes with file systems. You can also initialize disks, create fault-tolerant disk systems, leap tall buildings in a single bound . . . you get the idea.

Mounting drives

The Disk Management utility allows you to mount a local drive at any empty folder on a local NTFS-formatted volume. When you mount a drive, you make it accessible to the system as a whole, which in turn gives you more flexibility to manage your data storage.

Using dynamic disks

Dynamic disks are one of the best things to come along (in the technical sense) since mouse pads. Dynamic disks allow you to go about your administrative tasks without shutting down the system. Because you won't be interrupting users, using dynamic disks is another example of user transparency, as discussed in Chapter 7.

With this new system, you can work in the Disk Management utility to create, extend, mirror a volume, or add a new disk without rebooting the system. From any networked Windows 2000 computer, you can manage any other computer running a variant of Windows 2000 (as long as you have administrative privileges to run Disk Management, of course).

TECHNICAL STUFF

Da wiz, da wiz, da wunnerful Wizard of Oz

What is a wizard? In the technical sense, a *wizard* is a person with a lot of networking and administrative know-how. (True techno-geeks may call me on this definition, claiming that true masters are called *gurus,* but I won't get into that level of hair splitting.)

Taking advantage of this magically and technically enhanced term, Microsoft and many other companies have taken to calling any program that takes your input and automatically performs a task for you a wizard program.

You won't use wizards much. As stated before in this book's Introduction, you need to know how and why something is done, which won't happen if you rely on wizards to do the dirty work for you. Later on, when you're in a rush and don't feel like digging around in a reference book, feel free to click the button or rub the magic lamp to call out your personal wizard program.

Better yet, the Disk Management utility is, on the whole, more simple and intuitive than the older Disk Administrator utility. As with group and user management, right-click menus now exist to show you which tasks you can perform on the selected object. In many cases, you even have wizards to steer you through tasks such as creating partitions.

Graphic, Shocking Displays of Disks and Volumes

As long as you're logged on as the Administrator account or a member of the Administrators group, you can view your disk settings graphically. To do so, you use the Disk Management utility, which displays your disks with all the relevant data. This feature is a real advance for Windows administrators because the graphic representations make your procedures and judgment calls more intuitive. It's also a logical extension of the GUI-based nature of the Windows product.

To start the Disk Management utility:

1. **On the main Windows desktop toolbar, click the Start button and choose Settings⇨Control Panel.**

2. **Double-click Administrative Tools and then double-click Computer Management.**

   Alternatively, you can click Start, choose Programs⇨Administrative Tools. In the Administrative Tools submenu, select Computer Management. Use whichever way you find more intuitive. You'll arrive at the same screen.

   The somewhat mislabeled Computer Management screen appears.

3. **Call up the Disk Management utility in the console tree residing in the left window pane. Click Disk Management (located under the Storage icon).**

   If you need to increase or decrease the size of each pane, drag the divider bars between the window panes.

If you see the Storage icon but not Disk Management, then click the plus sign to the immediate left of the Storage icon. Because Disk Management is stored in tree format underneath Storage, you'll be able to see it after you open the icon setting.

TIP

To hide or display the console tree, on the standard button toolbar, click the Show/Hide Console Tree icon. (This icon is not very intuitive, but then again, what kind of picture can you make that describes Show/Hide Console?) If you need to find it, just count over four icons down the toolbar from the left, past the Action and View menus. You shouldn't need to use this option unless you're unfortunate enough to have multiple disks to view, and you're on a cheapie 14-inch computer monitor.

If you select a volume in the list view of volumes in the top pane, the regions of the disks that make up that volume are selected in the graphical view of disks. In Figure 8-1, clicking Disk Management under Storage in the left pane brings up the Disk Management panes, displaying the volumes (top) and the available disks (bottom). According to the Disk Administrator, one disk is on this machine, in the NTFS format and weighing in at a little less than 2 gigabytes.

In the top pane, the only volume available is called C:. If you selected this volume, the entire disk graphic in the lower-right pane would be shaded, indicating that this volume takes up the entire drive.

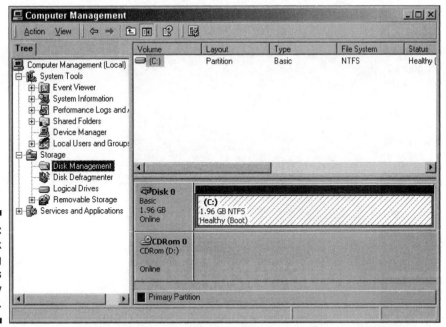

Figure 8-1: The disk being viewed is set up very simply.

Scoping out your disk properties

As in Group Management, you can call up the Properties screen by opening the Active Directory or Command Console, and selecting the disk object and using the Action menu. You can also get to it by right-clicking in the graphical view of the disk list (bottom pane) and then selecting Properties.

The Properties dialog box lists information about the physical disk as well as the volumes it contains. By default, you get the General information on the disk, including the file system on the disk, the label (if any), and a pie-chart representation of the used and free space left on the disk. Of course, all you number freaks out there can find the used and free space is also displayed in Bytes, Giga, Mega, and Econo-Pack.

See Figure 8-2 for an example of the detailed, yet easy-to-read, Properties screen.

Figure 8-2: The Properties screen defaults to the General setting, which displays data on the disk selected and a pie graphic showing disk space.

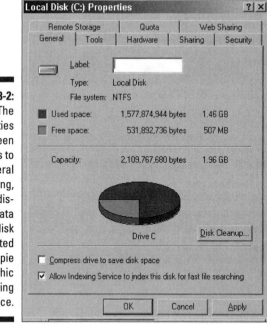

Similarly, if you want to view the properties of one of the volumes listed on the main Disk Management screen, right-click the volume and then select Properties.

The multiple panels in the Properties window give you information on everything you could possibly ask for. For starters, under the Hardware panel, you can see the company that manufactured the disk (a very helpful tool if things start slipping and you need warranty information before you rip the drive out of the box). Under Sharing, you can view the Sharing permissions enabled on the disk, and under Quota, you can see the system you've set up (if any) to regulate disk space.

Basic versus dynamic disks

Ready for another bash at new Windows 2000 terminology? There, there. Take another sip of java and come back when you're ready. Besides, what you're about to get in on is pretty darn cool.

Disk Management supports basic and dynamic disks. *Basic* disks use the partition-oriented scheme that should be familiar to anyone with Windows NT Server 4.0 administration experience. You can use both basic and dynamic disks on the same computer system, but a volume that spans multiple disks can only have one type of disk in it, basic or dynamic.

By default, when you installed Windows 2000, your hard disks were automatically initialized as basic disks. In the upgrade procedure, partitioned disks are automatically initialized as basic disks, so you can maintain partitions and volumes created with Windows NT Server 4.0 and not have your data boiled away into the silicon ether.

Tasks restricted to basic disks include

- ✔ Creating and deleting primary and extended partitions
- ✔ Creating and deleting logical drives within an extended partition
- ✔ Formatting a partition and marking it as active
- ✔ Deleting volume sets, stripe sets, mirror sets, and stripe sets with parity
- ✔ Breaking a mirror from a mirror set
- ✔ Repairing a mirror set or a stripe set with parity

You can initialize new or empty disks as basic or dynamic after installation. (As a rule, just assume that any data that you have on a basic disk will be blown away during a changeover to the dynamic format.)

A *dynamic* disk is a physical disk that contains dynamic volumes created using Disk Management. Unlike the garden-variety basic disk, dynamic disks can't contain partitions or logical drives. You also can't access dynamic disks using MS-DOS, primarily due to the disruption that a traditional partition would suffer if you removed or replaced the drive without shutting down the entire system first.

Tasks restricted to dynamic disks include

✔ Creating and deleting simple, spanned, striped, mirrored, and RAID-5 volumes

✔ Extending simple or spanned volumes

✔ Removing a mirror from a mirrored volume or splitting the volume into two volumes

✔ Repairing mirrored or RAID-5 volumes

✔ Reactivating missing or off-line disks

Both basic and dynamic disks allow you to

✔ Check disk properties such as capacity, available free space, and current status.

✔ View volume and partition properties such as size, drive-letter assignment, label, type, and file system.

✔ Establish drive-letter assignments for disk volumes or partitions and for CD-ROM devices.

✔ Establish disk sharing and security arrangements for a volume or partition.

✔ Upgrade a basic disk to dynamic or revert a dynamic disk to basic.

The Disk Management utility supports legacy volumes that exceed a single partition on more than one hard disk, but it doesn't allow you to create new ones.

Incidentally, a *legacy volume* (which sounds like something a deceased administrator would leave you in his will) is a volume created with a pre–2000 version of Windows.

Nobody's perfect: Limitations of dynamic disks and dynamic volumes

As a whole, dynamic disks and volumes sound like the way to go. However, although they may seem like the wave of the future, the dynamic duo of the Windows world do come with some problems. For example, dynamic disks cannot be supported on portable computers, which can be a serious limitation if you're part of a company or organization that has a large percentage of personnel on the go with laptops.

Luckily, this problem is a relatively benign one. Rather than creating multiple problems for you at present or in the future, it's more of a simple limitation. If you view a disk using the Disk Management utility on a laptop and right-click a disk in the graphical or list view, you won't see the option to upgrade the disk to a dynamic one.

In the following sections, I discuss several situations in which dynamic volumes have multiple limitations.

Installing Windows 2000

If a you create a dynamic volume from unallocated space on a dynamic disk, you won't be able to install Windows 2000 on that volume. The setup limitation occurs because Windows 2000 Setup only recognizes dynamic volumes that contain partition tables.

Partition tables are structures that appear only in basic volumes and in dynamic volumes that went through the upgrade process from basic to dynamic. Simply creating a new dynamic volume on a dynamic disk does not create a partition table.

Extending a volume

The flip side of the preceding problem is that if you have a basic volume that was upgraded to dynamic (by upgrading the basic *disk* to dynamic), then you can install Windows 2000 on that volume. However, you can't extend the volume if you need more space on the volume.

According to Microsoft, you can't use an extended volume because the boot volume, which contains the Windows 2000 files, can't be part of a spanned volume. If you extend a volume that was upgraded from basic to dynamic, then it contains a partition table. In that case, Windows 2000 Setup recognizes the spanned volume but can't install to it because the boot volume can't be part of a spanned volume.

Only a couple dynamic volumes allow you to install Windows 2000 on the volume itself. These include simple and mirrored volumes, and these volumes must contain a partition table, which in turn means that these volumes must complete the upgrade process from basic to dynamic. Luckily, you find out exactly how to do just that a little later in this chapter.

Volumes that span multiple disks

When you perform an upgrade of a basic to a dynamic disk, you can also use the Disk Management tool's graphic display to determine whether the basic disk resides on multiple disks. The Disk Management screen clearly displays the basic disk that contains any volumes that reside on multiple disks (such as mirrored, striped, spanned, or RAID-5 volumes). If this is the case, you need to upgrade all other disks that contain part of the volumes to dynamic.

Why the RAID? Are there bugs in the machine?

RAID really doesn't have anything to do with insecticide. RAID stands for Redundant Array of Inexpensive Disks. It's an almost foolproof — but very expensive and complex — way of storing data across multiple disks. It's only used by corporations with warehouses full of data and with huge data-storage needs, so it's a bit beyond the scope of what I cover in this book.

Also (to make things more complex), if these other disks *also* contain additional volumes that reside on multiple disks, you must then upgrade all disks that contain parts of these volumes. In a nutshell, you have to upgrade all of these disks together.

More details on the limitations, advice, and rules to keep in mind when performing a basic to dynamic disk upgrade are also a little further on in this chapter.

According to Microsoft's documentation, each of the disks in question must have at least 1MB of unallocated space at the end of the disk or else the upgrade will fail. This is often called the *1MB Rule.*

Locating a new disk

Adding a new disk to your system does not require you to use the Disk Management utility until after the disk's physical installation. After you install the disk, open the Disk Management utility. On the utility screen, choose Action⇨Rescan Disks. If you're from the UNIX side of doing things, Rescan operates very much like the probe-scsi command you're used to seeing on your Linux, Sun, or HP boxes.

If the Disk Management utility doesn't detect the new disk after you select Rescan Disks, you may need to restart your computer. Remember that newly added hard disks are added to the computer as basic disks. Of course, you can always upgrade the new disk to a dynamic one using the upgrade process described in this chapter.

Moving disks to another computer

Before you disconnect the disks, make sure the status of the volumes on the disks is Healthy. You can determine the status of the disk by opening the Disk Management utility. By default, the disks and volumes are listed with the size, type, and status. If the status of the volumes are not Healthy due to some physical failure of the disk drive, disk head, or corruption of the data, repair the volumes immediately before the disks are physically moved.

After the disk checks out as healthy, shut down the computer. Next, turn off the computer (*shutting down* and *powering down* are two separate ideas . . . but you knew that). Remove the physical disks for installation on the other computer. Complete your installation. Restart the original computer that contained the hard disks you moved.

Open Disk Management and choose Action⇨Rescan Disks. Right-click any disk marked Foreign, click Import Foreign Disks, and then follow any instructions that appear on your screen.

After you import a dynamic disk from another computer, you can see and use any existing volumes on that disk. Whenever you remove or import disks to a different computer, you must choose Action⇨Rescan Disks, and then verify that the disk information is correct.

Managing Disks on a Remote Computer

When attempting to manage a disk on a remote computer, remember that both the client and server computers must be members of the same domain. Alternatively, the computer must be within a trusted domain. The user of the client computer must be a member of the Administrators or Server Operators group on the remote computer.

To begin the remote administration process,

1. **Click the Start button and select Run.**

2. **In the box that appears (see Figure 8-3), type** mmc **and click OK.**

   The Console menu appears.

3. **Click Add/Remove Snap-in.**

   The Snap-In screen appears.

4. **Click the Add button.**

   As shown in Figure 8-4, the Add Standalone Snap-In screen appears, asking which snap-in to add.

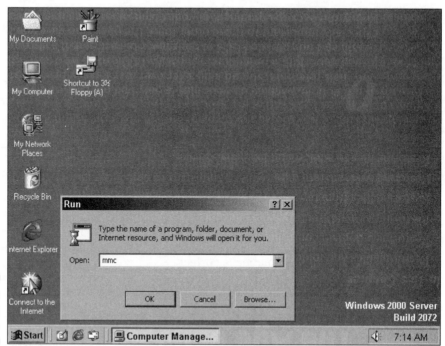

Figure 8-3:
The Run
dialog box.

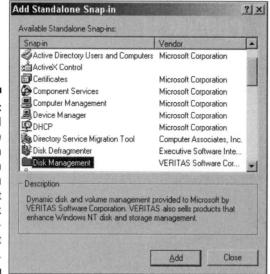

Figure 8-4:
The Add
Standalone
Snap-in
screen
allows you
to select
the Disk
Manage-
ment
snap-in tool.

5. **Click Disk Management and then click the Add button.**

   The Choose Computer screen appears, asking you to select the computer that holds the remote disk you want to administer (see Figure 8-5).

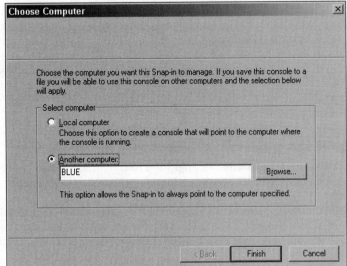

6. **Select Another Computer and then type the name of the remote computer in the empty field immediately below.**

   If for some reason you can't remember exactly what computer you wanted to look at, click the Browse button to the right of the open field. You are rewarded with a list of the machines you can access.

7. **Click the Finish button to complete your task.**

Upgrading a basic disk to a dynamic one

The key to success? Bet you didn't know that 1 megabyte of free disk space is the answer, did you? That is, the answer to successfully upgrading from a basic to dynamic disk. The Disk Management utility automatically reserves this free space when creating partitions or volumes on a disk. However, if you created disks with partitions or volumes using a different operating system than the Microsoft standard, the free space needed for this operation may not be available.

Closing up shop

Before you begin upgrading a disk from basic to dynamic, close any programs running on those disks. Also be sure to make a complete backup of any data you have stored there. You'll sleep better at night knowing that you can undo any alterations you've made.

After you complete the upgrade of a basic disk to a dynamic disk, any existing partitions on the basic disk become (dynamic) simple volumes. You can't change the dynamic volumes back to partitions. Also, after an upgrade, a dynamic disk can't contain partitions or logical drives. Additionally, the disk can't be accessed by MS-DOS or by Windows operating systems other than Windows 2000. (Sound elitist? Maybe, but it does promote a single disk-to-operating system standard.)

Using the wrong side of the Force

System and boot partitions are upgraded to dynamic volumes after you restart the computer. All other partitions and basic volumes are upgraded immediately. However, if a partition or basic volume on the disk that you're upgrading is in use, an event known as *force dismounting* occurs, which means that any programs using the volume are automatically disconnected. If the volume can't be force dismounted, then you'll be forced to restart the computer.

Keeping in mind a few little rules

Here are some additional rules and limitations to keep in mind:

- ✔ **Boot and system partitions:** You can upgrade a basic disk containing the system or active partitions to a dynamic disk. After the disk is upgraded and the computer is rebooted, these partitions become simple system or active volumes.

  You can upgrade a basic disk containing the boot partition (which contains the Windows 2000 operating system) to a dynamic disk. After the disk is upgraded and you restart the computer, the boot partition becomes a simple boot volume.

- ✔ **Disks with sector sizes larger than 512 bytes:** You won't be able to upgrade a basic disk to a dynamic disk if the sector size of the disk is larger than 512 bytes.

- ✔ **Other operating systems:** You'll run into problems if you upgrade a disk with a partition that contains an operating system other than the Windows 2000 operating system. If that additional operating system is currently running, you're headed straight for trouble.

  You won't be able to start the computer from that operating system after the upgrade. Shut down the additional operating system before you continue down the upgrade path or you'll hit a brick wall of resistance.

✔ **Reinstalling the Windows 2000 OS:** You can perform a fresh installation of Windows 2000 on a dynamic volume if that volume was upgraded from a basic volume. Upgrading a volume from *basic* to *dynamic* reserves the partition table information. You'll need this table information to perform fresh installations of Windows 2000 on dynamic volumes.

✔ **Reverting to basic disks:** After you upgrade a basic disk to a dynamic disk, you can't simply change the dynamic volumes back into partitions. Instead, you have to delete every single one of the dynamic volumes on the disk. You have to use the Revert to Basic Disk command, which is located under the Action menu in the Disk Management window.

Performing the upgrade

Ready to go? Let's rock and roll!

1. **Open the Disk Management utility.**

2. **Right-click the basic disk that you want to upgrade.**

   A pop-up menu appears.

3. **Click Upgrade to Dynamic Disk and follow the instructions on your screen.**

   If you don't see the Upgrade command, you may be right-clicking a volume instead of a disk. Alternatively, the disk may have been previously upgraded to a dynamic disk, or the computer is a portable laptop computer.

Keep in mind that dynamic disks just aren't supported for laptops, no matter how powerful and important they may be to your organization.

After you upgrade a basic disk to a dynamic disk, you can't change the dynamic volumes back to partitions. Instead, you must delete all dynamic volumes on the disk and then use the Revert to Basic Disk command.

Re-scanning disks

Whenever you change your disk configuration, use the Rescan Disks command. The changes will likely not appear in Disk Management (that same old creature, *user transparency,* raising its ugly head again). When the Disk Management utility re-scans disks, it scans all attached disks for disk configuration changes. It also automatically updates information on removable media, CD-ROM drives, basic volumes, file systems, and drive letters.

To use the command, open the Disk Management utility and choose Action⇨Rescan Disks.

Reverting a dynamic disk to a basic disk

Does your dynamic disk want to go out dancing all the time? Flirt too much when you do? You can change your dynamic disk back into a basic disk if you like — but be prepared to spend lots of time watching movies at home.

1. **Open Disk Management.**

2. **Right-click the dynamic disk you want to have turned back into a basic disk.**

3. **Select the Revert to Basic Disk command.**

   Alternatively, choose Action⇨Revert to Basic Disk.

Remember that you must remove all volumes from the dynamic disk before you can change it back to a basic disk. After you change a dynamic disk back to a basic disk, you can create only partitions and logical drives on that disk.

Restoring disk configuration information

Luckily, for this segment of administration, restoration of a previous configuration is pretty easy.

1. **Insert a floppy disk into the machine's floppy disk drive.**

   The floppy disk must contain the disk configuration information from a previous version of Windows 2000 (Windows NT 4.0 and other earlier versions of Windows).

2. **Open the Disk Management utility and choose Action⇨Restore Basic Disk Configuration, as shown in Figure 8-6.**

   Follow the instructions on your screen, being sure to click the Finish button at the end of the procedure.

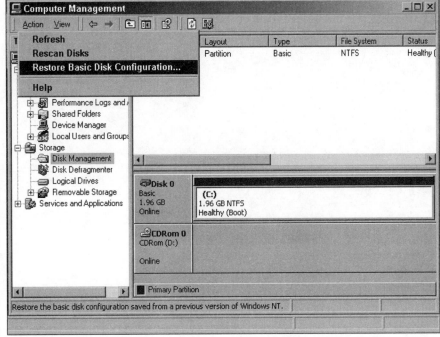

Figure 8-6:
In the Disk Management Utility, the Restore Basic Disk command is found under the Action menu.

If you perform a restoration, this procedure overwrites existing basic disk configuration information with a previously saved configuration.

Chapter 9

Putting Up Partitions

● ●

In This Chapter

▶ Brushing up on some terminology

▶ Choosing between NTFS, FAT, and FAT32

▶ Multiple operating systems and file-system compatibility

▶ Planning disk partitions

▶ Working with volumes

▶ Mirroring volumes

● ●

*I*f you've just come from Chapter 8, you now have a good handle on all the real estate that you have under your control. Whether you have 500 megabytes to play with or 500 gigabytes, it's yours to do with as you see fit. Why think of it as real estate? Because—much like real property—the size of the estate is a major determinant of what you'll be doing with it, whether constructing mini-malls or skyscrapers.

The real estate scenario is also useful because as the mayor of your user community, you're back to putting on your zoning commissioner hat again. Now that you know the boundaries of your power, it's time to decide what to put on the property. How to divide the space into *parcels* (called partitions or volumes in the Windows 2000 world) is the topic of this chapter. So put away the surveying equipment, compass, and plumb bob — it's time to find out how you can make most efficient use of the space you have available to you, whether it's the (virtual) size of the state of Alaska, or the dimensions of a broom closet.

Dipping into the Terminology Well

Yes, it's time to bash away at Windows terminology again. But sending you forward into the chapter without this information would deprive you of what you're going to need in the upcoming chapter. And as the old saying goes, you don't want to show up at a gunfight with a Swiss Army knife.

Are file systems saturated FAT, polyunsaturated FAT, or trans-FAT?

Regardless of how much you stuff into a given file system, its dimensions don't change. So FAT isn't an indication of how big or small a given file system actually is. FAT stands for the more sensible acronym, *File Allocation Table.*

The Microsoft folks, when building NT and Windows 2000, could have stuck with one of the older, more established file-system types. But

did they? Nooooo, that wasn't good enough for Microsoft. So they developed their own standard, called NTFS. NTFS, which stands for (logically enough) NT File System, has several extra capabilities, the main one being that it causes a real pain in the neck to anyone who wants to use some other kinds of file system on a Windows NT or Windows 2000 network.

File system

Whether you know it or not, you probably already have several kinds of file system in your house or office. A *file system* is nothing more than a structure, whether physical or virtual, that provides organization to a group of objects. Your office Rolodex is one. Your phone book is another. And if your bedroom is anything like mine, you have a file system for your dirty clothes, called a *pile.*

The file system on a computer keeps your data organized, tracks where it resides, and acts as a gatekeeper by checking the permissions of anyone who tries to access the files under its control. File systems come in several flavors, such as DOS FAT, FAT32, and other types.

Partition

You create a partition whenever you split the physical disk into two or more parts. Most people, unless they own a 100-gigabyte hard drive or are on a network, never need to split their disk. For them, they may have just the C: drive, which consists of one partition (that spans the whole disk) filled with directories and files within the directories.

Partitions fall into one of two categories: either *primary* or *extended.* A primary partition is one used by the operating system itself. An extended partition is one you create with the remaining free space on your drive. You may only have one extended segment on any given physical hard disk.

A gaggle of gigabytes

Incidentally, you'll see references to disk space crop up again and again through this whole section. The strangest measurements are cited next to disk numbers: MB, GB, and TB.

No, these aren't blood types or the results of allergy tests. They're the most common abbreviations for an amount of data that a physical disk can hold. A *byte* is a piece of information (and for you technical types, no, I'm not getting into what a *bit* or a *chomp* is).

MB, or *megabyte,* stands for enough space to hold one million bytes. GB, or *gigabyte,* is enough space for one billion bytes. TB stands for *terabyte,* which is so incredibly huge that you only find it on a handful of the largest machines. Suffice it to say that if you're administering one of these monsters, you'll soon find out why it's called a "terror-byte"!

Volume

A volume is a partition or group of partitions that has been set aside. Aside for what? Volumes can only be allocated for use by file system flavors NTFS and FAT. One could say that *volumes* are a fancy, Microsoft-centric name for partitions, but that's not really the case. With volumes, you can use the disk space for special uses, such as *mirroring*, which you discover more about later in this chapter.

The Menu of Choices in Windows 2000: FAT, FAT32, and NTFS

Like a diner at a four-star restaurant, you have three main courses to choose from in the Windows 2000 world when it comes to formatting your hard drive. Which file system should you format it as? Windows 2000 supports NTFS, the File Allocation Table (FAT), and FAT32. Whichever you ultimately choose will be affected by what you want, what you need, and what's actually available. NTFS, the specially designed Microsoft file system, is, of course, the recommended choice for those administering Windows 2000 systems because it supports several special features that the others don't have (see the later section "Why choose NTFS?" for more).

NTFS has always been a more powerful file system than FAT and FAT32. Windows 2000 Server includes a new version of NTFS, with support for a variety of features including Active Directory, which is needed for domains, user accounts, and other important security features. You can use the Setup program to convert your partition to the new version of NTFS from FAT or FAT32.

Keep in mind, however, that choosing NTFS is slightly limiting because Windows 2000 is the only operating system that recognizes NTFS! Therefore, your main consideration must be whether you'll ever realistically plan to access files on that volume or partition from other operating systems, such as Windows 95, 3.1, or MS-DOS.

Always remember that formatting a partition *erases all data* on that partition. Take the time to go through a partition with a fine-toothed search engine and determine where anything valuable is that you want to move off the partition (such as the company payroll). Doing so can save you innumerable gray hairs, heart palpitations, and sweaty runs from the building as the user community hunts you down with torches and pitchforks.

Unlike reformatting the partition, *converting* a file system doesn't place your files at risk. Of course, if you don't have any files on the partition — or the ones there are of very limited value, like out-of-date Pokemon trading cards — you're best off formatting the partition with NTFS rather than converting it. You're better off doing this because a partition that's formatted with NTFS, rather than converted from FAT or FAT32, has less fragmentation and better performance. (Of course, NTFS has better performance all around than FAT and FAT32, whether the partition has been formatted or converted.)

Additionally, you can convert a partition to NTFS after the Setup procedure by using the Convert.exe utility. If you've inherited a Windows 2000 system that could use a conversion or two, follow the Convert.exe instructions when running it. To start Convert.exe:

1. **Click the Start button and select Run.**

   The Run dialog box appears.

2. **Type** cmd **in the Open field, and press Enter.**

   A DOS shell command window appears.

3. **At the command prompt, type** help convert **and press Enter.**

   The first of a series of help screens appears to guide you through the conversion process (see Figure 9-1).

```
Select C:\WINNT\System32\cmd.exe                                    _ □

Microsoft Windows 2000 [Version 5.00.2072]
(C) Copyright 1985-1999 Microsoft Corp.

C:\Documents and Settings\Administrator>help convert
Converts FAT volumes to NTFS.

CONVERT volume /FS:NTFS [/V]

  volume       Specifies the drive letter (followed by a colon),
               mount point, or volume name.
  /FS:NTFS     Specifies that the volume to be converted to NTFS.
  /V           Specifies that Convert should be run in verbose mode.

C:\Documents and Settings\Administrator>
```

Figure 9-1:
The first of
Convert's
help
screens.

Why choose FAT and FAT32?

FAT and FAT32 are sort of default file-system options. I say *sort of* because they are system defaults for any Windows product except for Windows NT and 2000. If you've inherited a system that pre-dates the recent releases of Windows NT, you're sure to find some machines with partitions that are formatted with FAT or FAT32.

If you truly want to format a file system as FAT or FAT32, use FAT32 on partitions that are 2GB or larger or regular old FAT on partitions that are smaller than 2GB. In the big scheme of things, FAT and FAT32 are similar to each other, except that FAT32 is designed for larger disks than FAT. Of course, although FAT32 is more efficient at keeping things in order on a large partition, the fastest all-around file system for large disks is still NTFS.

During Setup, if you choose to format a partition as FAT, Windows automatically detects whether the size of the partition is over 2GB in size. If the partition is larger than 2GB, Setup automatically changes to format the file system as FAT32.

Although NTFS is the *de facto* standard for today's Windows environment, you may want to choose FAT or FAT32 as your file system in the following situation — if you have a computer that will sometimes run an earlier operating system along with Windows 2000. If you're going to keep a computer that runs Windows 3.1, 95, or 98, you have to keep a FAT or FAT32 partition as the primary partition on the hard disk so it can start normally.

According to Microsoft, Windows NT Version 4.0 with Service Pack 4 has access to partitions with the latest version of NTFS. But beware! Windows NT 4.0 can't access files stored using NTFS features that exist on Windows 2000 but not Windows NT 4.0. (You can see the list of new features in the next session.)

Why choose NTFS?

Aside from being the new standard in file systems (at least as far as Mr. Bill is concerned), NTFS has a number of advantages. NTFS has been proven to be much more scaleable for large (20GB and counting) hard drives. Overall, the maximum NTFS drive size is much greater than the limit for FAT and FAT32. Furthermore, as drive size increases, performance with NTFS doesn't suffer the same lag time as a comparable FAT- or FAT32-formatted partition.

The following sections describe the all-new options that are some of the NTFS-specific features that you can use if you plan to format the disk as NTFS.

Active Directory

To begin with, NTFS is a critical component when using Active Directory (which itself I cover in more detail in Chapter 22). You can use it to view and control network resources easily. You can use domains, which are part of Active Directory, to fine-tune security options while keeping administration simple. Domain controllers require NTFS.

Encryption

NTFS also allows file encryption, which greatly enhances security. NTFS also allows you greatly increased *granularity* — that is, security control that uses finer units of measurement to meet your specific needs. You can set permissions for reading, writing, and executing on individual files rather than just folders.

Quotas

Disk quotas, which I cover in excruciating detail in Chapter 12, allow you to monitor and control the amount of disk space used by the users on your system.

Recovery logging

Recovery logging is another very helpful feature, particularly if your organization isn't providing you with a budget for a portable generator. This NTFS recovery option allows you to restore information that was potentially lost or damaged in case of a sudden, improper shutdown due to a nearby nuclear explosion, attack of killer bees, or someone pulling the wrong plug.

Remote storage

Remote storage is also a new option under NTFS. This option provides you with additional disk space. With remote access, you can more easily get to and access removable media such as writable CD-ROMs and storage tapes.

Sparse files

NTFS allows the creation of what are called *sparse files*. A sparse file (so called because it takes up a small amount of disk space) is a file created by an application that starts out huge but is saved to take up less space than a file that would result from a normal save process.

The Odd Couple (s) Among Operating Systems — File System Compatibility

Although it tends to cause more headaches than a jackhammer applied to the cerebral cortex, some people insist on running more than one operating system on a machine at one time. If you're set up with two operating systems (say Windows 98 and Windows 2000), you get the option to start with one or the other at boot time. This option is known as a *dual-boot* system. (Of course, you can have triple-boot, quadruple-boot, and quintuple-boot systems, but that moves beyond silliness and into masochism very quickly.)

Multiple operating systems on a machine or network tend to increase administration hassles a quantum leap because certain operating systems simply refuse to acknowledge the NTFS/FAT/FAT32 hegemony. (In plainer words, they just don't get it.)

For this reason, the recommended file system is a pure NTFS setup with Windows NT or 2000. However, if you're still interested in running other operating systems, the following sections contain the information you need to at least make an informed decision about what challenges you're going to face.

Windows NT series

If you have a computer running Windows NT 4.0 with Service Pack 4 or later, you might be able to access some files from NTFS for Windows 2000. Note the word *might*, and beware!

No ambiguity exists regarding other operating systems, however. NTFS allows no access from any other operating system at all. What's more, if you set up a computer so that it starts with Windows NT 3.51, and you also have Windows 2000 Server on a local NTFS partition, when that computer starts with Windows NT 3.51, the NTFS partition won't even be visible, let alone accessible.

Windows 95, 98, and 3.1

They're in the same operational family, but they don't get any favors from the NTFS file system. Instead, you'll be on steady ground if you stick to FAT or FAT32.

OS/2

For some odd, obscure technical reason, OS/2 reads FAT easily, but doesn't handle FAT32 well. Come to think of it, it doesn't *read* FAT32 at all!

DOS

Once again, FAT works fine on DOS. The jury's out on whether it will handle FAT32, because DOS was never really designed to work with huge disk drives (mostly because they didn't exist at the time DOS came into being).

Readability doesn't equal feature access

Files that use any new features with the Windows 2000 NTFS are completely usable or readable *only* when the computer is started with Windows 2000 Server. For example, Windows NT 4.0 lacked the encryption capacity. A file that uses the new encryption feature simply won't be readable from NT 4.0.

According to Microsoft, if you want to set up a computer with both Windows NT and Windows 2000, you have only one option — running Windows NT 4.0 with the latest released Service Pack (Service Pack 4 or better).

That said, in my experience, even running the latest NT Service Pack doesn't seem to help matters much. Rumors exist that a later service pack for NT will provide access to files using the new features in Windows 2000 NTFS. But as the administrator's saying goes, "You can't administer a system with vaporware." *Vaporware*, of course, is any software that a company promises to deliver at an "undisclosed time in the future."

FAT32 is by far the most rare of the file systems in the Microsoft world. However, in case you use it, keep the following in mind:

- ✔ FAT32 can't be used on floppy disks.

- ✔ Domain support is nonexistent.

- ✔ Volumes can range in size from 512MB to 2TB.

- ✔ Windows 2000 allows you to format a FAT32 volume for no more than 32GB.

Planning Out Your Disk Partitions

When you partition a disk, you take the active role as zoning commissioner and dividing your physical disk into sections. No, you won't need to get out the pizza cutter for this job. Partitions are logical separations that act as effectively as a physical divider like a wall, barbed-wire fence, or those little plastic separators you use when you're in the supermarket checkout line.

Each section, or *partition,* on a disk functions as a separate unit. You can format every one of these separate areas for use by a file system, such as FAT or NTFS. Although you can set up your computer to use more than one operating system, you won't be able to set up more than one style of file system per disk partition.

You only need to plan your disk partitions before running Setup when you first install Windows 2000. If you're upgrading, then you won't need to worry about it.

One of the partitions you create is especially important — the *primary* partition, on which you install the files needed to load an operating system, such as Windows 2000. Primary partitions are sometimes called *system* partitions, because they can play a role in starting the operating system.

Before you create or delete hard disk partitions, *always* back up the disk's contents beforehand. Mucking about with partitions *will* destroy any existing data. Backing up the contents of the hard disk before any major change to disk contents is a good policy, even if you don't plan on changing every available partition.

I wish I could give you a magical formula to determine the size of your partitions as you plan out your disk use, but no set way exists to divide up your disk. There are only a couple principles you should follow. First, fewer partitions of a larger size are generally more efficient than many partitions of a smaller size. Second, give the operating system, applications, and important files plenty of room, so make their partitions extra spacious. Finally, use up all of your disk space. Waste not, want not!

Whenever you start to perform a new installation, you need to determine the size of the partition where you're going to install Windows 2000 Server. Windows 2000 Server requires at least 1GB of free space on the disk. (If you can't remember that figure, don't worry — it's described in System requirements both on the internal documentation and on the outside of the box.)

However, 1GB is the absolute minimum. If you can, have more disk space than the minimum amount. Doubling or tripling the amount of space you'll allocate will allow you to install optional components you may find helpful. In addition, you'll find it easier to allocate space for user accounts, Active Directory information, logs, and future service packs used by the operating system.

During the Windows 2000 Server installation process, you select the partition on which to install (thereby making that partition the *system* or primary partition). If you specify a partition on which another operating system exists, you are prompted to confirm your choice. However — and trust me on this one — you're far better off taking the system defaults that Windows 2000 wants. Not following what Windows 2000 wants annoys it, makes it pouty, and boy, will you pay for it later on down the line!

If you want to set up a computer so that it contains multiple operating systems, you must give Windows 2000 its own primary partition. Placing Windows 2000 on another operating system's primary partition leads to the overwriting of critical files needed by that other operating system.

Instead, during the Setup process, create and size a partition that you want to designate as the Windows 2000 primary or system partition. After you're up and running, you can use the Disk Management utility (which I cover in Chapter 8) to manage new and existing disks and volumes.

As a rule, this method is the better — and safer — way of creating new partitions from unpartitioned space. It's also a better way to delete, rename, and reformat existing partitions. You'll also find it better for adding disks, removing disks, and upgrading or reverting hard disks between a basic and dynamic format.

Never install Windows 2000 on a compressed drive unless the partition was compressed with the NTFS file system compression feature. The operating system won't install properly. In fact it will complain, quite loudly, during the entire process, and you may not be able to run the system.

Remote Installation Service requirements

If you plan to use your Windows 2000 server to install operating systems onto other computers, you need a separate partition for use by RIS, the Remote Installation Service. RIS allows you to install the Windows system on remote computers over the network so that you don't need to physically go to the computer and pop a CD-ROM in the disk drive. To begin with, you have to use NTFS on the partition. Windows 2000 NTFS is required for the Single Instance Store feature of Remote Installation Service.

If you plan on creating a new partition for Remote Installation Service, do it only after you complete the Setup process. Microsoft recommends that you use at least 2GB of space for your RIS partition.

Working with volumes

Luckily, managing volumes with Windows 2000 is a relatively flexible task. The number of volumes (also known as partitions that are made by and for Windows 2000) you can create on a disk is limited only by the amount of available free space on the disk. Keep in mind, though, that from a general administrative standpoint, administering fewer, rather than a greater number of volumes on a given disk is easier. You can also create volumes that span two or more disks.

As with partitions on earlier installations of Windows, each volume on a disk can have a different file system, such as FAT, FAT32, or NTFS. If you use only the Windows 2000 operating system (not a bad choice as far as I'm concerned), you can create one volume that occupies your entire disk. Of course, if you want to use other operating systems, you have to budget disk space during Setup when you specify the size of the volume that is to contain Windows 2000.

 If you want to use multiple file systems and your existing hard disk has only one volume, you have to create a second volume on the disk. Unfortunately, if the disk lacks free space, you have to take the drastic step of reinstalling Windows, this time leaving room on the disk for additional volumes.

Whenever you make changes to your hard disk, the changes are immediately available. You won't have to quit Disk Management to save them or restart your computer to implement them, although you may have to Refresh the Disk Management window to view the changes. As with most things in life, there is an exception to the rule. When upgrading a boot disk to a dynamic disk, or if a volume is in use on the disk that you attempt to upgrade, you must restart the computer for the upgrade to be successful. Plan accordingly.

Creating a volume that a Mac can use

You can create a volume on a Windows 2000 server that can be made available to Macintosh clients. In a nutshell, you create a folder on the server that has been made available to Macintosh clients. You do so by using Computer Management. Just follow these steps:

1. **Click the Start button and choose Programs⇨Administrative Tools⇨Computer Management.**

2. **In the console tree on the Computer Management window's left pane, double-click Shared Folders, then right-click the Shares option.**

3. **Next, select New File Share from the pop-up menu.**

   The Create Shared Folder dialog box appears, as shown in Figure 9-2.

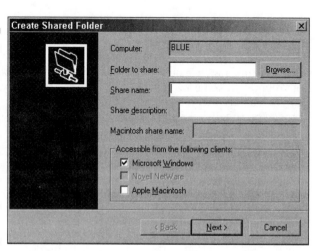

Figure 9-2: The Create Shared Folder window. Note the Accessible from the following clients section at the bottom of the window.

4. **In the Folder to share field, type the drive and path to the folder you want to make Macintosh-accessible.**

   If you're not sure, you can click the Browse button to locate the folder.

5. **Make sure to enter the Share name and Share description.**

6. **Finally, select the Apple Macintosh check box in the Accessible from the following clients section at the bottom of the window.**

7. **Click Next, and then follow the instructions as the Create Shared Folder Wizard starts up.**

Seven years' good luck: Using mirrored volumes

Mirroring disks is a fairly complex method of ensuring an additional layer of fault tolerance. Most of the time, you won't need to resort to using mirrored volumes, unless you work in an environment where you have a continual stream of data coming in. This data must be valuable enough and time-critical in the utmost degree — otherwise, you can rely on daily or weekly backups to cover most of your needs.

Mirror, mirror, on the wall . . .

If you're from the Windows NT 4.0 world, you may have encountered mirrored volumes, known as mirror *sets*. Although you can provide some support with Disk Management for mirrored volumes on basic disks, you won't be able to repair, resynchronize, break, and delete existing mirrored volumes. Also, you won't be able to create new mirrored volumes on basic disks. The only place you'll be able to create new mirrored volumes under Windows 2000 is on a dynamic disk.

A *mirrored* volume is one that duplicates your data onto two physical disks. The redundancy of the data is provided by the copy, or *mirror* of the volume. The mirror volume should always be located on a different disk, preferably on a different machine that is preferably in a different country on a different continent, but hey, work with what you have available.

The idea is that if one of the physical disks fails, the data on the failed disk becomes unavailable. However, the system continues to operate using the unaffected, or *mirror* disk.

When creating a mirrored volume, you create a volume using free space on another disk to match the first volume you want to mirror. The same drive letter must be used for both volumes. In fact, when creating mirrored volumes, you're best off if you can use hard disks that are the same size, manufacturer, and even model, if you can manage it. Any volume you choose, even a system or boot volume, can be mirrored onto another volume of the same size or greater on another disk.

Mirrored volumes provide a duplicate set of data, but they also double the number of disks required. Mirroring also doubles the number of input/output (I/O) operations when writing to the disk, because instead of saving something once, you're really doing it twice. But that's the price paid for increasing your level of redundancy.

Incidentally, in clinical tests (similar to the ones used for dental products, except it's hard to floss with a hard drive), mirrored volumes scored better overall in read and write performance than RAID-5 volumes. Although I'm not a corporate accountant, the cost of using mirrored volumes is initially lower because mirroring requires only two disks at minimum, whereas RAID-5 volumes require three or more disks to start out.

Finally, if you ever want to use the space in a mirrored volume for other purposes, you must first break the mirrored volume relationship. You also have to delete one of the mirrored volumes. Breaking the mirrored volume won't necessarily mean that you'll lose the information, but to be on the safe side, you should still perform a complete backup. (Think *users, torches,* and *pitch-forks*, in that order.)

Creating a mirrored volume

Creating mirrored volumes isn't too onerous a task as long as you're logged on as the Administrator or a member of the Administrators group. Much like a recipe, you need certain ingredients before you begin:

- ✔ Administrative rights that you've begged, borrowed, or assigned to yourself
- ✔ One or two computers running Windows 2000 Server, depending on whether the dynamic disks will be on the same machine
- ✔ Two dynamic disks to create a mirrored volume
- ✔ The same drive letter, used for both copies (mirrors) of the mirrored volume

After you have all the ingredients, follow these steps:

1. **Open the Disk Management utility by clicking the Start button, pointing to Programs⇨Administrative Tools, then clicking Computer Management. Once in Computer Management, click Disk Management in the window's left pane.**

2. **Right-click the unallocated space on one of the dynamic disks where you want to create the mirrored volume, and then click Create Volume.**

   The first screen of the Create Volume Wizard appears.

3. **Click the Next button, select Mirrored volume, then follow the instructions on your screen.**

Removing a mirror

Alas, there are times when you'll need to dismantle your mirrored system to gather more space, or to change the mirroring to different volumes on different machines. Luckily, removing mirrors is fairly straightforward, but you must keep in mind that several changes will result from your actions.

After you remove a mirror from a mirrored volume, the removed mirror becomes unallocated space. The remaining mirrored volume becomes a simple volume that's no longer fault tolerant, because no mirror exists to be fault tolerant to. Also, be sure to do your backups, because all the data on the removed mirror is deleted.

First, open the Disk Management utility. Right-click the mirror you want to remove. Because Windows 2000 is smart enough to recognize a mirrored volume, the new option Remove Mirror appears on the pop-up menu. Selecting this option starts the removal procedure. After it starts, you're best off following the instructions on your screen.

Resynchronizing a mirrored volume

If you lose one face of a mirrored volume set, data is still being written to the remaining face of the mirror. When you resurrect the disk that had crashed (whether due to a power failure or a mechanical error), you no longer have a fault-tolerant system. In other words, the data on your newly resurrected disk is *out of date* or *stale*. You want to correct this situation as soon as possible, because stale data tastes bad, and looks funny, too.

To make the mirrored volume fault tolerant again, you must resynchronize the mirrored volume to update the information on the reconnected disk. Begin by opening the Disk Management window. Right-click the mirrored volume you want to resynchronize, and then select the Resynchronize Mirror command.

Normally, you shouldn't even have to do this much. Mirrored volumes on dynamic disks are designed to resynchronize themselves in case of outages automatically.

Chapter 10

To Go Forward, You Must Back Up

*T*hroughout this book, I preach about how important it is to make backups. And make backups of your backups. And while you're at it, make
backups of the backups of those backups you backed up. Some very good
reasons exist for this obsession with backups.

One, you get to keep your job. Two, you get to keep your hair from falling out,
or at least turning prematurely gray. And three, you get emotional satisfaction knowing that you've done the right thing as a Windows 2000 administration professional.

You can use several methods for backing up your data, depending on your
budget, available equipment, and most importantly, your needs. Although
some may disagree with my opinion that needs are more important than
equipment or budget, I've found that any organization that underspends on
its backup needs only does so until the first outage that causes a loss of a significant amount of data.

A word to the wise: If you see a situation such as I just described developing
and you can't change it, try to get as far out from the blast radius as you can,
as soon as possible! However, if you do have some control over the situation,
be sure to read through this chapter. You can then abscond with a treasure
trove of excellent techniques for developing and setting up your own effective backup strategies.

Windows 2000 Backups — A Polite Way to C.Y.A.

Windows comes with an excellent Backup utility with which you want to get very familiar. Using the Backup utility on your hard disks allows you to protect yourself and your data from accidental loss if your hardware or software decides to take an impromptu vacation.

You can use the Backup utility to archive your data on another storage device such as a second hard disk or a tape. In a disastrous situation, your *original* data can be corrupted by a virus program, rendered inaccessible by a disk head failure, or erased by a maniac wielding a large electro-magnet. In any of the preceding cases, you can easily restore the data from the archived copy you've created with the Backup utility.

You can use Backup to back up and restore data on either File Allocation Table (FAT) or NTFS file systems. However, be sure that whatever file system type is used for a backup, the same system is used for restoration. If you back up data from an NTFS volume used in Windows 2000, Microsoft recommends that you restore the data to an NTFS volume used in Windows 2000.

Restoring the data (which I cover in detail in Chapter 11) in an NTFS volume on, say, Windows NT 4.0 would be crippling. Not only would you likely lose data, you may also lose file and folder features such as permissions, encryption settings, disk quota information, mounted drive information, and remote storage information.

Although the Backup utility no longer manages the storage devices and media, you can now use it to back up files to tape drives, removable disks, or recordable CD-ROMs. If you don't have a separate storage device, you can back up to another hard disk or to a floppy disk.

Now that Backup no longer manages the storage devices themselves in Windows 2000, tasks such as mounting and dismounting a tape or disk are now done with the *Removable Storage* utility.

Location, location, location

Incidentally, if your backup needs can be placed on a floppy disk, you're pretty lucky. If you plan to back up to another hard drive, at least make this drive on a different machine, in preferably a different location. That way if the machine sparks up or your building's fire sprinklers short out your computer banks, you still have a workable backup.

In addition, the Backup utility allows you to archive and restore what's known as the Windows 2000 System State, which is a mouthful to say, but is appropriate, because the System State includes the system files, Registry, Component Services, Active Directory database, file-replication service, and the Certificate Services database. In other words, the most critical of the critical files you want to save (unless you want to rebuild your system from the ashes up).

Finally, Microsoft has done a slam-bang job in the integration of the Backup utility with a couple of desperately needed Windows 2000 programs. The Backup utility now works hand-in-hand with the Remote Storage utility, used for archiving data. Even more useful is the integration made with the Windows 2000 Task Scheduler, used for automating backup jobs (such as "cron" in the UNIX world).

Types of Backup

If you're looking to perform a backup, it's always good to know the scope of what you have to save. Ideally, you want to perform the most complete backup you can, but sometimes it's not an efficient choice to make on a daily basis. The Backup utility allows you a bit more flexibility by providing you with five methods of backing up data on your Windows 2000 network.

Copy backup

A *copy backup* copies all the files you've manually selected. It doesn't mark each file as having been backed up. This method is useful because if the Archive attribute isn't cleared, then the normal or incremental backup process that you schedule won't *skip* this file just because you decided to make a copy between scheduled backup operations.

Daily backup

A *daily backup* copies all selected files that have been modified on the day the backup is performed. As with a copy backup, the selected files are not marked as having been backed up, which keeps the scheduled incremental backup from skipping them.

Incidentally, the *day* that a file is modified under this system means "any file that was modified after midnight, the day that the daily backup is performed."

Incremental backup

An *incremental backup* backs up only those files created or changed since the *last* normal or incremental backup. Unlike the previous incarnations of backups, this backup procedure clears the Archive attribute, meaning that it marks files as having been backed up.

Incremental backups taste great and are less filling to your hard drive. But they take up less space on your drive because they back up less — only selecting the files and directories that have been altered since your last incremental backup!

Therefore, if you back up your system with a combination of normal and incremental backups, you absolutely cannot rely on incremental backups to restore your system from the ground up in case of a truly monumental disaster, such as the entire hard drive failing, the flooding of your computer lab, or the release of another Steven Seagal movie. To restore order to your universe, you need the last normal backup set as well as all incremental backup sets.

Differential backup

A *differential backup* copies all files created or changed since the last normal or incremental backup. Like the daily backup, it doesn't mark the Archive attribute. Unlike the daily backup, it saves files changed one day, one week, one month ago, or more.

As with incremental backups, restoring your system from the ground up requires that you have the last normal as well as the last differential backup.

Normal backup (as opposed to an abnormal backup)

A *normal backup* is the fullest backup in every sense of the word. This backup copies all selected files, in the process filling up the most hard drive space (or tape spool, depending on what you're using).

This backup marks each file as having been backed up. If you're lucky enough to have a recent normal backup, you can restore the system from ground zero in case of a major outage. Unfortunately, if you have a system that adds truly critical data on a daily basis, you may have to rely on a combination of normal and incremental backups to retain the freshest data if you need to restore the system.

On the whole, you can make the most economical use of your storage space by backing up your data using a combination of normal backups and incremental backups. Also, due to the time-consuming nature of normal backups, interspersing these backups with quick incremental ones is by far the most time-efficient backup method. On the flip side (isn't there always one?) recovering files is more time-consuming and difficult because the backup set will be stored on a minimum of two disks or tapes with this system.

Permissions and Rights to Back Up Data

It goes without saying (but here goes anyway) that you have to be an administrator or a backup operator in a local group to back up any files or folders on machines belonging to a local group. Similarly, if you have administrative rights on a Windows 2000 domain controller, you can back up files or folders on any computer in the domain.

However, you're still not allowed to back up System State data, as I discuss shortly.

If you're not an administrator or a backup operator, you can still perform backups, albeit in a more limited fashion. You must be the owner of the files and folders you want to back up. Alternatively, you must have one or more of the following permissions for the files and folders you want to back up: Read, Read and Execute, Edit, or Full Control. Unless you're the administrator, you can't magically acquire these permissions — the Windows 2000 administrator must assign them to you.

If you're not the administrator (or have access to the administrative account), you may also run afoul of disk-quota restrictions that may restrict your access to a hard disk. If you can't access a needed hard disk, completing the back up process is simply impossible for you. You can check whether you have any disk quota restrictions by right-clicking the disk you want to save data to. Select Properties from the pop-up menu, and then click the Quota tab. (You can find out more in Chapter 12.)

As an administrator, you can restrict access to a backup file by selecting Allow only the owner and the Administrator access to the backup data in the Backup Job Information dialog box. By selecting this option, only an administrator or the person who created the backup file will be able to restore the files and folders. On the whole, this option is good to set because it prevents users from playing with and possibly damaging your precious backup file.

Finally, note that you can only back up System State data on a local computer. Even if you're an administrator, you won't be able to back up System State data on a remote computer.

System State Data

You've probably seen the term a few times as you flip through this chapter, and you're surely wondering: What is this mysterious thing called *System State data*? Windows 2000 refers to the following system components as the System State data:

- ✔ Active Directory directory service
- ✔ Boot files
- ✔ Certificate Services database
- ✔ Cluster service information
- ✔ COM+ Class Registration database
- ✔ Registry information
- ✔ SYSVOL directory

By contrast, the Windows 2000 Professional operating system designates relatively few components as the System State data. These include the following short list:

- ✔ Boot files
- ✔ COM+ Class Registration database
- ✔ Registry information

You can back up and restore all of these system components using the Backup utility. When you back up or restore System State data, you can't choose to back up or restore individual components of the System State data. It's an all or nothing deal. This restriction is due to dependencies among the System State components — if even one of the components is missing, then your system either won't run or will be in a bad state if it is able to run at all.

 If you want to, you can restore the System State data to an alternate, or remote location. However, only the registry files, SYSVOL directory files, Cluster database information files, and system boot files will be restored.

The Active Directory directory services database, Certificate Services database, and COM+ Class Registration database won't be restored if you designate an alternate location for restoring the Windows 2000 System State data.

If you have more than one domain controller in your organization, and the Active Directory directory service is replicated to any of these other servers, you may have to authoritatively restore any Active Directory data that you want to restore. Without authoritative restoration, many distributed objects will never get replicated or distributed to your other servers because they will appear to be *older* than the objects currently on those servers.

You can perform this authoritative restoration by using the Ntdsutil utility. The Ntdsutil utility allows you to mark Active Directory objects for an authoritative restore. This restoration process ensures that any restored replicated or distributed data is properly replicated or distributed throughout your organization.

You can run the Ntdsutil command line utility from the command prompt after you have restored the System State data but before you restart the server on the network. You can find help for using the Ntdsutil utility at the command prompt by typing **ntdsutil /?**, as shown in Figure 10-1. (I, for one, made sure to ntdsutil vigorously today — how about you?)

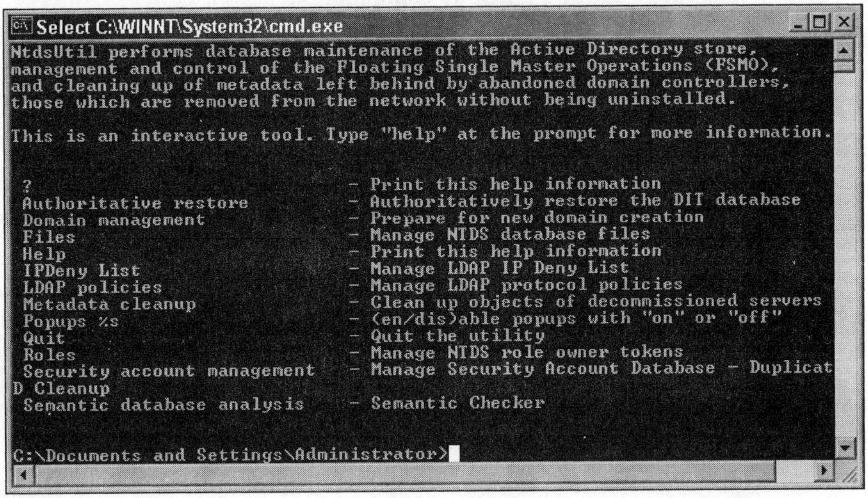

Figure 10-1:
Typing
ntdsutil /?
in the DOS
prompt
window
takes you to
the help
menu for the
utility.

Developing Backup and Restoration Strategies

Good backup planning allows you to recover quickly when your data gets lost somewhere between your monitor and the electronic ether. If you run a low-security to medium-security network, granting backup rights to one user and restore rights to a different user can sometimes be best. On a high-security system this method is not advisable because it doubles the chance that a password could be cracked. As a rule, on a high-security network, only administrators should back up and restore files.

If you manage people, train the junior administrators with access to the restore rights to perform all the restore tasks. Doing so is a good *personnel* backup policy if you're sick, late, or sunning yourself on the beach in the Bahamas. And for some further suggestions, consider implementing as many of the following strategies into your backup plan as possible.

✔ **Perform normal backups:** Back up an entire volume with a normal backup to prepare for the unlikely event of a complete system or disk failure. Murphy's Law says that during a period where the most valuable data is stored on your computer, the chances are highest that it will crash. So if you're aware of some major data that will be saved on your machine, initiate a full backup as soon as you can.

✔ **Back up directory services:** Back up the directory services database on a domain controller to prevent the loss of user account and security information.

✔ **Intersperse incremental and daily backups:** If you find yourself the victim of backup fatigue with the lengthy normal backup time, don't just stop backing up. Start using incremental or daily backups to cover the gap between normal backup times, particularly if you plan to make some important structural changes to the system or the network.

✔ **Create a backup log:** Always keep a book of logs to make it easier to locate specific files. This record is exceptionally helpful when restoring data. What's important is that you keep a *hard copy* somewhere you can find it, in case the alleged disaster has also claimed your print server as a casualty. If the tape containing the backup set catalog becomes corrupted, a printed log can help you locate a file.

✔ **Retain triplicate copies of all media:** When you make media copies, keep at least one copy off-site in a properly controlled environment. By properly controlled, I mean an environment that's both secure to thievery (placing the tape on your desktop is not a good idea) and to the elements (leaving a tape in your car on a hot sunny day will turn your tape into a plastic Slurpee).

✔ **Physically secure both devices and media:** Secure both the storage device and the backup media. A cartridge tape can easily be smuggled out of a building and the possibility exists for someone to access the data from a stolen medium by restoring the data from a stolen tape. If possible, keep your tape drive and media in a secure location. A locked storage room is appropriate for the drive, and a locked cabinet is adequate for a tape or writable CD-ROM.

Setting backup options

Start the Backup utility by clicking the Start button and choosing Programs⇨Accessories⇨System Tools⇨Backup to open the Backup window and set the backup options (see Figure 10-2).

After the Backup screen opens, choose Tools⇨Options. The default panel in this screen is Backup Type, where you select one of the five types of backup discussed earlier in this chapter. To set the Backup options, click the General tab to get to the General pane, shown in Figure 10-3, where you can actually set a whole raft of available options:

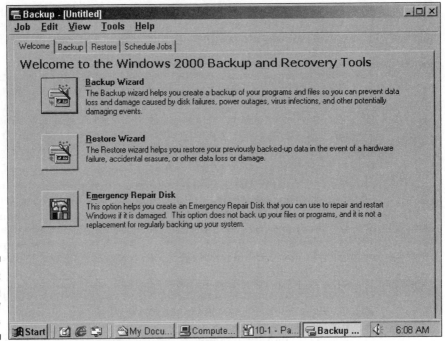

Figure 10-2:
The Backup utility screen.

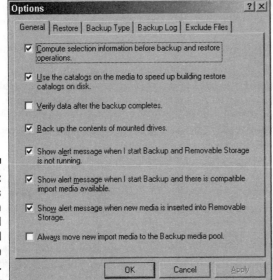

Figure 10-3:
The Options screen with the General panel selected, in all its glory.

✔ **Compute selection information before backup and restore operations:** Selecting this option instructs the computer to estimate the number and size of the files to be backed up or restored. This information is calculated and displayed before the backup or restore begins.

✔ **Use the catalogs on the media to speed up building restore catalogs on disk:** This option indicates that you want to use the on-media catalog to build the on-disk catalog for restore selections. However, if you want to restore data from several tapes, and the tape with the on-media catalog is missing, or you want to restore data from damaged media, you shouldn't select this option. The restoration procedure could take several hours if your backup set is very large.

✔ **Verify data after the backup completes:** This option checks the backup data and the original data to be sure that the data matches. If it doesn't match, a problem may exist with your media, the transmission method you are using, or some other kind of corruption. You should immediately attempt to locate the source of the problem. If need be, you may want to use new media, a new tape drive, or even new cabling if it seems to be the source of the problem.

✔ **Back up the contents of mounted drives:** This option instructs the machine to back up the data on a mounted drive. If you neglect to select this option when you decide to back up a mounted drive, only the path information for the mounted drive will be backed up, not the contents of the drive itself.

✔ **Show alert message when I start Backup and Removable Storage is not running:** If you back up data to a tape or to other media managed by Removable Storage, check this box. It displays a dialog box when you start Backup and the Removable Storage utility is malfunctioning (or just plain not running).

✔ **Show alert message when I start Backup and there is compatible import media available:** Again, if you back up data to a tape or to other media managed by Removable Storage, check this box. It displays a dialog box when you start Backup and you have new media available in the Import media pool.

✔ **Show alert message when new media is inserted into Removable Storage:** If you back up data to a tape or to other media managed by Removable Storage, check this box. (Is there an echo in here, or is it just me?) This displays a dialog box when Removable Storage detects new media.

✔ **Always move new import media to Backup pools:** If you back up data to a tape or other media that's managed by Removable Storage, you don't need to check this box. Selecting this option automatically moves any new media detected by Removable Storage to the Backup media pool.

Backing up files to a file or a tape

You can use the Backup utility to back up data on either FAT or NTFS volumes. Compared to the earlier Backup utilities that Microsoft provided, this new utility is markedly faster, leading to more efficient backups. (Well, okay, my sophisticated benchmarking utility *was* a watch with an actual second hand, but overall you should see a difference.) To complete a backup, complete the following tasks:

1. **From the Backup Utility screen, choose Job⇨New.**

2. **In the Backup panel, select the files and folders you want to back up by clicking the box to the left of a file or folder in the directory tree.**

3. **Next, click to select the check box for any drive, folder, or file that you want to back up.**

4. **To select your Backup destination, do one of the following:**

   • Choose a tape device if you want to back up files and folders to a tape.

   • Choose File if you want to back up files and folders to a file. (If Windows 2000 doesn't detect an installed tape drive, this option is selected by default.)

Note that I said *installed,* not *attached,* tape drive. If you have an external, portable tape drive that you've just plugged into your machine, Windows 2000 probably won't automatically detect it. You can either restart the machine so that it detects the drive, or you can take the smarter, less labor-intensive option and manually select the drive for the Backup destination.

5. **Choose Tools⇨Options to select the backup options you want, such as the backup type, log file type, and the selections under the General panel.**

6. **When you finish selecting your backup options, click Apply or OK to exit from the Options screen.**

7. **If you want to set advanced backup options such as data verification or hardware compression, click Advanced.**

   When you finish setting advanced backup options, click OK.

8. **Click the Start Backup button on the Backup screen (make sure to click the tab labeled Backup in the Backup utility's main screen) to start the backup operation (see Figure 10-4).**

If you're feeling, lazy, you can also use the Backup wizard to back up files by choosing Tools⇨Backup Wizard. And if you're feeling *exceptionally* lethargic, you can even click the large Backup Wizard button on the Backup utility's main screen (complete with magic wand and graphic sparkles).

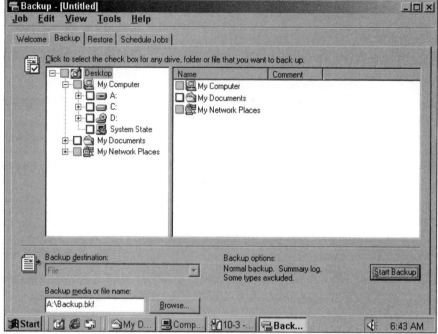

Figure 10-4:
The Backup
screen,
where you
can click
the button
labeled —
wait for it —
Start
Backup!

If you're managing media or storing data using the Removable Storage utility, then you should back up the files that are in the following folders:

✔ Systemroot\System32\Ntmsdata

✔ Systemroot\System32\Remotestorage

Following this recommendation ensures that you can restore the Removable Storage and Remote Storage data in case of a serious outage.

Formatting a tape

You only need to use this procedure if you're using a DC-2000-type tape drive, which requires that you format a tape before you use it. Simply open the Backup utility and click the Restore tab. On the Restore screen, simply right-click the tape you want to format, choose Format from the pop-up menu, and you're off and running.

Retensioning a tape

I'm not even sure that *retensioning* is a word (well, if *permissioning* is, then why not?), but at least I can explain what it means. Essentially, it's using the computer to order the tape drive to take up the slack in your magnetic tape so that it's ready for use. (And no, this technique is not going to help you retension your old Def Leppard audio tapes. You can still use a pencil or a handy forefinger to do that.)

Open the Backup utility and click the Restore tab. On the Restore screen, click the tape you want to retension. Choose Tools⇨Media Tools⇨Retension.

You can also access the Retension command by opening the Backup utility and clicking the Restore tab. After you're in the Restore screen, simply right-click the tape you want to retension, select Retension from the pop-up menu, and you're off and, um, retensioning.

Erasing a tape

If you're running out of tape room and your budget doesn't look like it's going to expand as fast as the national debt, you'll eventually have to erase a tape to get it ready for reuse. Erasing a tape moves the tape from the backup media pool to the free media pool.

Keep in mind that you can only erase a tape if the tape is physically in the tape drive or in a loader slot of a tape change. (I know that sounds pretty simple but you wouldn't believe some of the questions I have fielded on this one. Windows is good at remote storage, but not *that* good.)

Open the Backup utility and click the Restore tab. On the Restore screen, click the tape you want to erase. Choose Tools⇨Media Tools, and then select Erase. Of course, as before, you can also access the Erase command by right-clicking a tape on the Restore tab.

Backing up System State data

Remember how System State data covers everything that is, well, *important* on your system? If you want to back up the System State data, you have to select the System State option in the Backup panel after you're in the Backup Utility window. Click the box next to System State to back up the System State data along with any other data you have selected for the current backup operation.

Note that when you move the mouse pointer over the selection, it turns into a check mark. Note also that you can only back up the System State data on a local computer. You won't be able to do the same for the System State data on a remote computer. To see an example of what objects make up a System State backup, see Figure 10-5.

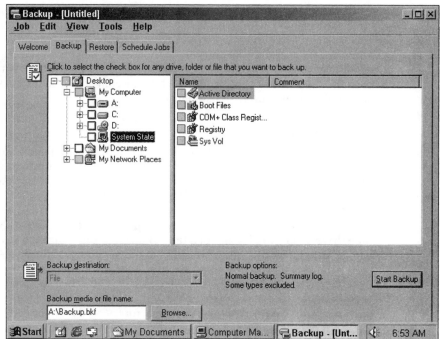

Figure 10-5:
Clicking
System
State in the
left-hand
pane of the
Backup
Utility
(under the
Backup
panel)
shows you
the objects
that will
comprise
the backup
of the
System
State data.

Scheduling backups

For those of you from the UNIX world, scheduling backups is a familiar task, at least if you edited the "crontabs" and worked with the "cron" daemon. If you're not familiar with scheduling backups on any kind of platform, then you should get familiar as quickly as possible, because doing so will save you a lot of work in the long haul.

The term *scheduling* really means *automating*. When you hear the term automating you should perk up, because that means *less work*. Now, to schedule a backup, you must have the Task Scheduler service running. To do this, you can open the DOS command prompt window and type **net start schedule**. A better way is for you to use Services in the Computer Management window to start, stop, and view the status of services (see Figure 10-6).

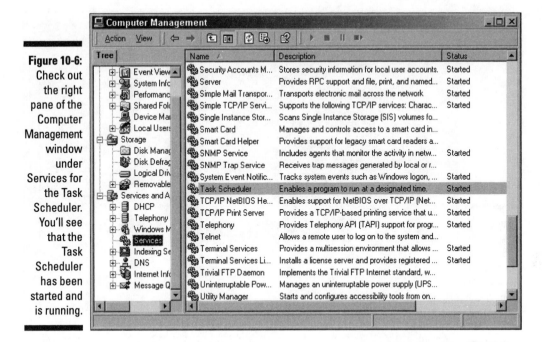

Figure 10-6:
Check out
the right
pane of the
Computer
Management
window
under
Services for
the Task
Scheduler.
You'll see
that the
Task
Scheduler
has been
started and
is running.

After you have the Task Scheduler service running, follow these steps:

1. **In the Backup utility, click the Schedule Jobs tab to get to the Schedule Jobs panel, shown in Figure 10-7.**

2. **Click the Add Job button to begin the scheduling process.**

3. **In the Scheduled Job Options dialog box, type a name for the scheduled backup job under Job name.**

4. **Click Properties to set the date, time, and frequency parameters for the scheduled backup.**

5. **When you have finished, click OK twice to complete the process.**

You can change the settings of a scheduled backup job after you schedule it by clicking the Schedule Jobs tab and then clicking the Backup icon that is displayed on the calendar.

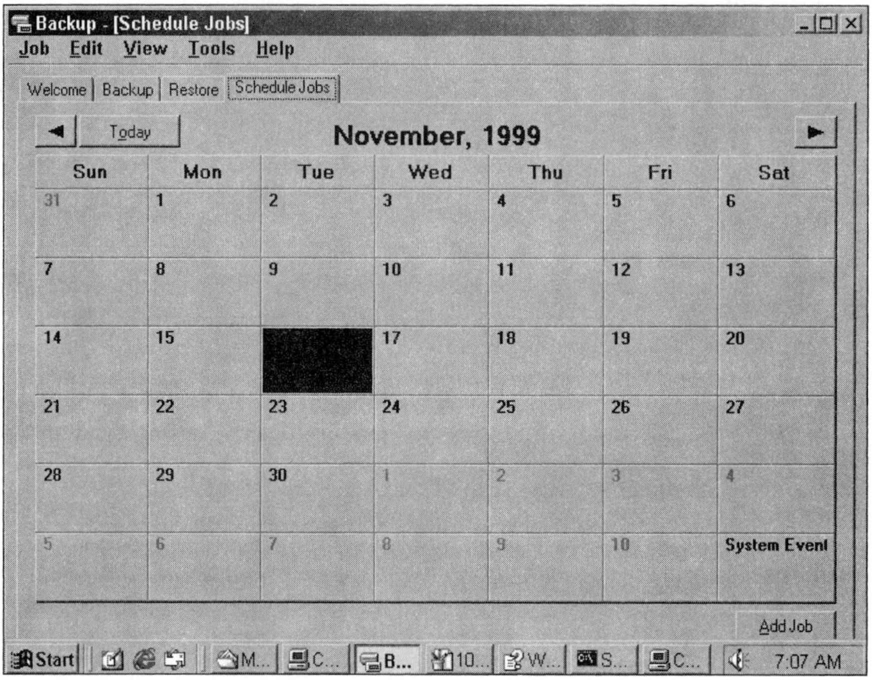

Figure 10-7:
The
Schedule
Jobs panel.
The Add Job
button is in
the lower
right.

Backing up files on a Microsoft Exchange server

According to Microsoft, you can back up files on a Microsoft Exchange Server as long as you're running Version 5.5 or earlier. The later versions of the server will be using a different backup system, presumably faster and more intuitive than the current method. To begin the backup:

1. **Open the Backup utility.**

2. **Click the Start button and move your mouse pointer so that it points to Programs, and then in the submenu that comes up, point to System Tools and click Backup.**

   The Backup screen appears.

3. **To get to the Backup panel, click the tab marked (ready?) Backup.**

4. **When you're in the Backup panel, click to select the Exchange Server, or type the name of the Microsoft Exchange Server that you want to back up.**

   The name must begin with two backslashes, as in \\Backmeup or \\Xchange_Rate.

5. **Click Connect to Organization, and then click OK to complete the task.**

Note that when you initiate the restoration process on a Microsoft Exchange Server, the Information Store service and Directory service are stopped. Make sure that you start the services after the restore is complete! To do so, choose Tools⇨Microsoft Exchange, click Start Service, select Directory or Information Store, and then click OK to finish.

Chapter 11

The Age of Restoration

*O*f course, backing up your files is only half the battle for your sanity and hair retention, should a disaster ever rear its ugly head. Restoration is just as important a procedure, especially to the folks who have valuable data, e-mail, and downloaded GIFs of their favorite rock star. It's also going to be especially important to those other folks, the ones who gave you the budget to buy the backup equipment at your disposal (such as it is, at least in the vast majority of cases).

If you want to sleep better at night knowing that the backup system you sweated and slaved over all week is, in fact, doing what it's supposed to, then I highly recommend a trial run. Schedule a Saturday, Sunday, or time out of the main schedule and away from a Superbowl or a *Star Trek* marathon. Run through the restoration procedure you have set up. If nothing else, it will prevent you from having a very nasty surprise should you actually have to restore the system from a major crash and discover that your magnetic tapes have been storing Barry Manilow's favorite tunes to sing in the shower.

In this chapter, you plunge headlong into restoring files, folders, and critical system data — and then into how to set up an effective restoration process. Which should help ensure that the right stuff is on those tapes — and, in the event of an emergency, make you very happy (unless you're a really BIG Barry Manilow fan).

Restoring Files and Folders

Although you'll be choosing different menu choices and selecting different operations depending on your choice of media and backup routine, the basic procedure for a restoration is remarkably the same. The basic restore operation can be broken down into a series of steps. In each case, you manually select the files you need resurrected, picking the most useful options, and actually kicking off the entire process.

Starting the Backup utility and moving to the Restore panel

Because Microsoft has embedded so many new options and choices for backups and restorations, the Backup utility has separated the Backup screen from the Restore screen. When you open the Backup utility, you get a series of tabs which, when clicked, take you to function-specific panels. Obviously, for this exercise, you use the panel labeled Restore.

Selecting the files and folders you want to restore

The Restore screen in the Backup utility provides you with two separate panes. In the left-hand one, a tree view of the files and folders that you have backed up is displayed. You can use this tree view in much the same way you use Windows Explorer to open drives and folders and select files, simply by clicking them.

Selecting the restoration location for your backed-up files and folders

The Restore function in the Backup utility provides you with three choices for the location of your restoration.

First, you can restore your backed-up data to the original folder where the data was located when you initiated the backup procedure. This option is a real advantage if you really are trying to restore a system, in the truest sense of the word. Replicating the exact structure of a directory is the surest course to making the restoration as *transparent* as possible, given the circumstances.

Second, you can select an alternate location for your backed-up data. As in the first option, you retain the structure of the backed-up folders, even if it's in an alternate folder. If you don't want to overwrite or change any of the current files or folders on your disk, but you want to retain a copy of the older file structure, this option may be your best bet.

Finally, you can elect to restore your backed-up files to a single folder. Instead of retaining the structure of the saved directories, the files are all dumped into the location without any reference to their prior order. This option is useful if you have no plans on restoring the old file structure, and want to find a file without hunting through a myriad of old folders. (After all, the files will still be listed alphabetically, making your search all the easier.) If you want to see the options you have available, check out Figure 11-1 for enlightenment.

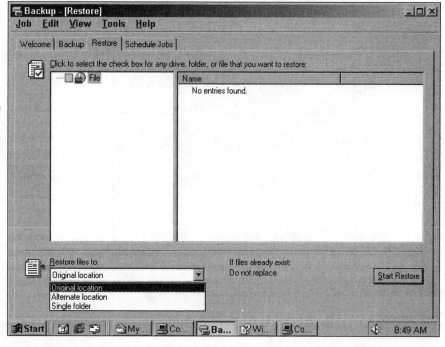

Figure 11-1:
A view of the Restore panel in the Backup utility showing the three choices you have available in the Restore Files to: drop-down list.

Setting the restore options

The Backup utility provides a Restore tab in the Options dialog box that lets you select how you want your files and folders restored, as shown in Figure 11-2. Once again, you can choose from one of three options:

- **Do not replace file on my computer:** This selection prevents files on your hard drive from being overwritten. On the average, this method is safest for restoring files, which is probably why it's appended with the Recommended label.

- **Replace the file on disk only if the file on disk is older:** If you're worried about losing changes that you made to your files since the last restoration, this will be your best option. Of course, if you've been mucking about with the system dates, this option could get a little tricky, which is a good argument against playing around with the system date utility without a good reason.

- **Always replace the file on my computer:** Flat out, this option replaces all the files on your hard disk with your backup copy. If you've made changes to files or the directory structure since you last backed up your data, this option erases those changes. For this reason, this option is a fairly risky one to select (compared to the first two candidates).

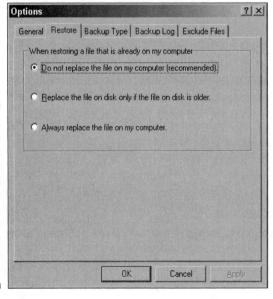

Figure 11-2: Clicking the Restore tab of the Options screen gives you the three available restore selections.

Starting the restore operation

The Backup utility prompts you with a dialog box to confirm that you're ready to restore data. You also have the opportunity to set advanced restore options, such as whether you want to restore security settings and the Removable Storage database before you actually begin the restoration process.

As I discuss in Chapter 10, the Registry, Active Directory directory service, and many other key components are contained in what is called the System State data. You must specifically back up this System State data if you want to back up and restore these components from a file, tape, or other media. If you restore the System State data but fail to designate an alternate location to restore the data, the Backup utility erases the System State data currently on your computer and replaces it with the System State data you're restoring.

You can only restore the System State data on a local computer. You won't be able to restore the System State data on a remote computer.

Administrators and Backup Operators can restore encrypted files and folders without having to decrypt them. So you can put away your Ovaltine secret decoder ring and save it for the upcoming chapter on the Registry.

Restoring a Domain Controller

Losing a domain controller is a particularly serious occurrence. Your first move should be to attempt to repair the system using the Emergency Repair Disk (ERD). Your system should either come with a repair disk (sometimes labeled as a *boot and restore* disk) or you should have made one yourself. If you lack an ERD and need to make one, consider bookmarking this page and turning to Appendix D to make yourself a backup disk in case tragedy strikes.

If the system cannot be repaired using the ERD, or if you have suffered a major hardware malfunction, then you'll likely need to reinstall the Windows 2000 operating system. Be careful to duplicate the number and size of disk volumes as before, or if in doubt, make it larger than the previous system. After you've done that, proceed with either of the next two steps:

✔ If no domain controllers were in the domain, then you can restore Active Directory from your backup media, whether it's a file, tape, or writable CD-ROM.

✔ If you had an additional domain controller on your network, you can restore the Active Directory using replication with another domain controller. (You can still restore the Active Directory from backup media if that makes you more comfortable.)

Using Backup Media to restore the Active Directory

As I mention in Chapter 10, the Active Directory is part of the list of files that compose the System State data. As long as you've used the Backup utility to back up the System State, you should be able to restore the files that make up the System State similarly.

Restoring the System State recovers the Active Directory, File Replication Service (including Sysvol) and Certificate Services. Keep in mind that if the domain controller computer has been replaced, you may need to reconfigure the network settings manually, or the client computers on your network will become very confused about what is where.

Restoring the Active Directory from a replica

If you're not feeling too ambitious and you were lucky enough to have an additional domain controller, you have an easy task ahead of you. Use the Active Directory Installation Wizard to reinstall Active Directory, promoting the server to a domain controller. Active Directory and Sysvol will be brought up-to-date through an automatic replication process from a domain controller.

Restoring files from files or tapes

The actual restoration process may end up being a little more involved than the backup process, but that's only because you have to take time to consider the consequences of how you're going about the restoration. To begin:

1. **Open the Backup utility and click the Restore tab.**

2. **On the resulting Restore screen, select the check box in the left-hand pane for any drive, folder, or file that you want to restore.**

   For further granularity of control, select the files and folders you want to restore in the right-hand pane by clicking the box to the left of a file or folder.

3. **Next, make sure you take your time and select the right one of the three Restore files to options:**

   • **Original location:** Choose this option if you want the backed up files and folders to be restored to the folder or folders they were in when they were backed up, replicating the same file and directory structure.

- **Alternate location:** Choose this option if you want the backed up files and directory structure to be restored to a different folder that you designate.

- **Single folder:** Choose this option if you want the backed up files and folders to be restored to a folder that you designate. As stated previously, this option doesn't preserve the folder structure of the backed up data. Instead, you get all the files dumped into one location.

4. **If you selected Alternate location or Single folder, you'll be prompted to type a path for the folder under Alternate location.**

   If you're not sure of the exact location or have carpal tunnel syndrome from all your keyboard work, click the Browse button to locate your folder.

5. **Choose Tools⇨Options, then select the Restore tab. On the Restore panel, select one of the following three choices to continue with your Restoration process:**

   - **Do not replace the file on my computer:** Choose this option if you don't want the restore operation to copy over files already on your hard drive.

   - **Replace the file on disk only if the file on disk is older:** Choose this option if you want the restore operation to replace the chronologically older files on your disk with newer files stored on your backup copy.

   - **Always replace the file on my computer:** Choose this option if you want the restore operation to replace files on your disk regardless of whether the backup files are newer or older.

6. **Click OK to accept the restore options you have set, then click the Start Restore button.**

If you want to change any of the advanced restore options, such as restoring security settings, the Removable Storage database, and junction point data, click Advanced. When you finish setting advanced restore options, click OK to keep your settings; then click the Start Restore button on the Restore screen.

Of course, you can also use the Restore Wizard to restore files by choosing Tools⇨Restore Wizard.

If you restore the System State data without designating an alternate location for the restored data, Backup erases the System State data that's currently on your computer and replaces it with the System State data you are restoring.

Restoring System State data

Open the Backup utility, click the Restore tab, and then click to select the check box for any drive, folder, or file that you want to restore. In this case, make sure to click the box next to System State. Selecting this option ensures that you restore the System State data along with any other data you have selected for the current restore operation. (It's a misconception that you can only restore System State data by itself in a separate restoration procedure.)

Remember that if you restore the System State data to an alternate location, only the Registry files, SYSVOL directory files, Cluster database information files, and system boot files are restored to the alternate location. The Active Directory directory services database, Certificate Services database, and COM+ Class Registration database are not restored when you specify an alternate location.

When you restore the System State data to a domain controller, you must choose whether you want to perform an *authoritative* restore or a *nonauthoritative* restore. The default method of restoring the System State data to a domain controller is nonauthoritative. In the nonauthoritative mode, any component of the System State that's replicated with another domain controller, such as the Active Directory directory service or the File Replication service (including the SYSVOL directory), will be brought up to date by replication after you restore the data.

Authoritative restoration: Electronic white-out for mistakes

Of course, you may not want to duplicate the changes that you may have made after the last full System State backup operation. In other words, you may have instances where you want all replicas to have the same state as the backed up data. To do this, you'll have to perform an authoritative restore.

You have to perform an authoritative restore in certain situations. For example, if you inadvertently deleted users, groups, or other incredibly important objects from the Active Directory directory service, you want to restore the system so the deleted objects are recovered (and, well, *restored* to the way they were before you messed them up). To do this task, you need to run the Ntdsutil utility after you restore the data but before you restart the domain controller.

The Ntdsutil command lets you mark objects as authoritative, which ensures that any stored replicated or distributed data on the system is properly replicated or distributed throughout your company or organization. You can run the Ntdsutil command-line utility from the DOS command prompt. As stated in Chapter 10, you can find help for the Ntdsutil utility by typing **ntdsutil /?** at the DOS command prompt.

To restore the System State data on a domain controller, you must first start your computer in a special safe mode called *directory services restore* mode. This option allows you to restore the SYSVOL directory and Active Directory directory service database. And remember, you can only restore the System State data on a local computer. You can't restore the System State data on a remote computer.

Restoring files to a Microsoft Exchange server

As stated in Chapter 10 on the Backup process, this option primarily applies to Microsoft Exchange Version 5.5 and earlier. Later versions will be working with new procedures that are in the works up in Microsoft HQ.

To begin the restoration, follow these steps:

1. **Open the Backup utility and click the Restore tab to get to the Restore screen.**

2. **On the Restore screen, click to select the check box for any drive, folder, or file that you want to restore, then select the Microsoft Exchange data you want to restore.**

3. **Click the Start Restore button.**

   The Restoring Microsoft Exchange dialog box appears.

4. **If you are restoring Information Store data, type the name of the server to which you are restoring data in the Restore screen to field.**

5. **Choose any other Restore options you want, and then click OK.**

If you designate a server that's different from the original server the data was backed up from, you must also choose Erase all existing data.

If you restore data back to a Microsoft Exchange Server, the Information Store service and Directory services are stopped. Start the services after the restore is complete. Choose Tools⇨Microsoft Exchange, click Start Service, select Directory or Information Store, and then click OK to complete the task.

Chapter 12

Meeting Your Quotas

● ●

In This Chapter

▶ Disk quotas overview

▶ Why you should enable disk quotas

▶ Documenting and auditing disk use

▶ Enabling disk quotas

▶ Assigning, viewing, and modifying quota settings

▶ Adding and deleting quotas

▶ Importing and exporting quotas

▶ Disabling quotas

● ●

*T*wo kinds of people populate the world of 2000 A.D. — those who need more disk space and those who don't use computers. If you've come this far in the book, I can pretty well guess that you don't fall into the latter category. So, by default you fall into the first — the type of person who needs more disk space, whether it be today or (more likely) yesterday.

It seems odd that in this day and age, when you can buy a gigabyte's worth of space for the price of a nice lunch, that disk space issues are still key for Windows administrators. Apparently, some things just never change. Suppose that you just doubled your disk capacity, thanks to your unceasing efforts to deflect user complaints to the upper management folks who determine your technology budget. Problem solved, right? Well, it's more like your problems took a quick visit to their relatives in Kalamazoo. To paraphrase the great action movie star (and rumored Windows user), Ah-nold Schwarzenegger, "They'll be back."

Solving space problems by buying scads of disk space is at best a delaying tactic against the inevitable. Granted, if you're independently wealthy and you can slap in an extra 100GB whenever you take the time to visit the local Radio Shack, then this strategy will work. But for the more normal folks, this strategy is a dead end for two reasons.

First, extra dollars to buy more disk space are allocated on a strict *need* basis in most organizations, whether you're part of a government laboratory or a corporate technology center. So, when you're handed 100GB, it's not usually to play with and allocate as you see fit. Instead, it's usually tied into an ulterior motive, such as to provide the database group a new disk to store the accounting files on, or a new drive for the CEO to store the digital pictures of him and his golfing buddies at Pebble Beach. Very, very rarely will you be able to swing a major upgrade for something as *minor* as keeping your user community happy.

Second, even if you do place more space out on the drive for the user community, it will fill up more quickly than you realize. To paraphrase a physics term this time, *data abhors a vacuum*. All that lovely space works out to an extra what, 5 or 6MB per user? That space will easily be filled up after they realize they can store their favorite *Baywatch* or *Melrose Place* pictures off the Web. And then they'll complain to you when they can't seem to find the space for those pesky project reports.

The answer to your dilemma is the basis of this chapter — the enabling and administration of disk quotas.

Understanding Disk Quotas

According to the faithful and ever-accurate dictionary by Mr. Webster, a *quota* is "a proportionate part or share of a fixed total amount or quantity." It's not a bad description of what a quota system on Windows 2000 really is. Any kind of *quota system* on a computer network is designed to track and control disk space usage for volumes.

Windows 2000 follows up this idea with a few special Microsoft twists. For example, you can use the quota system to prevent further disk space use and write to a log whenever a user exceeds her amount of specially allocated disk space.

Windows 2000 disk quotas allow you to set two main values around which the system pivots. First, you can set the absolute disk quota limit that a user is allowed to claim for file storage. Second, you can set the level at which the disk quota system gives the user a warning. This *warning level* is the point at which a user account is coming close to the allocated disk quota limit.

Suppose that you can set a user's disk quota limit to a rather miserly 20 megabytes on the hard disk. This means that the user can store no more than 20MB of files (word files, graphics files, sound files, whatever) on her allocated section of the disk. However, suppose that you set the disk quota warning level to 18MB. If the user stores more than 18MB of files, the event triggers the set warning level and the disk quota system logs it as a system event for you to deal with.

At what level below the absolute limit of quota storage should you make the warning? Judging from experience, the rule of thumb that I've learned to live with is to set the warning at 10 percent below the absolute threshold.

I've actually specified the preceding example (the 20-18MB example) because it takes this advice a little too literally. My feeling is that you need a little *wiggle space* to allow you to make other arrangements — or chastise the user — before she runs into serious problems. A margin of error only 2MB wide is a little small for my tastes. Similarly, if you're overly generous with your users and they have 500MB quotas, a 50MB limit is a bit too wide to get concerned about!

Overall, I suggest a minimum space of 5MB and a maximum of 25MB. Normally, users won't fill up a 5MB area too quickly, unless they're trying to save streaming video files of the latest Marilyn Manson or Rolling Stones concert.

Of course, if you want to be the *kinder and gentler* sort of administrative tyrant (come on, it's the fun side of the job), you can specify that users are allowed to exceed their quota limit. Just don't encourage it! When you enable the quota system but don't set a hard limit on disk space, you're effectively removing the teeth from the quota system. However, this technique is useful if you want to simply track disk space use on a per-user basis.

Windows is flexible enough that where you can also specify that when a user exceeds her warning level, nothing is logged. Of course, doing that reminds me of the drink made popular (or at least memorable) in the San Francisco espresso bars.

It's a decaf, non-fat cappuccino topped with sugar-free whipped cream. To all the knowledgeable espresso servers, this concoction is known as a Why Bother? — which is what comes to my mind if you decide not to use the limiting or logging capabilities of the superb Windows quota system that you've chosen to enable.

When you enable the Disk Quotas system, volume usage is automatically tracked for new users from that point on. But existing volume users have no disk quotas applied to them! This situation exists for two reasons. First, quotas do add more *overhead* to your CPU, so Windows naturally limits the blanket use of the quota system.

Second, your operating system would go into conniptions and roll itself into a fetal position if it had to sort out all the log messages that could come rolling in if it automatically applied quotas to existing users. After all, existing users had *no* limits to adhere to, so it's likely that all previously existing users are flagrantly disobeying the new quota rules! In order to apply the newly enabled disk quotas to existing volume users, you have to add new quota entries in the Quota Entries window.

To support disk quotas, you must format a disk volume with the version of NTFS used in Windows 2000. You can enable quotas on both local volumes and network volumes, but again, those volumes must be formatted with the NTFS file system. Volumes formatted with the version of NTFS used in Windows NT 4.0 are upgraded automatically by Windows 2000 Setup to handle the Windows 2000 quota system.

If the volume you've selected is not formatted for NTFS, you won't be able to even get to the quotas screen. You run into a similar quandary if you're not logged in as the Administrator account, or at least an account within the Administrators group on the local computer.

Because Microsoft is trying to help avoid frustrating users, instead of allowing users to progress through the Quota screens and then forbidding them to apply their choices, the Quota tab isn't even displayed on the volume's Properties page. On the whole, I'd say that this feature is a very humane way to reduce the stress and frustration level that often accompany high-tech items like computers, cars, printers, and fax machines.

User actions that affect the quota limit

To users, a quota limit is very much like a credit card limit — easy to spend, hard to bring back into trim. In order to be charged against their allocated limit, users copy or save a new file to a volume formatted with the NTFS file system. For example, suppose a user decides one evening to write the sequel to *War and Peace*, a longer and more in-depth work called *Peace, then Back to War Again*.

The file, when saved, is 40MB in size (just the prologue). Saving it to an allocated disk quota of 50MB reduces the remaining space to 10MB, and possibly sets off the limitation alarms, if you follow the 10 percent rule quoted earlier in this chapter.

Another sort of action that affects the quota limit is when the user takes ownership of a file on an NTFS volume. For example, one user takes ownership of the 5MB appendix file to *Peace, then Back to War Again,* because this user has a thing for appendixes. The original author, desiring to get rid of this file, copied it to a volume where someone could take ownership. End result at the end of the game: The author's disk use decreases by 5MB and the appendix-phile's disk use increases by 5MB.

What counts for the quota

Ever been in the express line at the supermarket and wondered whether you're breaking the ten-items rule by buying a dozen eggs? Luckily, common sense allows the egg container to be considered *one* item.

Similarly, use common sense when figuring out quota statistics. Suppose that you're limited as a user to 20MB of space. You compress a 40MB file into a file that's only 12MB in size. Will the quota level block you? Of course not — whatever the full, expanded size of the file, quotas only care about what amount of space that's truly being used at the given moment.

Quotas on folders and disks

Bear in mind that *quotas* on folders or disks is something of a misnomer. Disk quotas are independent of folder structures of volumes and their layout on physical disks, applying only to volumes. After all, the actual object called a *folder* is nothing more than a structural element. While the contents of the folder may expand in size, the object itself does not — it's there to help provide logical order.

Now, if a volume contains many different folders, the quotas assigned to the volume apply collectively to all the folders. For example, if \\Dummystuff\A and \\Dummystuff\B are shared folders on Volume IDG, users' utilization of both \\Dummystuff\A and \\Dummystuff\B are subject to what you've assigned for the quota on that volume.

By contrast, if you apply quotas to volumes that reside together on the same physical disk, each volume quota applies only to its *specific* volume. If Volume A and Volume B exist on the same disk, quotas are tracked independently for the two volumes, which allows you to apply different quotas for each volume, depending on how heavily the specific volume is being used, and the degree of your need for monitoring and enforcing space allocation.

Finally, if a given volume spans multiple physical disks, the same quota you create and apply for that volume applies to the entire spanned volume — regardless of whether a given volume resides on a single physical disk or whether it spans two, three, or a half-dozen disks (although that would give an administrator horrors just to think about).

Enabling Disk Quotas

Depending on how you plan out your quota settings, you may want to set your quota limits very specifically. For example, you could set a quota limit of 20MB for all users of the Database department, while making sure that the three database administrators who routinely work with large Oracle or Sybase files on the server have a 50MB limit.

When you enable quotas on a volume that already contains files, Windows calculates the disk space already used by user accounts who have copied, saved, or taken ownership of files on the volume up to that point in time. The quota limit and warning level you set are applied to all current users based on those calculations. Similarly, newly created users who begin using the volume from that point on are also given these quota restrictions.

Later on, you can then set different quotas, or disable quotas, for individual or multiple users. For example, if one or both users in the database administrators example cited previously do not have files stored on the server when you enable quotas, you need to use the Select Users property sheet to set their quota limit to a value higher than the default for new users. Otherwise, you may end up with some users who are very frustrated that your new and improved Windows 2000 administrative tools are preventing them from getting their jobs done.

To enable disk quotas, follow these steps:

1. **Open the desktop icon My Computer by double-clicking it.**

2. **Right-click the disk volume for which you want to enable disk quotas, and then select Properties from the resulting pop-up menu.**

   The Properties dialog box appears, showing seven or eight different tabs.

3. **Click the Quota tab to get to the Quota panel (see Figure 12-1).**

4. **On the Quota properties panel, select the Enable Quota Management with a click of the mouse.**

   Note that the grayed-out quota controls darken and become fully usable for you.

5. **When this happy event takes place, click OK.**

If you're not the administrator, you can still view the properties of a given disk or volume. But you won't be allowed to even see the Quotas tab — it'll be as if it never existed, giving a whole new meaning to the term *user transparency*.

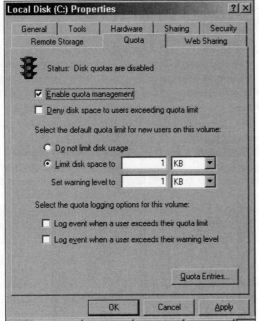

Figure 12-1:
The Quota
property
panel for a
local disk.

Documenting Disk Space Use

If you're more interested in finding out where your disk space is going to (as opposed to in a handbasket), you can specify a disk quota limit without denying users further disk space use. This setting is the most useful when you don't want to deny users access to a volume, but want to track disk space use on a per-user basis.

You can document disk space use via this feature, which is useful for

- ✔ Demonstrating additional disk space needs, particularly to those who hold the purse strings in your company.

- ✔ Showing distribution of disk space on a per-user basis, so you can demonstrate to an obnoxious user why you can't allow him to store ten CD's worth of MP3 files on his space.

- ✔ Keeping historical records of disk space use. (Who knows, maybe they'll use them to make a miniseries someday.)

- ✔ Notifying users of disk space over-utilization. Have fun and be creative with your e-mail warnings. It comes with the territory.

Auditing Disk Space Use

Luckily (at least for most of us), we're selected for the privilege of a thorough tax audit only once every few years, if at all. The government, in its infinite wisdom, realizes that things would grind to a halt if every single person were subjected to such detailed recording and record searching every single year. So audits are done almost at random, with a limited number of agents.

Similarly, enabling quotas causes a slight increase in server overhead, leading to a slight decrease in the performance of your file server. Usually, this slow-down won't be enough for you to notice, but if you're in an environment that's chronically overloaded and speed is of the essence, auditing is for you.

By periodically enabling and disabling the quotas you've set up, you can take advantage of the auditing capabilities provided by the Disk Quota system. Best yet, you can reduce the performance impact on your file server by following this pattern.

When you enable quotas for an audit, Windows calculates how much disk space is used by those users who have stored files on a volume, as per your pre-set quota standards. You can then contact those users who are using more disk space than they should as you see fit, normally with a scathing e-mail. (I hope some of you out there know that I am joking — kind of.) If you don't want to impede your file server performance by continually monitoring disk usage, don't forget to disable quotas after you're done viewing the data.

The best way to keep a detailed audit record is to save a copy of the data to another application, such as Microsoft Excel. For information on how to do that most effectively, grab a copy of *Excel For Dummies* (IDG Books Worldwide, Inc.).

Exceeding Disk Quota Limits

Depending on the options you select for your Disk Quota system, you get the following results when the disk quota limits are exceeded. Trust me, someday very soon, they will be!

- **Deny disk space to users exceeding the quota limit:** With this selection, users who exceed their quota limit receive an `insufficient disk space` error from Windows and cannot save data to the volume without first deleting, moving, or otherwise expunging some existing data.

  If you leave this option cleared, users can exceed their quota limit, but you can still track the usage statistics.

✔ **Log event when a user exceeds his quota limit:** With this option, an event is written to the Windows system log on the computer running disk quotas whenever users exceed their disk quota limit. Administrators can view these events with Event Viewer. If you have a lot of messages, be sure to filter for disk event types.

✔ **Log event when a user exceeds his warning level:** With this option, whenever users exceed their quota warning level, an event is written to the Windows system log on the computer running disk quotas. Again, if you have a lot of messages, be sure to filter for disk event types.

Assigning the Default Quota Values

As a rule, you can use the default quota values that Microsoft has assigned to the Quota utility. Try running with defaults when you start it — unless you're severely short of disk space. If you experience system slowdowns or other problems, you can either adjust the Quota system manually or you can purchase more disk space.

To assign the default quota values, follow these steps:

1. **Open My Computer by double-clicking it.**

2. **Right-click the volume for which you want to assign default quota values, and select Properties from the pop-up menu.**

   The Properties dialog box appears.

3. **Click the Quota tab and select the Enable Quota Management check box in the Quota panel.**

4. **Select the Limit Disk Space To option by clicking the button to the left of the open fields, as shown in Figure 12-2.**

   Doing so darkens the fields, allowing you to edit the disk space limit and warning levels. You can type numeric values in the text fields, using decimal values such as 5.5 or 1.8MB if you feel like it. Alternatively, you can select a disk space limit unit from the drop-down list. MB, KB, GB, and the other settings are abbreviations for various disk space measurements you can use.

5. **Click OK when finished.**

When you enable the disk quotas on a given volume, users with write access to the volume who have not exceeded their quota limit can store data on the volume. The first time a user writes data to a quota-enabled volume, default values for disk space limit and warning level are automatically assigned by the Quota system.

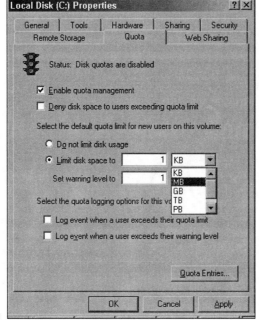

Figure 12-2:
In the
Quota panel,
you can
select an
amount of
disk space
with the
drop-down
list on
the right.

Viewing Disk Quota Information for Volume Users

If you're inheriting a Windows 2000 system from another administrator, it's worth checking out the Disk Quota information your first go-around. You should also consider checking your quota information whenever you have some dead time in your schedule. If a gang of malicious users has cracked your Administrator's password, this is a prime place for them to go; from there they can increase or remove the Disk Quota on their own account, leaving all the space they want for their Metallica sound clips.

To view disk quota information for volume users, follow these steps:

1. **Open My Computer by double-clicking it.**

2. **Right-click the volume for which you want to assign default quota values, and select Properties from the pop-up menu.**

3. **Get to the Properties dialog box of the volume you want and click the Quota tab.**

4. **On the Quota properties page, click the Quota Entries button, located in the lower right of the window.**

The Quota Entries window appears, as shown in Figure 12-3.

Each row in the window contains information for a volume user.

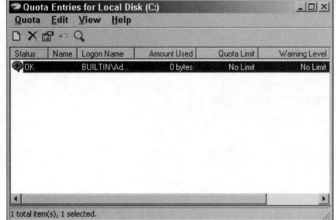

Figure 12-3:
The Quota
Entries
screen,
ready to
display
available
quotas.

Keep in mind that when the Quota Entries window is opened for the first time, volume quota information must be obtained from the network domain controller. After the information has been obtained from the domain controller, it is saved so that it's immediately available the next time the Quota Entries window is opened.

If you're having problems with your network domain server at the time you begin this operation, you'll likely end up with incomplete or inaccurate data.

Modifying User Disk Space Limits and Warning Levels

If you find yourself running out of space or getting larger-than-normal warning messages, you might consider editing one or both of these parameters. Of course, the ideal solution is to buy more disk space. If you don't control the company purse strings, this is a viable alternative. To modify the limits and warning levels, do the following:

1. **Open My Computer by double-clicking it.**

2. **Right-click the volume for which you want to assign default quota values, and select Properties from the pop-up menu.**

3. **In the Properties dialog box, click the Quota tab.**

4. **On the Quota properties panel, click the Quota Entries button in the lower right.**

   The Quota Entries window appears.

5. **Select the entries for the users whose options you want to modify by clicking them.**

6. **Choose Quota⇨Properties in the upper-left toolbar.**

   The Quota Settings dialog box appears, as shown in Figure 12-4.

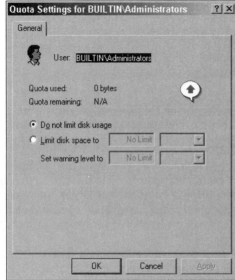

Figure 12-4:
The Quota
Settings
screen, set
to Do not
limit disk
usage.

7. **Modify any of the options you want to change and then click OK.**

If you want to track disk space usage without limiting disk space, do not limit disk usage. Make sure that you click the Do not limit disk usage button to select this option.

On the flip side, clicking Limit disk space to activates the open fields for limiting disk space and setting warning levels. As in the main Quota panel, you can type a numeric value in the text field or select a disk space limit unit from the drop-down list. Again, if you want, you can use decimal values.

The value you enter in the disk space limit cannot exceed the maximum capacity of the volume. Of course, if you can figure out a way around this, let me know — you may have broken some obscure law of physics and I can use the press coverage.

Creating quota reports

After you have your Quota system up and running, you should consult it every now and then. A periodic review of your quota setup can help you identify problem areas before they mushroom into major crises. If you're truly interested in getting a good night's sleep, be sure to do this at least every three to four months. You can create quota reports by doing the following:

1. **Open My Computer by double-clicking it.**

2. **Right-click the volume for which you want to assign default quota values, and select Properties from the pop-up menu.**

3. **In the Properties dialog box, click the Quota tab.**

   The Quota Properties window appears.

4. **On the Quota Properties panel, click the Quota Entries button.**

   The Quota Entries window appears.

5. **While the Quota Entries window is open, open a document in the program that you will use to create the report.**

   You can use Word if you want, but your best bet is to use Microsoft Excel. Having a spreadsheet available here is very handy.

6. **In the Quota Entries window, click the entries you want to include in your quota report and insert them into the document by clicking and dragging.**

   The rows set in the Quota window will match the program you use to create the report, particularly if you're using Excel, because the transferred data retains the same column and entry order as in the Quota Entries window.

Adding new quota entries

Adding new quota entries is simple. You should add new entries whenever your hard drive space expands — which is normally when you add a new hard drive.

Unless you fence in the open country on the new drive, it *will* be taken over by disk-rustlers who want that extra 10 gigabytes to store those extra Western novels they've been writing in their spare time.

Meanwhile, pardner, here's the lowdown on ridin' fences on your drives:

1. **Open My Computer by double-clicking it.**

2. **Right-click the volume for which you want to assign default quota values, and select Properties from the pop-up menu.**

3. **In the Properties dialog box, click the Quota tab.**

4. **On the Quota properties panel, click the Quota Entries button in the lower right.**

   The Quota Entries window appears.

5. **Choose Quota⇨New Quota Entry from the toolbar menu.**

6. **In the Add New Quota Entry dialog box, specify one of the following options and then click OK:**

   • **Do not limit disk usage:** Tracks disk space usage without limiting disk space.

   • **Limit disk space to:** Activates fields for limiting disk space and setting warning levels. Type a numeric value in the text field and select a disk space limit unit (MB, GB, KB, or whatever) from the drop-down list.

   As a rule, you're pretty safe if you follow the default disk space limit and warning level values established by the volume administrator.

7. **In the Select Users dialog box, in the Look In list box, select the name of the domain or workgroup from which you want to select user names.**

   Note that you can change the area to look in by clicking the down-arrow to the right of the Look In box, which shows a menu with the other available locations.

8. **Click Add, and then click OK to apply your changes.**

Deleting quota entries

Be sure to delete a quota entry if you remove a disk from your system for any reason. You should also remove a Quota system setup if you're reallocating the disk from user account usage to, say, applications. This prevents problems with applications, such as running out of space to store valuable log files.

1. **Open My Computer by double-clicking it.**

2. **Right-click the volume for which you want to assign default quota values, and select Properties from the pop-up menu.**

3. **In the Properties dialog box, click the Quota tab.**

4. **On the Quota properties panel, click the Quota Entries button in the lower right.**

   The Quota Entries window appears.

5. **Click the entries for the users you want to delete, and then choose Quota⇨Delete quota entry.**

6. **When the Disk Quota dialog box appears, click the Yes button.**

7. **Click the files that you want to take action on, then click one of the following buttons:**

   - **Delete:** Deletes selected files from the volume.

   - **Take ownership:** Gives you ownership of selected files on the volume.

   - **Move:** Moves selected files to a specified volume.

8. **Click Close to apply your selection.**

Before you can delete a record, all files owned by the selected user on the volume must either be deleted or moved to another volume. Alternatively, ownership of the files can be transferred to another user but it must be done prior to starting the delete process. You are prompted to delete, take ownership of, or move a file only if the user still has files on the volume at the time that you begin the deletion process.

Importing quota settings

I can hear some readers thinking, "But I already have the perfect quota system set up on the machine in the other lab — why do I have to redo all my hard work over here?" How can I hear that? Well, as the guys patrolling Area 51 are supposed to say, *I could tell you, but then I'd have to kill you.* (Kidding!) Call it an astute guess: Nobody likes to redo work.

Cheer up — the folks at Microsoft have foreseen this unhappy situation and remedied it. If you want to *import* your settings from a remote machine, you can now do it. Just follow the handy-dandy instructions and you're ready to go.

1. **Open My Computer by double-clicking it.**

2. **Right-click the volume for which you want to assign default quota values, and select Properties from the pop-up menu.**

3. **In the Properties dialog box, click the Quota tab.**

4. **On the Quota properties panel, click the Quota Entries button in the lower right.**

   The Quota Entries window appears.

5. **Select Import from the Quota Entries pull-down menu.**

   The Import Quota Settings dialog box appears, as shown in Figure 12-5.

Figure 12-5:
The
amazingly
non-
eye-catching
look of the
Import
Quota
Settings
screen.

6. **Select the name of the file that contains the quota settings you want to import, and then click Open.**

   A dialog box warns you if an imported setting will overwrite existing settings for a volume user. Be careful before you decide whether you want to overwrite existing user settings.

7. **After you click Open, exit the Quota Entries menus by closing the windows or clicking Close. Your import setting is saved.**

As an alternative to all this foofaraw, you can open two instances of the Quota Entries window: one for the volume *from* which you are importing the quota records, and one for the volume *into* which you want to import quota records. Then, in classic Windows fashion, you can click and drag quota records from the source volume's Quota Entries window to the destination volume's Quota Entries window.

Exporting quota settings to another volume

The flip side to importing quotas is exporting them to other machines. After all, when you have the perfect system set up, why waste time duplicating your effort? Save yourself the hassle and export your work in the following manner:

1. **Open My Computer by double-clicking it.**

2. **Right-click the volume for which you want to assign default quota values, and select Properties from the pop-up menu.**

3. **In the Properties dialog box, click the Quota tab.**

4. **On the Quota properties panel, click the Quota Entries button in the lower right.**

   The Quota Entries window appears.

5. **Select Export from the Quota Entries pull-down menu.**

6. **In the Export Quota Settings dialog box, select the name of the file that contains the quota settings you want to export, and then click Open.**

7. **In the Export Quota Settings dialog box, shown in Figure 12-6, specify a destination folder, type a filename for the saved settings, and click the Save button.**

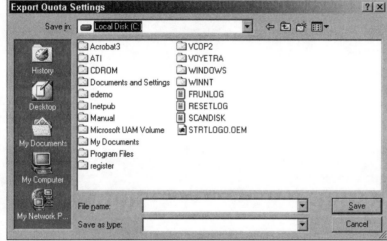

Figure 12-6:
The even
snazzier
look of the
Export
Quota
Settings
screen.

Disabling disk quotas

Of course, there may come a time when you realize that you've outgrown the need for disk quotas. Truth be told, the only time I've seen this was when the users threatened to mob the administrator — but that's a story for another time. If you're threatened with bodily harm, complete the following tasks to disable your Disk Quota system:

1. **Open My Computer and right-click the disk volume for which you want to disable disk quotas.**

2. **Select Properties from the menu that appears.**

3. **In the Properties dialog box, click the Quota tab.**

4. **Deselect the Enable quota management check box and then click OK.**

See? I told you that being a Windows 2000 Administrator wasn't that hard.

Part III
Configuring Hardware and Software

The 5th Wave   By Rich Tennant

"Oh sure, it's nice working at home, except my boss drives by every morning and blasts his horn to make sure I'm awake."

In this part . . .

Proceed with care! This part covers subjects that can make you and break you as an effective Windows 2000 system administrator. Within the following pages are such career-killers as printing and the Registry. But I'll be gentle.

Chapter 13

Management Console Miracles

A new feature to Windows 2000 is the *Microsoft Management Console*, called *MMC*. (Why MMC? Well, try saying Microsoft Management Console ten times really fast and you'll see.) Officially, it's supposed to be a new framework in which to display your administrative utilities in Windows 2000. Unofficially, I think you'll agree that it serves a similar purpose to an old-fashioned peg board you hang tools from.

You can administer your entire system without ever touching, clicking, or laying eyes on the Microsoft Management Console. However, by providing you with a place where you can access every single utility more directly and efficiently, MMC more than proves its worth. Instead of laboriously going through the Start buttons multiple pop-up and pull-down menus, you can start and stop administrative functions with a few mouse clicks.

MMC — Administrative One-Stop Shopping

Microsoft Management Console (MMC) is called a *console* because it allows you to create, edit, and save administrative tools in a similar formula and window frame. You may also think about it as a *one-stop shop* for your administrative needs, or at least a conveniently located mall with the various consoles as the shops you need to visit. (If you've ever wanted to roll up your sleeves and redesign the local mini-mall, here's your chance.)

MMC is a relative newcomer to the Microsoft line of business. MMC is really a new feature bundled with the Windows 2000 operating system. However, because it's not as integral to the core of the system as, say, the NTFS file system, you can also run MMC on the later versions of other Microsoft products, such as Windows NT 4.0, Windows 95, and Windows 98. (No official word exists as to whether it works on Windows 3.1, but my advice is this: Don't even think about it.)

MMC itself doesn't provide any administrative functions, but it provides (like the mini-mall example I'm talking about) a convenient place to get to everything and do whatever you have available to you in one location. Most of the tools you'll be adding into the MMC are called *snap-ins*. You can also add ActiveX controls, folders, and taskpad views, as well as hyperlinks to Web pages.

MMC has two modes — user and author — that you'll need to use in order to make effective use of the utility.

User mode

User mode allows user accounts access to work with existing MMC consoles. You can grant user access mode fully (that is, the user can access all window commands, but may not add or remove a snap-in) or with limited access.

Author mode

Author mode allows you the equivalent of full access in user mode. Of course, in addition to full access, you're allowed to add or remove snap-ins, create new windows and tasks, and generally act like an administrator. If you're from the UNIX side of doing things, you may recognize these modes as similar to the Command and Edit modes in the vi text editor.

You can access these modes by choosing Console⇨Options. A drop-down list allows you to switch between modes, complete with a description of the mode's powers, in case you should forget. You can see an example of an options screen in Figure 13-1.

Opening MMC

Opening MMC is simple, but it's not just a matter of mousing around. Yes, for once in a long while, to open MMC you'll have to actually do some typing. (It's a sort of discouragement factor for any casual user who may want to play around with MMC.)

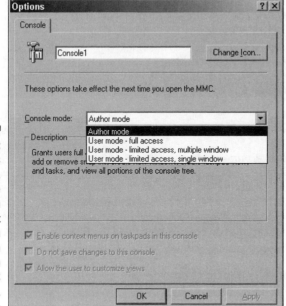

Figure 13-1:
The Options
screen.
Note the
drop-down
list that
allows you
switch
modes in
the MMC
console.

Click the Start button and select Run. In the Open field, type **mmc**, and click OK to start MMC.

Another way to bring up MMC is to bring up a DOS command prompt. The complete command-line syntax is

```
mmc path\filename.msc [/a]
path\filename.msc
```

I, Author

Note the /a option listed in the preceding example. This option opens a saved console in the *author* mode, but does not permanently change the default mode setting for files. When you omit this option, MMC opens console files according to their default mode settings, although normally the default mode for an administrator is the author mode.

Of course, you shouldn't worry if you're unable to remember the saved console locations when typing in the DOS window. After you open MMC or a console file in author mode, you can open any existing console by choosing Console⇨Open.

If you've saved some consoles, you need to specify the complete path and filename for the saved console file. By default, if you don't specify a console file, MMC opens a new console.

Creating a Desktop Shortcut to Open MMC

If you belong to the *terminally lazy* classification of administrators (join the club — at least if you have the energy), then you'll want to simplify matters by making MMC available to you in the simplest fashion. The best way to do this is to create a shortcut to MMC right on the desktop:

1. **Right-click an open area on the Windows desktop.**

2. **Select New⇨Shortcut.**

3. **Follow the instructions on your screen.**

   A specially named shortcut appears on your desktop.

   Double-clicking this shortcut opens up the MMC console without your having to go through the Start button and its subfolders or Run command.

You can drag a shortcut that you create on the desktop to other folders in the operating system, such as the folder where you keep your .msc files or the folder for the Start menu.

You can also create a shortcut to MMC in folders by using Windows Explorer:

1. **Open Windows Explorer and click the folder where you want the shortcut.**

2. **Choose File⇨New.**

3. **Select Shortcut, then follow the instructions on your screen.**

   Windows completes the task for you, and you'll have your shortcut in no time.

Getting to Know the MMC Console

Yes, saying MMC console is sort of redundant. And repetitive, too. But Microsoft Management Console is really the name for the utility, not the screen that displays the information you need to make use of MMC properly.

The MMC console consists (as many of the Microsoft administrative tools do) of a window divided into two panes. The left pane contains two tabs: Tree and Favorites. The Tree tab displays the administrative tools you have allocated to the MMC when you were in author mode in a tree directory format. The Favorites tab allows you to further organize your selected snap-ins and other MMC items. (For a better idea of how this looks, see Figure 13-2.)

In the right-hand pane, you have the *details* of the utilities listed in the tree format. The details pane shows you detailed information about each item (yes, I know you're surprised as I was) listed in the tree pane on the left. Click different items in the console tree to see the information in the details pane change to match your selection.

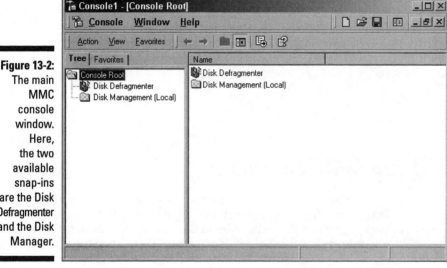

Figure 13-2:
The main
MMC
console
window.
Here,
the two
available
snap-ins
are the Disk
Defragmenter
and the Disk
Manager.

The MMC window also has several menus and a toolbar that are specific to the MMC utility. These menus and toolbars provide commands to open, create, and save MMC consoles. The most useful of these commands are under the Action, View, and Console pull-down menus.

And, of course, each console (such as Disk Defragmenter and Disk Manager) has its own menus and toolbar, separate from those of the main MMC window, that help a user perform tasks. For reference on any of these functions, be sure to look at the chapter specific to the console's function. (For example, boogie on over to Chapter 8 for Disk Management.)

Finally, a description bar runs along the top of the details pane. Depending on how much information you want to see, you can select what to hide from the View menu. After you add items to the main MMC console, you can choose to hide the main menu bar, main toolbar, description bar, and status bar to prevent users from making unnecessary changes to the console. Choose View➪Customize and select what you want to show or hide by selecting the check boxes to the left of the offered options. To view the Customize View window (is there an echo in here?), view Figure 13-3.

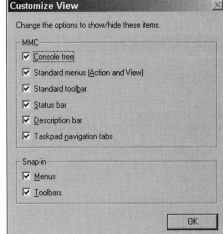

Figure 13-3:
The
Customize
View
window, for
customizing
the MMC
view.

Using MMC consoles

If you're not in the mood to author new consoles, you may never need to build custom consoles of your own. Preconfigured consoles are usually available in the Administrative Tools folder in Control Panel or from the Start menu. You just need to check these locations for these snap-ins, and you're in business.

Preconfigured consoles that come as part of your operating system are configured to open in one of the three user modes. In Windows 2000, the default mode is user mode — limited access, single window. If you save a custom console to a per-user Administrative Tools folder, it's available in the Administrative Tools folder on the Programs menu for that particular user.

Custom consoles, if saved to the default location, are located at the end of the following path:

```
\\systemdrive\Documents and Settings\user\Start
        Menu\Programs\Administrative Tools
```

Using columns in saved consoles

In saved consoles that display columns in the details pane, you can customize how the columns and rows appear. As long as you're displaying icons in the right-hand pane in detail, you can reorder or hide columns.

You can also reorder rows alphabetically or chronologically, all by clicking the column heading at the top of the pane. You can also export the contents of columns to a text file in WordPad or Microsoft Word.

In addition, with certain snap-ins, you can filter columns based on additional attributes. If you enable this feature, a row of drop-down list boxes that contain options for filtering appears beneath the column headings.

 When you customize the columns in a console, your settings are automatically saved from session to session. This nice touch saves you from a bunch of repetitive clicks, sore fingers, and embarrassing expletives.

Working with Snap-Ins

The *snap-in* is the basic component of an MMC console. The key concept is that a snap-in always resides in an MMC console. Snap-ins, like plug-ins downloaded from a Web site, don't run all by themselves. By default, when you install a component that has a snap-in associated with it on a computer running Windows, the snap-in is available to anyone creating a console on that computer.

You can add a single snap-in to a console, or you can add multiple instances of a snap-in to the same console to administer different computers. Each time you add a new instance of a snap-in to a console, any variables for the snap-in are set at default values until you configure the snap-in.

So, if you configure a particular snap-in to manage a remote computer and then add a second instance of the snap-in, don't take it for granted that your new settings are in place. You have to manually reconfigure the new instance to manage the second remote computer.

As a general rule, you can only add snap-ins that are installed on the computer you are using to author a console. However, in Windows 2000, if your computer is part of a domain, you can use MMC to download any snap-ins that are not locally installed, but that are available from the Active Directory directory service. From the Active Directory, you can click and drag (or select copy) to move the snap-ins you want.

The MMC supports two types of snap-ins: standalone and extension.

Standalone snap-ins

You can normally add a standalone snap-in, usually called a *snap-in,* to a console tree without adding another item first. (Hence the term *standalone.*) The vast majority of snap-ins fit into this category.

To add a snap-in, open the MMC and choose Console➪Add/Remove Snap-In. Of the two tabs in the Add/Remove window, the default is Standalone, as shown in Figure 13-4. Simply click the Add button and select the snap-in from the resulting window.

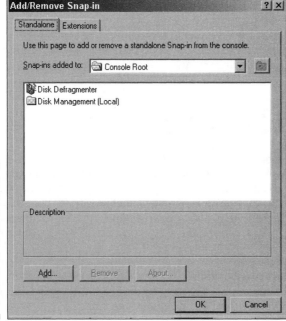

Figure 13-4:
The
Add/Remove
screen is
set by
default to
the
Standalone
tab.

Extension snap-ins

An extension snap-in, usually called an *extension,* is always added to a standalone or extension snap-in that's already on the console tree. When you add a snap-in or extension to a console, it appears in one of two areas.

It may appear as a new item in the console tree on the left-hand pane. On the other hand, it could add context-menu items, additional toolbars, additional property pages, or wizards to a snap-in already installed in the console. If it appears, it shows up underneath an existing snap-in on the MMC console. An example of this situation appears (though not at all mysteriously) in Figure 13-5.

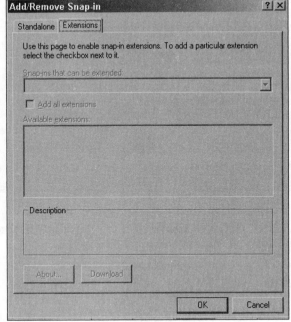

Figure 13-5:
Select the
Extensions
tab on the
Add/Remove
screen to
locate
and add
extension
snap-ins.

Adding a published extension snap-in to an MMC console

You can add a published extension snap-in by following the procedures outlined here. Luckily, most of your work is designed to get you to the Windows 2000 installation wizard programs as quickly as possible.

1. **Begin by opening a saved console in author mode by doing any one of the following three things:**

   • Right-click a file with an .msc extension, and then click Author.

   • Click the Start button, select Run, type **mmc path\filename.msc /a**, and then click OK.

   • Choose Console⇨Add/Remove Snap-in.

2. **Select the Extensions tab. In the Snap-ins that can be extended field, click the arrow on the right.**

3. **Select, from the drop-down menu, the snap-in that you want to extend.**

Snap-ins that aren't as much of a snap

If you select the Add all Extensions check box on the Extensions tab, only extension snap-ins that are *locally* installed and registered are added to the console.

You have to specifically download extension snap-ins from the directory service to make them available in a console. Whenever adding all published extensions for a given item, do not select the Add all Extensions check box. You'll be better off selecting the check box next to each published extension instead.

4. **In the Available Extensions field, select the check box next to the published extension you want to add. Click Download.**

   One or more of the wizard programs starts.

5. **Follow the instructions on your screen, and then click OK.**

You'll only be able to access extension snap-ins published in the directory if the computer you are using is

 ✔ Running Windows 2000

 ✔ A member of a Windows 2000 domain (not just a member of a workgroup)

Using the MMC Help system

Help is everywhere you want it (or need it) in the MMC system. You can access Help for MMC from a multitude of areas: the Help menu on the main toolbar, the button on the toolbar of a console window, on the System menu of the MMC window or a console window, or by right-clicking an item in either the console tree or details pane. If that isn't simple enough, try pressing the F1 key.

Help for MMC displays a table of contents, an index of topics, and a topic search engine. The MMC Help utility also includes general help for MMC and help that's specific to each console snap-in. If you decide to author a console, you may want to provide additional documentation for tasks associated with the console. This provides excellent backup material for a junior administrator who may be filling your shoes on the day you're off sick or catching rays in Acapulco.

Chapter 14

Cut! Print It!

*I*f you go by what you read, most books tell you that Group Administration, or maybe File Partition Administration, is the most time-critical, all-around most important thing to know about effective Windows 2000 administration. Baloney. Talk to any administrator worth his weight in silicon chips and he'll tell you the truth: that printing is by far the most important topic you can learn.

I can hear some readers thinking, "Printing? You mean that process where ink is sprayed on or burned into little pieces of paper and spit out of a machine? Isn't that a little . . . you know, *beneath* a Windows 2000 administrator?" On the contrary! Printing is your be-all and end-all (well, okay, next to the servers blowing up) of your job. Here's a rundown on why that's the case:

✔ **Printing is time critical to all users.** No matter how long it takes to get a file re-permissioned or to have more space allocated for their slice of the disk, people generally print out what they need, right when they need it. Unfortunately for you, that's generally *yesterday*.

✔ **Printing is egocentric.** Unlike being able to access a faceless accounting file, poor printing reflects badly on the users' creations. So they seem to take it as a sign that the universe is personally raining on their parade if the print services start acting up.

> ✔ **Printing is what's known as a *visible task*.** Nobody really notices when the tape backups break down. No one usually notices if you're suffering a 5 percent reduction in speed by running disk quotas. But everybody seems to notice when the printer isn't printing — and they'll come running to you, making you wish you had pursued an acting career or entered law school instead of trying your hand at administration.

The Printing World Under Windows 2000

Microsoft likes to talk about Windows 2000 printing capabilities by proclaiming that "With Windows 2000, you can share printing resources across your entire network!" Well, is it true? Absolutely. However, is it worth really talking about? No, not unless you're completely new to the technical world, because this capability has been around for quite some time now, even in (gasp!) non-Microsoft operating systems!

In any reasonably well-networked system running under Windows, Macintosh, or UNIX, the idea of network printing is fairly similar. Clients on various computers hooked up to your network can send *print jobs* (the documents they want to print) to printers attached locally to their computer, a remote print server, or to printers connected to the network using internal or external network adapters.

Where Windows 2000 differs, and gives Microsoft's sales reps something to truly crow about, is that Windows 2000 supports several advanced printing features that you won't find elsewhere. I look at some of the best of the pack a little further on in this section. I have to say, though, that one of my favorites is the feature that enables a sort of *plug-in*–style printer driver. That is, you don't have to install a printer driver on a Windows 2000 client computer to enable it to send print jobs to a given printer. The driver is downloaded automatically whenever the client connects to a Windows 2000 print server, saving you the hassle of copying over the print server.

Keep in mind that although you have access to this nifty feature, it's only a stopgap measure so that you don't have to start copying over printer drivers on the fly in the middle of an important print job. (And as I say at the start of the chapter, every print job is an important print job, at least to your users.)

After you identify that this feature is being used, think of it as a warning flag to do a little administration after hours. Because this feature necessarily slows down the print time and puts more load on the network (from downloading the driver, among other things), be sure to install printer drivers ASAP on the machine that needs it. You can follow the directions later on in this chapter on installing drivers.

The *print server* that you keep hearing about is basically any Windows 2000 machine that you've set up to receive print jobs and hand them off to the printer. A print server acts as sort of a central receiving area for print jobs, which it keeps in a *print queue,* also known as a *print spool* to those of you who are more familiar with Linux or UNIX.

A print server doesn't have to be a machine that's close to the printer, or even attached to it. About the only requirement for making a machine a print server is that it has to be visible to everyone on the network, and it has to have the disk space and available RAM to store and process the print spool in less than geologic time scales.

While we're on the subject of terminology, keep in mind that a *logical printer* is a different silicon animal than a *regular* printer, even if people get sloppy about the terminology. The logical printer is the software interface to the print server. The regular, everyday printer is the actual hardware device that does the dirty deed of spitting out paper with sprayed on or burned-in ink patterns. Whenever you send in a print job, the logical printer spools the job before it's sent to the printer itself to be collated and printed.

Windows 2000 improves on many features that were found in a more limited form on the earlier versions of Windows NT, particularly NT 4.0. For example, remote administration includes the ability to remotely administer printer ports, something that was only easier to do on UNIX machines before now! Similarly, some of the new and improved features you're going to find on Windows 2000 include the following list of services.

Applications printing

Your ability to print from an application has been spruced up. When you print from an application, the standard Print dialog box now allows you to search for printers in the Active Directory. You can even add entirely new printers on the fly from the Print dialog box, instead of backing up and using the Add New Printer utility. Figure 14-1 shows you how to find printers in a standard Microsoft application.

Keep in mind that this new Print dialog box facility may offer reduced functionality when you use older, non-Microsoft programs that aren't especially made to work with the new feature.

User settings

Windows 2000 Server and Windows 2000 Professional clients are now able to set their own document settings. Prior to this feature, flexibility was sharply limited on several Windows products, such as 95 and 98, where users had to petition their administrator to make the changes, resulting in extra *busy work* for you.

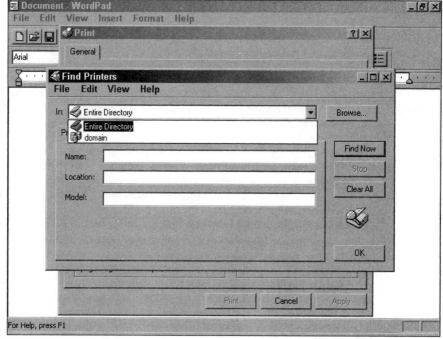

Active Directory services

Windows 2000 Server now lists all shared printers in the domain as objects in Active Directory. Because shared printers are in the Active Directory directory now, you can use the Active Directory search tools. This tremendous advantage helps you locate the most convenient printing resources that match your needs, such as location of the printer, or its capability to print in color.

A new default port

The new standard, default port in Windows 2000 replaces the older LPRMON for TCP/IP printers connected directly to the network or through a network adapter. According to the latest Microsoft benchmark testing, this new standard port transfers data up to 50 percent faster than LPRMON.

LPRMON isn't quite 100 percent obsolete yet, though. It's still required for a printer connected to a UNIX or Linux host. Again, those of you from a UNIX background may recognize the LPR naming convention applied to this print monitor port.

Detailed print queue monitoring

The new print queue monitoring application allows you to monitor both local and remote printers via the System Monitor's new Print Queue object. You can monitor a variety of performance benchmarks, such as bytes printed per second, number of job errors, and total pages printed by each machine.

Internet Printing — Quite Possibly the Wave of the Future

In a truly farsighted move, the Windows 2000 operating system now offers printing across the Internet. You can print from clients using Windows 2000 Server and Windows 2000 Professional to Windows 2000 print servers using a Uniform Resource Locator, also known as a URL (pronounced *Earl* by the Net-surfing crowd). You can actually use a Web browser to pause, resume, or delete print jobs, or to install new print drivers from a Web site. In fact, you can even use a Web browser to view and manage the printer and print job status.

You can use any Web browser to manage printers. However, you must be using Internet Explorer Version 4.0 or later to actually connect to a printer. The fact that Internet Explorer happens to be a Microsoft product is completely incidental, of course.

To install a printer from the Internet or intranet, you need to use the printer's URL as the printer's name. Windows 2000 Server can process print jobs that contain URLs as long as it's running Microsoft Internet Information Services (IIS). If the print server is being implemented on Windows 2000 Professional, the Microsoft Peer Web Services (PWS) must be running. Internet printing uses Internet Printing Protocol (IPP) as its low-level protocol, which is encapsulated within the HTTP protocol packet.

Print server security is provided by the IIS or the PSW, depending on whether you're running Windows 2000 Server or Windows 2000 Professional as listed previously. However, ways exist for someone to *hack* around this protection from the outside. Consider using a secondary authentication system, such as Kerberos. Kerberos is quite secure, and what's more, it's supported quite well by the Microsoft Internet Explorer application.

At Your Service: The Print Servers

You can implement printing through a printer that's attached directly to the network through a network adapter in a couple different ways. You can follow the standard procedure of working through a computer designated as a print server. Alternatively, you can bypass the server route and add a printer directly to each user's computer.

Printing without using a print server

If you decide to set up your print environment without a print server, each user on the network can add the printer to his or her Printer folder without sharing the printer. The users can set their own driver settings and their own document print settings.

Taken as a whole, this method works on a relatively small network of machines such as a Windows 2000 workgroup, but the reasoning behind it is outdated. For example, one prior advantage to this setup was that in the bad old days before Windows 2000, users of certain Windows products such as Windows 98 weren't able to set their own printer settings without an administrator's help. That's not the case anymore with the new Windows 2000 print services.

The lack of real advantages is added to a couple of real disadvantages latent in this printer configuration. Because each computer has its own print queue displaying print jobs sent from itself and *no other computer,* you can't really determine the status of a local print job relative to all the print jobs from other computers.

In case of a slow-down, the user can't determine whether the application's gone brain dead or if multiple print jobs have been spooled ahead of her job. And if she can't tell that, who will she run to, complaining? I'll give you a hint. It's not the local Better Business Bureau office.

Printing with a print server

The other, preferred way to set up printing is to have one Windows 2000 Server computer function as a print server. The selected computer adds the printer and shares it with the other users via the Find Printers interface in the print application.

You can also designate a computer running Windows 2000 Professional as a limited print server, but I wouldn't really recommend it as anything more than a temporary measure. A print server running 2000 Professional can't support Macintosh or NetWare services. What's more, it's limited to only ten connections within the same local area network (LAN), which could lead to major network traffic jams on a large network if you have a sudden surge of printing needs.

Sacrificing a machine to the printer gods

Some administrators who are short on good, high-quality hardware treat allocating a machine as a print server like selecting a person to be fed to Pele, the volcano goddess. It shouldn't be quite so drastic a move. True, using a print server does require a computer to function as the print server, and that at the very least has an impact on its performance to do other tasks.

However, a print server doesn't need to be a 100 percent, fully dedicated machine. Print servers are implemented on servers that also perform other duties, so you can count on running different tools on your print server without considering it as a *sacrificed* machine. For putting up with this extra drain on CPU cycles from this computer, you get some pretty hefty advantages from your print server, including:

- A central point to manage the printer driver settings.

- A single print queue that appears and is updated on every computer connected to the printer, letting each user see where his or her print job is in relation to others waiting to print.

- Similarly, error messages appear on all computers, so everyone knows the state of the printer (such as broken, running, or some other state of the Union).

If you're running into print slowdowns or you want to use the server for other tasks at a speed somewhere above banana slug, throw as much RAM onto the computer as you can. Microsoft's minimum is 64MB, but that is a base level only. Tripling or quadrupling this amount can make your life much easier for a much smaller chunk of change than buying a new machine.

Back in the Driver's Seat: Reviewing Printer Drivers

Calling a program a *printer driver* is something of a misnomer. The driver doesn't run the printer, let alone actually take it anywhere interesting. A printer driver is simply a program used by word processing and other applications to communicate with printers. Printer drivers, because they're usually designed to run a specific piece of hardware in mind, are some of the most *specific* programs around — they don't have much flexibility, because they're tailored for a single type of printer. You may have some luck running a *generic* print driver, but you may be disappointed with the formatting or quality of the output. You have been warned!

Most printer drivers contain three types of files:

- **Data file:** Provides information about the capabilities of a specific printer, including its resolution capability, whether it can print on both sides of the page, and what size paper it can accept. You can find a clear indicator of what price segment your printer was in by looking at the relative size of the file, because the more complex the printer's options, the more data this file has inside.

- **Printer graphics driver file:** The graphics driver translates device driver interface (DDI) commands received from an application such as Word or Excel into commands that a printer can use. Whenever you start to print, the graphics driver file works with the configuration file to translate the DDI files into the proper printer commands.

- **Printer interface file:** Displays the Properties and Preferences dialog boxes when you configure a printer. Depending on the driver you're using, you may see more or fewer options than if you use the specific printer driver for your printer. If you need to search for it, the file has a .dll extension.

Discovering a Fount of Fonts

If you're running a printing program that's less than a decade old, you likely have the capability to print everything from 6-point pica to 80-point Gothic Heavy Metal Banner text. Note that I said you had the *capability,* not that you could do it right away! Printers, whether they're laser, ink-jet, or dot-matrix, normally support a fixed set of resident fonts. You can expand by installing font cartridges or loading fonts from software, but in today's Internet-savvy world, you can often download new fonts from the Web.

If you're new to printer fonts, it's time for a little font terminology before you go any further.

- **Cartridge fonts:** Much like the latest offering for Nintendo or Sega, cartridge fonts are stored in a cartridge or a card that plugs into your printer.

- **Downloadable fonts:** These font sets are sent from the printing computer to a printer's memory when needed for printing. You may hear them referred to as *soft fonts.* Some printers have the capability to store multiple selections of soft fonts. If your printer supports this feature in its Properties menu, enable the feature to increase printing speed.

- **Internal fonts:** Internal fonts have already been loaded into the printer's ROM. Internal fonts are always available for printing, although if you have a low-end printer, this set may be very limited. Internal fonts are also sometimes called *resident fonts* because they (sensibly enough) reside directly on the printer.

Not all kinds of printers can use all three types of fonts. The pen plotters beloved by engineers, architects, and seismologists normally can't gag down those downloadable fonts.

If you use downloadable fonts that print to Windows 2000 print servers, consider installing the fonts locally to the print server. You take a big CPU cycle hit to perform this task.

Any Port in a Storm: Choosing and Configuring a Port

The print monitor program, also called the *port* monitor, controls the I/O port to the printer. (I/O stands for *Input/Output*, not Garbage In/Garbage Out as some may have told you.) The *printer port* is a communications interface through which a printer communicates with a computer. Also, it is really a logical structure inside your software code; the physical analogy is the spot where you plug in the cable.

You add printer ports using the Add Printer Wizard. You can also perform this task from the Ports tab in the printer's property page. Finally, you can perform this task via the print server's property page.

If you're actually physically plugging the printer into the print server machine, you need to select the appropriate local port. LPT1 through LPT3 represent parallel ports; COM1 through COM4 represent serial ports. The process of selecting a port and the subsequent options that are displayed depends on how your printer is connected to the server or network and what software (including protocols) you have installed.

If you're not sure whether you're using a parallel or serial port, check the back of your computer. Parallel ports are a large, bar-shaped plug, so big that sometimes the printer cable is held on by a pair of wire braces at each end of the plug socket. How big? The biggest on your machine, measured lengthwise from one end to the other. In the immortal words of every person giving street directions, *you can't miss it.*

An interesting feature that you may have on your machine relates to Universal Serial Bus (USB) and IEEE 1394 printers. These printers support what's called *hot* plug-and-play. Don't get too excited here; all it means is that the correct port monitor automatically installs when you plug a printer into the correct physical port (and USB or IEEE 1394 port). Windows 2000 automatically detects the device, displays the settings, and prompts you to confirm.

Adding a Port

You can actually add a printing port right when you add a new printer using the Add Printer Wizard. The wizard prompts you to select a new or existing port for your printer. Of course, you can also perform this task separate from the wizard process. You need to actually go into the Printers window on your print server:

1. **Click the Start button and choose Settings⇨Printers.**

   The Printers window appears.

2. **Choose File⇨Server Properties.**

   The Print Server Properties window appears, as shown in Figure 14-2.

3. **Click the Ports tab, and then click the Add Port button.**

   You have a myriad of port types to choose from on the Available port types list.

4. **Simply click the appropriate port name, and then click New Port.**

5. **Configure the port you added and click Close to shut the Printer Ports dialog box.**

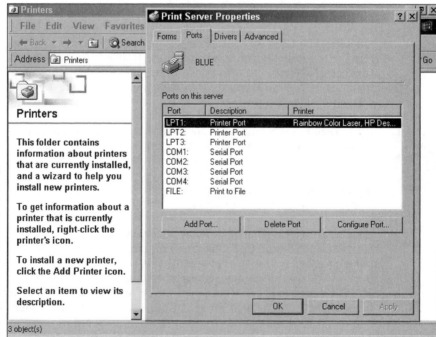

Figure 14-2:
A view of the Printers window and the Print Server Properties window, set to the Ports tab.

By default, only Local Port and Standard TCP/IP Port appear in the Available port types list. For more esoteric port types, you may need to click New Port Type and enter the path to the compact disc or the local file location containing the necessary files.

Adding a standard TCP/IP port

A computer that acts as a print server must run TCP/IP protocol to communicate with and send print jobs to the printer. (Luckily for you, TCP/IP has become the standard for network communications, so you don't need to install anything in that regard.) An LPR port is best for print servers that need to communicate with host computers (such as UNIX or VAX).

You can add ports through the Print Server Properties dialog box. The standard TCP/IP port simplifies connecting remote printers with TCP/IP protocol. The overwhelming majority of directly attached network printers currently support TCP/IP protocol.

To add the port, follow these steps:

1. **Click the Start button and choose Settings. Click Printers in the pop-up menu that appears.**

   The Printers utility screen appears.

2. **Double-click the Add Printer icon.**

   The Add Printer Wizard program appears.

3. **Click the Next button.**

4. **Select Local Printer, deselect the Automatically Detect My Printer check box, and then click Next.**

5. **Select Create a New Port and then click Standard TCP/IP Port.**

6. **Click Next to continue running the Add Standard TCP/IP Printer Port Wizard.**

   Follow the wizard's instructions on the screen to finish installing the TCP/IP-based printer.

Adding an LPR port

The LPR port is the way to go when you're running servers that need to communicate with host computers such as UNIX or VAX. A network-connected printer must have a card that supports LPD for TCP/IP printing to work properly. Again, keep in mind that computers that need to submit print jobs to host computers should use the standard TCP/IP port in most cases.

Follow these steps to add an LPR port:

1. **Click the Start button and choose Settings. Click Printers in the pop-up menu that appears.**

   The Printers utility screen appears.

2. **Double-click the Add Printer icon.**

   The Add Printer Wizard program appears.

3. **Click the Next button.**

4. **Deselect the Automatically Detect My Printer check box and then click Next.**

5. **Select Create a New Port and then click LPR Port.**

6. **Click Next and add the following information:**

   • **Name or address of server providing LPD:** Type the domain name system name or Internet Protocol address of the host for the printer you are adding.

   • **Name of printer or print queue on that server:** Type the name of the printer as identified by the host, which is either the direct-connect printer itself or the UNIX computer. Avoid using strange symbols or long names, which another computer may not recognize.

7. **Complete the instructions on the screen to finish installing the TCP/IP printer.**

Adding an AppleTalk printing device port

Se habla Macintosh? Your system must use AppleTalk protocol if you want to add an AppleTalk printing device. You can easily tell whether this is the case, because AppleTalk Printing Devices is available only when the AppleTalk protocol is installed. If AppleTalk Printing Devices is not available, click Cancel to close the Add Printer Wizard and follow the procedures to add optional networking components. Otherwise, follow these steps:

1. **Click the Start button and choose Settings. Click Printers in the pop-up menu that appears.**

   The Printers utility screen appears.

2. **Double-click the Add Printer icon.**

   The Add Printer Wizard program appears.

3. **Click the Next button.**

4. **Select Local Printer, deselect the Automatically Detect My Printer check box, and click Next.**

5. **Select Create a New Port and then select AppleTalk Printing Devices.**

6. **Click Next.**

   An AppleTalk Printing Devices list appears.

7. **Select the AppleTalk printer that you want to add and then click OK.**

8. **Click Yes to capture the AppleTalk device.**

   Follow the remaining instructions in the wizard to finish installing the AppleTalk printer.

Adding a Hewlett-Packard network port

Hewlett-Packard printers are a world unto themselves. Their JetDirect cards support TCP/IP protocol, and should be added by using the standard TCP/IP port. However, the older HP-JetDirect cards do not support TCP/IP! Although thankfully HP got on the TCP/IP bandwagon with everyone else in the later years, the earlier Hewlett-Packard network port uses the DLC protocol, which also explains why HP uses its own specific set of printer cabling.

Because adding more protocols significantly affects network performance, verify that the HP JetDirect card you have cannot support TCP/IP protocol before adding DLC protocol.

Follow these steps to add a Hewlett-Packard network port:

1. **Click the Start button and choose Settings. Click Printers in the pop-up menu that appears.**

   The Printers utility screen appears.

2. **Double-click the Add Printer icon.**

   The Add Printer wizard program appears.

3. **Click the Next button.**

4. **Select Local Printer, deselect the Automatically Detect My Printer check box, and click Next.**

5. **Select Create a New Port, click Hewlett-Packard Network Port, and then click Next.**

6. **Click Refresh.**

7. **From the Card Address list, click the printer card address of the printer you have added to the network.**

8. **Type a name for the printer and then click OK.**

   Follow the instructions on the screen to finish the installation.

Adding a local port

When you're running a network environment, it's better to use a printer that's connected directly to the network through a network adapter. Using a parallel port impacts the speed and flexibility of your printing output.

To add a local port, follow these steps:

1. **Click the Start button and choose Settings. Click Printers in the pop-up menu that appears.**

   The Printers utility screen appears.

2. **Double-click the Add Printer icon.**

   The Add Printer Wizard program appears.

3. **Click the Next button.**

4. **Select Local Printer, deselect the Automatically Detect My Printer check box, and click Next.**

5. **Select Create a New Port, click Local Port, and then click Next.**

6. **Type the port name and then click OK.**

   Follow the instructions on the screen to finish adding a printer with the Add Printer Wizard.

Deleting a Port

Deleting a port is one of the simpler tasks in this chapter. You just need to follow along:

1. **Click the Start button and choose Settings. Click Printers in the pop-up menu that appears.**

   The Printers utility screen appears.

2. **Choose File⇨Server Properties.**

3. **Click the Ports tab.**

   The Ports screen appears.

4. **Click the port you want to delete and then click the Delete Port button.**

   Because this area is potentially sensitive, Windows 2000 prompts you with a confirmation dialog box.

5. **Click Yes to confirm.**

Deleting a port removes it from the available port list. Any printer that communicates through that port has been effectively disconnected from printing, so be sure to notify your user community via e-mail if this is a significant change.

Installing Printers and Plug and Play

Plug and Play technology has become the standard in today's faster computer environment. Also called *fire and forget* hardware by the technical set, P&P provides the benefit of automatic hardware detection and installation for many hardware devices. Lucky for you, that includes 99 percent of new printers today!

Universal Serial Bus (USB) and IEEE 1394 printers

Printers using the latest connector technology — such as printers with a Universal Serial Bus (USB) port or IEEE 1394 port — are detected immediately (which is called hot Plug and Play). When you insert the jack into the port, Windows 2000 detects the printer and starts the installation process without any user intervention.

Printers that are not Plug and Play

Some printer types are not Plug and Play and need to be installed using the Add Printer Wizard. These printers include

- **Printers connected through a serial (COM) port.**

- **Printers connected directly to the network with a network adapter.** See the "Adding a local port" section earlier in this chapter.

- **Parallel (LPT port) printers.** After you verify that the printer is turned on and ready to print, add the printer with the Add Printer Wizard. Make sure that you select the Automatically Detect My Printer check box, or you're in for some frustrating times. If you want to do things the hard way, you can also restart your print server; during the Windows startup process, the computer runs a program that detects new hardware and starts the New Found Hardware Wizard.

Setting and removing printer permissions

No more asking whether you can borrow the server Saturday night for your big date or losing Administrator privileges because you didn't do the dishes. You control the permissions here!

1. **Click the Start button and choose Settings. Click Printers in the pop-up menu that appears.**

   The Printers utility screen appears.

2. **Right-click the printer for which you want to set permissions.**

3. **Select Properties from the pop-up menu and click the Security tab.**

   - Want to change or remove permissions from an existing user or group? Click the name of the user or group.

   - Want to set up permissions for a new user or group? Click Add.

4. **In the Name field, type the name of the user or group you want to set permissions for, click Add, and click OK.**

   The dialog box closes.

5. **Click Allow or Deny accordingly for each permission. To remove the user or group from the permissions list, click Remove.**

   See Figure 14-3 if you want to be sure — with so many things labeled Permission, I permit you to be slightly confused.

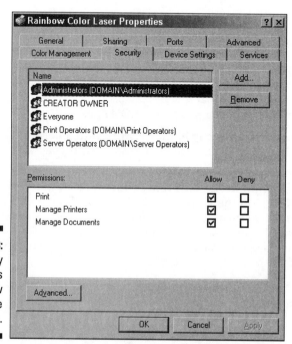

Figure 14-3:
The Security tab enables you to view and change permissions.

Specifying your default printer

If you take a quick glance at your Printer window, you'll see a check mark located next to only one of the added printers if you have multiple printers on your network. When you choose File⇨Print in many Windows-based programs, the default printer is used unless you specify otherwise.

The first printer you add to your Windows 2000 system becomes the default printer unless you specify otherwise. Follow these yellow brick steps to manually select the default printer:

1. **Click the Start button and choose Settings⇨Printers.**

2. **Right-click the printer you want to use as the default printer and then select Set as Default Printer.**

   A check mark appears next to the selected printer icon in the Printers window. See Figure 14-4 for an example.

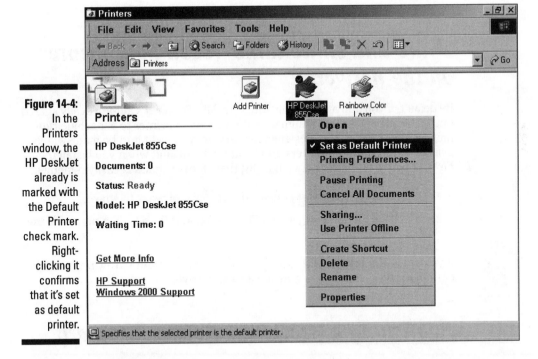

Figure 14-4: In the Printers window, the HP DeskJet already is marked with the Default Printer check mark. Right-clicking it confirms that it's set as default printer.

Updating printer drivers

You use the same commands to install a new printer driver and to update an existing printer driver with the latest 'n greatest edition.

1. **Click the Start button and choose Settings⇨Printers.**

2. **Right-click the printer for which you want to change drivers and click Properties.**

3. **Select the Advanced tab.**

4. **Click New Driver to install a new or updated version of the printer driver.**

   The Add Printer Driver Wizard starts.

   When you're working in the wizard, click the appropriate printer manufacturer and printer model if the new or updated driver is on the list. Sometimes, an updated driver comes on a floppy disk or CD-ROM. If so, click Have Disk if the printer driver is not included in the list. If you downloaded the new driver from the Internet, type the path where the driver is located and then click OK.

5. **Click Next after the information is in place.**

   Follow the instructions on the screen to finish installing the printer driver.

Share and share alike (even your printer on the network)

By default, if you add a printer on Windows 2000 Server, it's automatically shared out. (This is because it's assumed that if you add a printer to a machine running an operating system designed for servers, you want it to be made widely available.) In contrast, printers aren't shared by default when you install them on Windows 2000 Professional. Luckily, that state of affairs is easily remedied:

1. **Open Printers and right-click the printer you want to share.**

2. **Select the Sharing tab, select Shared As, and then type a name for the shared printer.**

If you share the printer with users who use very different hardware or different operating systems, you may need to add drivers.

Publishing a printer in Active Directory

If you're feeling ambitious, you can *publish* your shared printer in Active Directory (let the network know it's ready for shared use) as long as you're logged on to a Windows 2000 domain running the Active Directory utility. Active Directory is running when you see List in Directory on the Sharing property page. If Active Directory is, in fact, active, when you add a printer using the Add Printer Wizard and select to share the printer, the printer will also be published into the domain's Active Directory.

Keep in mind that you must have Manage Printers permission for the printer you want to share or publish. You can create long printer names that contain spaces and special characters. But as a general rule, avoid this practice. Some clients won't recognize printer THX-1138 or correctly handle a printer named 2xtreme.

To publish a printer, follow these steps:

1. **Click Start⇨Settings⇨Printers.**

2. **Right-click the printer you want to publish.**

3. **Click the Sharing tab.**

4. **Click Shared As and type in the name for the shared printer in the available field.**

   Be sure to select the List in the Directory check box to publish the printer in Active Directory. See Figure 14-5 for an example.

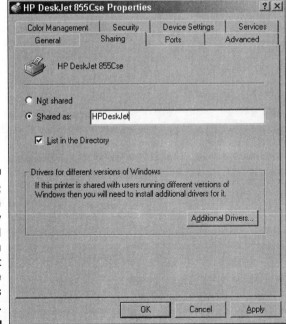

Figure 14-5:
List in the Directory isn't grayed out, so you know that Active Directory is running.

Only a shared printer can be published in Active Directory. If you stop sharing a printer, the printer vanishes from Active Directory, perhaps giving some of your users serious heart trouble.

Tracking printer usage

A useful but low-cost (in the CPU-cycles-are-time-which-is-money sense) process to monitor is the printer usage from a given group of users or computers. This way is a very good one to determine how to allocate your resources, particularly if they're in short supply.

For example, if you determine that the Accounting group ends up printing from their machines three times as much as the Facilities staff, you can hijack printers from the Facilities department (I'd advise you do it at night) and reallocate them to the accountants doing the bulk of the printing.

To track the usage of a printer, follow these procedures:

1. **Choose Start⇨Settings⇨Printers.**
2. **Right-click the printer you want to audit.**
3. **Select Properties from the pop-up menu.**
4. **Select the Security tab.**
5. **Click the Advanced button and then click the Auditing tab.**

   Figure 14-6 shows the resulting screen.

6. **Click the Add button. Select the user or group whose printer access you want to audit.**

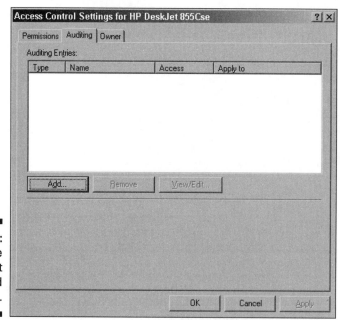

Figure 14-6:
Luckily, the IRS isn't involved here.

Monitoring print queue performance

If you want to be a truly proactive administrator, you should monitor print queue performance at select times of the day, whenever you've determined that the print requests to your server peak. To do so, follow these steps:

1. **Click Start⇨Programs⇨Administrative Tools⇨Performance.**

   The Performance screen appears.

2. **Click the + button on the Performance toolbar.**

3. **Select the print server computer from the Select Counters from Computer list box.**

4. **Select Print Queue from the Performance Object list box.**

   Be sure to click the counters you want to monitor.

   To view a detailed explanation of a counter, select it and then click Explain. To save yourself some time if you want to do this frequently, add this System Monitor to your Microsoft Management Console (MMC). Chapter 13 covers this topic.

Incidentally, monitoring printing queues is what's called in administrative lingo, *minding your Ps and Qs.*

Scheduling alternate printing times

By default, all printers added to a Windows 2000 network are set to maximum availability. That is, they're available 24 hours a day, 7 days a week. If you want to restrict printing times, perhaps to force a certain amount of load balancing on your printers, you can set this option in the printer properties. Keep in mind that doing so may not exactly improve your popularity with users!

1. **Click the Start button and choose Settings. Click Printers in the pop-up menu that appears.**

   The Printers utility screen appears.

2. **Open Printers and right-click the printer for which you want to change printing times.**

3. **Select Properties from the pop-up menu.**

   The Properties screen appears. It has a number of tabs for you to choose from.

4. **Choose the Advanced tab.**

   Take a peek at it; it's shown in Figure 14-7.

5. Click Available From to switch from the default Always Available.

To set the time period that the printer is available, simply click the up- or down-arrows next to the time fields.

If you want to change the minutes or the a.m./p.m. setting, click that part of the setting to shade it and then click the up- or down-arrows. You can also simply type in a start and end time, such as between 1:00 p.m. and 6:00 p.m.

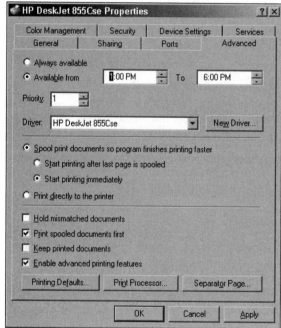

Figure 14-7:
The Advanced tab in the Printer Properties window.

Part IV

Administering Windows 2000 Server

The 5th Wave   By Rich Tennant

BIKER I.S. GUYS

SkinTight
TATTOOS

"Remember — I want the bleeding file server surrounded by flaming workstations with the word 'Motherboard' scrolling underneath."

In this part . . .

This is an exciting section because you'll be seeing some of the finest thinking to come out of Seattle since Starbucks' double espresso with an extra helping of whipped cream and chocolate shavings. Despite years of criticism from users and administrators alike, Microsoft hasn't decided to stay in one place. Instead, they've implemented a few new ideas — and improved on quite a few old ones — in areas that are quite specific to the Windows 2000 server.

Chapter 15

Your Registration, Please

*W*henever I write anything about the Windows 2000 Registry, I get a peculiar feeling: I want to stick a warning label on the edge of the page — one of those bright yellow labels that tell you not to operate your hair dryer "when partially or completely submerged in water." This is because the Registry is potentially hazardous to your system when edited by a user partially or completely submerged in inexperience. So here comes the warning label:

Editing the Windows 2000 Registry may not be brain surgery, but it can be nearly as disastrous if somebody does it wrong. Exercise extreme caution! Know what you're doing before you do it! *Please*.

The Brain of Windows 2000

(No, it isn't a movie. Yet. But I'm waiting.) The Registry , in effect, serves the Windows 2000 operating system as the equivalent of a brain (and better, I might add, than many other brain-equivalents I could name . . . but won't). It's where all those fancy graphical administration tools you've been using actually make their changes. So (potentially, at least) you may find the administration going quicker if you edit something in the Registry instead of getting at it through the old GUI-based system. On the flip side, the administration tools serve as natural safeguards against doing anything impulsive that could damage the system. Which takes you to Dire Warning Number Two:

Editing the Registry directly is, in effect, removing the safety net. To avoid making an awful mess, become familiar with what the Registry is and how to edit it (*if* you ever need to). If you must edit it, do so carefully. And rarely.

Oh, yeah — don't operate your computer partially or completely submerged in water, either.

Abandon All Hope, Ye Who Enter the Registry

Each computer running Windows 2000 stores its configuration information in the Registry — which serves as a kind of configuration database. Whatever computing background you come from, the Registry can show its teeth unless you treat it with *respect.*

Those of you from the UNIX side of the computer world can think of the Registry as a combination of the kernel with the system file. The Registry contains elements of both those features: It controls both the user-to-computer interface and the parameters under which the computer runs the commands you give it. Now, I would call those a couple of sterling reasons not to mess with it.

You can view and edit the Registry with special Registry Editor programs — though you don't absolutely have to do it that way. Windows 2000 has its own army of administration programs that automatically modify the system Registry when you use them — without running the added risk of human error (such as a typo or a mistaken directory).

The system constantly uses the Registry as a resource while it operates. For example, the user account settings that you create (via the various Windows 2000 editors) are stored in the Registry — along with vital information about system hardware, installed programs, and property settings. Windows 2000 continually refers to this information while the computer is in operation. (Otherwise, the system wouldn't know what it was doing.)

Because editing the Registry can damage your system, you should back up your data before making any changes. Otherwise, you face the penance of reinstalling Windows 2000. Reinstallation trashes important changes — such as any and all Service Pack upgrades that you may have made. You'd have to go back and make all the upgrades again! Oh, well. Back to Square 2000. . . . (Don't make that face — what if it froze like that?)

Do not replace the Windows 2000 Registry with the Registry of another version of the Windows or Windows NT operating systems. Trust me: This plain does not work. The Registry is as finicky about halting alien Registries at the gate as any Cold War border guard could be. Imagine it ringed with barbed wire and sporting a big sign: **Unregistered Registries Do Not Register.**

Overview of the Registry Editor(s)

A Registry Editor is the text-and-graphics-based tool for changing settings on your system Registry — without the terror of typographic hiccups. The Registry for Windows 2000 stores its configuration information in a database organized in a *tree* format, similar to the directory tree you'd see in Windows Explorer or (in those bygone days of high adventure) File Manager. So long as you have administrative permissions and know what you're doing (or at least get along tolerably well with it), you can edit and restore the Registry safely.

Numerical values that appear in the Registry are known as *value entries*. Your computer uses these entries as configuration settings that tell it how to run. The Registry stores these settings in folders called *keys* — which you can see in the *navigation pane* of the Registry window (you know, that real pane that tells you where to go). Opposite the navigation pane, the *topic pane* displays the value and tells you what's what. Whenever you double-click one of the value entries, it opens a dialog box and humbly invites you to edit it.

You can use the Registry Editor for many system tasks. These would include, for example:

- ✔ Eliminating duplicate entries for programs, which could confuse the computer.

- ✔ Deleting entries for programs that have been uninstalled or deleted but not properly removed from the Registry.

- ✔ Correcting system errors that prevent your computer from functioning or shutting down properly.

Incidentally, if you get an error in the Registry that causes your computer to stop functioning properly, you can restore the Registry to its previous state when you last successfully started your computer. A later section of this chapter unfolds that invaluable secret.

Using Registry Editors (Would You Like the Axe or the Chainsaw?)

Though some administrators don't know it, they really have *two* versions of Registry Editor available for use: *Regedt32.exe* and *Regedit.exe*. (Of course, you're in the know because you bought this book. Wise, very wise.)

- ✔ **Regedt32.exe** not only would make a cool name for a Seattle rock band, but it is actually an executable file that Windows 2000 installed in the systemroot\System32 folder — which is why its name bears the mystic number 32.

✔ **Regedit.exe** was also automatically installed (in a slightly different location — the Systemroot folder) when you installed Windows 2000. And I'll bet it didn't even tell you so.

You can use either utility to modify the Registry. Keep in mind, however, that doing so is a fairly wild-frontier approach; both editors lack features found in any self-respecting administration tool. Worse, although they operate in a text-based format, they lack even the most rudimentary features of a true word processor. Neither of the Registry Editors can check for garbled syntax, banana-fingered typing, weird grammar, or other language errors — which means you can make major mistakes with one typo. But wait, there's more — the results of an incorrect edit made with Registry Editor are unpredictable and may impair (or disable) your Windows 2000 operating system in highly unusual ways.

Fortunately, abject terror is unnecessary. A little common sense and caution go a long way — for example, getting your first view of the Registry by using the *Read-Only Mode* that is available on either editor.

UNIX and Linux folks may be glad to know that their favorite operating system does indeed have features analogous to Read-Only Mode: Command Mode in the vi editor, or a restricted permission file.

Because the Registry settings are so bound to each other (for example, a group setting impacts all the user settings under that group), any change that is made leads to multiple changes elsewhere that you cannot see. This is called the *ripple* or *cascade* effect. Always be aware of this before you make a serious change.

You can access the Registry to make changes to the Registry by using a Registry Editor, depending on your permissions. If you belong to the Admins group (as the Administrator account or other similarly endowed user), you can view the Registry of remote computers when you use the Select Computer option available on the Registry menu. One other handy feature: Every time you start using the Registry Editor, you see an associated icon appear on your taskbar.

There's an easy way to remember what you can do in the Registry. As a rule of thumb, you can make the same kinds of changes with Registry Editor that your permissions allow for other administrative tools.

Opening the Registry Editor

Because the Registry exists apart from the GUI (either "behind" or "outside" it, depending on which guru you ask), it makes a dandy place from which to start the Registry Editor. You have two ways to start the program. One is a relatively new method, which utilizes the Programs menu to get to a command prompt. To try out this fashionable new technique, follow these steps (illustrated in Figure 15-1):

1. **Click Start**

2. **Select Programs⇨Accessories⇨Command Prompt.**

3. **At the prompt, type** regedt32 **or** regedit.

4. **Press Enter.**

To open Registry Editor the old-fashioned way, use the Start button and the Run option:

1. **Click the Start button.**

2. **Select Run and type** regedit **or** regedt32 — **depending on which Registry Editor you want to open.**

   (No, it's not a typo — one really is regedit and the other regedt for regedt32.)

3. **Click OK.**

4. **The Registry Editor, shown in Figure 15-2, opens before you and rumbles, "What is your wish, O Master?"**

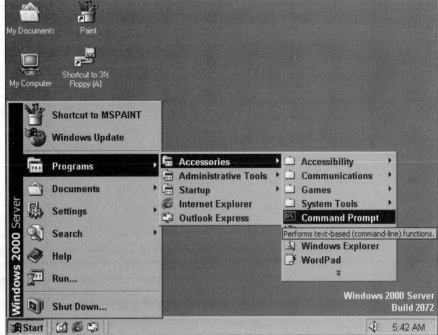

Figure 15-1: The new-and-improved way of getting to your command prompt.

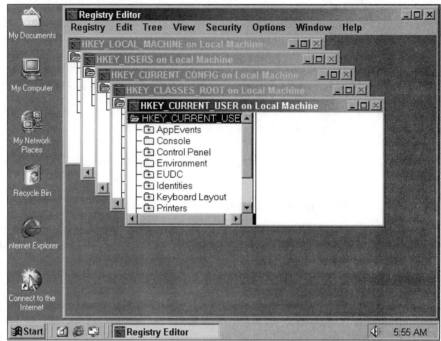

Figure 15-2:
The Registry
Editor and
its myriad
directories.

Opening the Registry of a local computer

When you edit the Registry on a local computer, the process is pretty simple (as shown in Figure 15-3):

1. **Click the Registry pull-down menu in the window's toolbar.**

2. **Click Open Local on the Registry menu, as Figure 15-3 sumptuously illustrates.**

Opening the Registry of a remote computer

The process for getting at the Registry on a remote computer is almost as simple as the local method:

1. **As you would do for a local computer, select the Registry menu.**

2. **Click Select Computer from the pull-down menu.**

   The computer shown in Figure 15-4 is named CYAN.

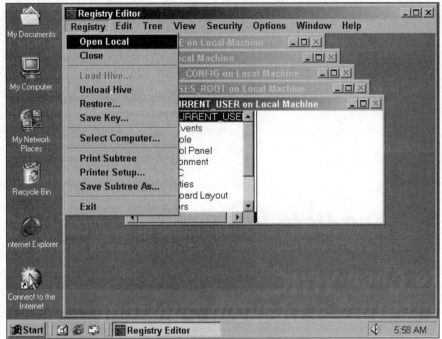

Figure 15-3:
Using the
Registry
menu to
select Open
Local.

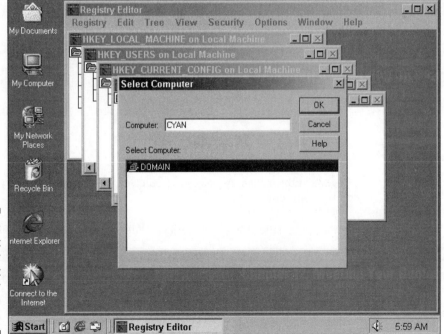

Figure 15-4:
The Select
Computer
screen, set
to look for
machine
CYAN.

3. **In the Computer field, type the name of the computer.**

   You can also move the mouse to the Select Computer field and click the domain(s) displayed.

   This bit of abracadabra displays the names of the computers under each domain.

4. **Select the Registry you want to open and then click OK.**

You can open only two predefined keys on a remote computer's Registry: HKEY_USERS and HKEY_LOCAL_MACHINE. It's a security measure. I could tell you more, but I would have to arrest you. (Kidding. This time.)

Viewing Data in Read-Only Mode

Read-Only Mode essentially gives a user permission to read the Registry, but not to write to it or execute permissions. This little touch of paranoia protects your Registry data from accidental changes that could wreak havoc on your machine. Note also that when you work in Read-Only Mode, the Editor doesn't save any changes you've made (because that would amount to the same thing as changing the Registry by writing to it).

To get into Read-Only Mode, follow these steps:

1. **Open the Registry Editor in one of the two ways mentioned earlier in this chapter.**

   The method you choose depends on whether you're working with a local or a remote machine.

2. **Select Options⇨Read-Only Mode.**

Registry Editor Keys

The Registry Editor displays windows, each of which represents a predefined key on the local computer.

Windows 2000 displays the following predefined keys, in order from back to front:

✔ HKEY_LOCAL_MACHINE

   This key contains configuration information that is particular to the computer but universal to each individual user account that makes use of that machine.

✔ HKEY_USERS

This key holds the root of all user profiles on the computer.

✔ HKEY_CURRENT_CONFIG

Stores information about the hardware profile used at the systems startup.

✔ HKEY_CLASSES_ROOT

This key is really more of a subkey to the following key:

HKEY_LOCAL_MACHINE\Software

The information here ensures that only the correct program opens when you use the Windows Explorer to open files and executables.

✔ HKEY_CURRENT_USER

This key contains the root of the configuration information for the user who is currently logged on. Unlike HKEY_USERS, this key holds information that changes depending on which user is making use of the machine. Taken as a whole, such identifying information is referred to as a *user profile*.

The key HKEY_CURRENT_USER is in actuality a subkey of HKEY_USERS.

You can use the Registry Editor to assign or change the value entries for each key. Value entries appear in the Registry Editor as character strings that consist of three components separated by colons. For example, Last Username : REG_SZ : 0x1 corresponds to the following values:

Entry name	Last Username
Entry type	REG_SZ
Entry value	0x1

If you're used to working in Linux or UNIX, you can think of Registry keys as the Windows version system variables — and the value entries as the variable settings you would get by typing in **echo $VARIABLE** or **env**. If you're more of a Windows habitué, don't worry if these UNIX-dialect terms seem a bit obscure. If you're interested in finding out more about running a Linux network, page through *Linux Administration For Dummies* by Michael Bellomo (IDG Books Worldwide, Inc.).

Closing the Windows in Registry Editor

If you don't plan to edit keys in multiple windows, you can close selected windows in the Registry Editor. This keeps your workspace a little clearer and prevents you from making mix-ups or losing windows behind other windows that are stacked behind it.

1. **Click the Registry Editor window you want to close.**
2. **Select Registry⇨Close.**

Updating Registry Information

By default, the Registry Editor automatically updates the Registry when anyone makes a change to Registry data. You can do so with the Auto Refresh setting, located under the Options pull-down menu. When Auto Refresh is on, no other method is available for updating the Registry. Other options that would otherwise be available to you are grayed out in the different pull-down menus.

If you switch off the Auto Refresh option, you have two new options available for updating the Registry with the Registry Editor:

✔ **Refresh All.** You can select this by clicking (you guessed it) Refresh All in the View pull-down menu. Selecting this option updates all information in every one of the Registry Editor windows, whether displayed or not. Auto Refresh works similarly.

✔ **Refresh Active.** You can select this by clicking (wait a minute, don't tell me) Refresh Active in the View pull-down menu. This option updates only the information in the Registry Editor window that is active at the time.

It's the Auto Refresh fake-out! Although Auto Refresh *appears* to be working when you access a remote Registry, the contents of the remote Registry are *not* automatically refreshed. Use the Refresh options mentioned earlier to do the job.

Switch it off, or forever hold your peace. If the manual refresh options are grayed out on a remote machine's Registry Editor, then look for the Auto Refresh setting. If it's turned on, then it grays out the other methods — even though it doesn't actually work! (Wait a minute . . . is this some sort of a psych test?) Deselect Auto Refresh to get the other options working.

Adding a New Subkey to the Registry

Well, no, a *subkey* won't unlock a fridge full of foot-long sandwiches. You can use Add Key command to add subsidiary keys (subkeys) to an existing key — but only if you *own* that key or have permission to open it. (Of course, you already have one or the other by default if you're the Big Kahuna of the Administrative account or are part of the Administrative group.)

If the HKEY_USERS or HKEY_LOCAL_MACHINE window is active, Add Key is unavailable at the root of the key. To add a Registry key to the root of these predefined keys, use Load Hive on the Registry menu.

1. **To select the key or subkey under which you want the new key to appear, click it.**

2. **Choose Edit⇨Add Key.**

   The Add Key screen appears, looking suspiciously like Figure 15-5.

Figure 15-5:
Give the new key a name or the addition won't be successful.

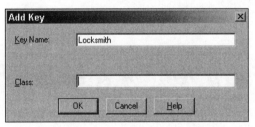

3. **In the Key Name field, type the name you want to assign to the new key. (In the example, the name used is Locksmith.)**

4. **In the Class field, type the class that you want to assign to your key, if necessary.**

Adding a Value Entry to a Registry Key

When you work in existing Registry keys, you can edit their contents or add new values. To add a new value (or add one to replace an old value) follow these steps:

1. **Select the key to which you want to add a value entry: Highlight it by clicking it once.**

2. **Choose Edit⇨Add Value.**

3. **In the Value Name field, type the name of the value entry you want to create (as shown in Figure 15-6).**

   Click the arrow to the right of Data Type. A pull-down menu with various selections appears. Select the date type you want to assign to your value entry.

No matter how much fun it might be, you can't just make up a data type. If you've suddenly kindled a passion for data types (hey, different strokes . . . .), you can get more info on which data types can be used — and get it straight from the horse's mouth: Search for *Windows 2000 data types* on the Microsoft Web site, at www.microsoft.com.

Figure 15-6:
You can type in the value name and select the data type.

Deleting a Registry Key or a Value Entry

You can delete both keys and value entries when you're in the Registry Editor. Of course, you can't delete predefined keys such as HKEY_CURRENT_USER or HKEY_USERS, because even the Registry Editor tries to safeguard against some idiocy! In fact, you won't be able to change the name of the predefined keys either. For the rest of the keys, it's open season. Follow these steps:

1. **Click the key or value entry that you want to delete.**

2. **Choose Edit⇨Delete. That little hummer is outta here.**

Confirming a Delete Action

Ah, but you're not done yet! (Technology is such a slave-driver.) As long as you're not in the safe Read-Only Mode, you need the Confirm on Delete setting to protect your Registry data from accidental deletions. This setting is the default; although you *can* switch it off (by deselecting it under the Options menu), actually doing so is bad form in most situations.

When Confirm on Delete is selected, the Registry Editor presents a dialog box that asks for confirmation any time you delete a Registry key or a value entry. Simply click Yes to make the big leap into deletion. And congratulate yourself on your caution.

Registry Security

You can also determine who can open your Registry keys in the Registry Editor. The Editor allows you to assign permissions to user accounts so that they, in essence, have limited Administrator privileges.

1. **Click the key to which you want to assign permissions.**

2. **Choose Security⇨Permissions.**

   The Permissions screen appears, showing the kindly features of Figure 15-7.

3. **Assign an access level to the selected key for either just Reading (as in Read-Only Mode) or Full Control for permission to add, alter, and delete.**

4. **If you want the permissions assigned to the parent key to also apply to the subkeys under the parent, select the check box by Allow Inheritable Permissions from Parent to propagate to this object at the bottom of the screen.**

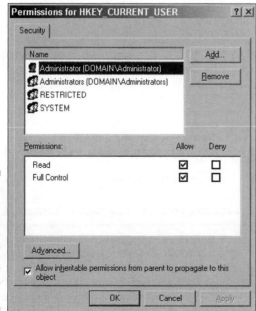

Figure 15-7:
The Permissions screen, here for the key HKEY_ CURRENT_ USER.

The Permissions List: Adding Users or Groups

If you want to expand the list of user accounts that have permission to edit the Registry, you can do that from the Permissions screen. First, be sure to log in as the Administrator (or as part of the Administration Group that can access the Registry). Open the Registry Editor and perform the following steps with all due solemnity:

1. **Click the key whose Permissions list you want to change.**

2. **Choose Security⇨Permissions⇨Add.**

   The Select Users, Computers, or Groups dialog box appears.

3. **Find Look In and click the computer or domain that holds the accounts of the users and groups you want to see.**

4. **Click the name of the user or group, click Add, and then click the OK button to confirm the new setting.**

5. **In the Permissions dialog box, under Permissions, assign a type of access.**

   Choose Read if you want the user to be able to read. Choose Full Control if you want the user to be able to read, edit, and delete its settings.

(Trouble)shooting the Registry

Sorry, but the Information Age isn't a safe place, either; as an administrator, you had best learn to shoot. Troubleshoot, that is. Your computer could be in serious trouble if it exhibits any of the following danger signs:

- Missing files
- Components that don't behave as expected
- Frequent error messages or stop errors
- A tendency to write bad checks to Microsoft

Your Registry could have become corrupt or damaged. You may have to put it out of its misery.

If you've made changes recently to the Registry, try undoing the most recent change. Keep going until the symptoms stop. If you're getting specific messages that point to certain components, determine what the correct Registry settings are for those components — and then realign the system's current settings to match the correct ones.

Restoring the Registry

If recent upgrades turned up some problems — say, a newly added driver that may be incorrect for your hardware — you can try returning your system to its *last known good configuration* before it turned to a life of corruption and shame.

To put your Registry on the road to recovery, start eliminating the usual suspects:

- ✔ Select Last Known Good Configuration.

- ✔ Alas, if the information is corrupted in this setting, it won't be much use. Ditto if your problem is really a hardware failure.

- ✔ If you have a backup copy of the Registry (as part of your backup of System State data) and you can open Backup, try restoring your Registry settings from there.

- ✔ If neither of the previous approaches has the decency to actually work, go to the final remedy and reinstall Windows 2000.

- ✔ Any remaining problems are normally the results of hardware failures — another whole fine kettle of fish.

If you can't start Windows 2000, try repairing the operating system with your Emergency Repair Disk — the handy-dandy disk in Appendix D. For more information on creating and using Your Emergency Repair Disk, see (yep) Appendix D. Utility belt and cape optional.

Final Tips on Working with the Registry

The Registry is so indispensable to the correct operation of your Windows system that harping on caution won't hurt: Treat the Registry with kid gloves when you can. To reduce the likelihood of running into serious Registry trouble, consider the following timely and practical suggestions:

- ✔ **Put big yellow warning labels everywhere, warning people not to edit the Registry.** KIDDING! (I think.)

- ✔ **Limit the number of people who have access to the Registry.** The Administrator account (and members of the Admins Group) always need full access to the Registry. But most other users shouldn't need Admins Group privileges, especially if they don't actually do any administrating. Don't tempt fate or the egos and ethics of your users.

In the words of one famous Windows 2000 administrator, "Never under-estimate the power of the Dark Side of the Force."

✔ **Keep Registry Editor in Read-Only Mode.** If you use Regedt32.exe, verify that the Read-Only Mode box on the Options menu is checked.

When you need to make changes to the Registry, turn off Read-Only Mode by clicking it — and then verify that Confirm on Delete is checked. When you're done making changes and have saved your edits, turn on Read-Only Mode again by clicking it.

✔ **Never leave Registry Editor running unattended.** You're just inviting trouble if you do. (Who knows *what* it'll get up to? And with whom?) If you work in a busy laboratory or company office, think of the Registry Editor as if it were a roll of $100 bills. (Why not? The damage that may occur you could cost at least that much.) If you wouldn't leave that bankroll out in plain view in the commons area, then don't leave the Editor wide open for mischief on just any workstation — not even on yours.

Chapter 16

It's a Control Thing

*Y*ou can think of the Control Panel as the dashboard of your car — it has your basic, everyday functions. The Control Panel is a veritable compendium of controls (that's a lot of 'em). The difference between the dash and the Control Panel? When you tune into that rockin' oldies station in the car, your 14-year-old reaches over and flips it back to the shriekin' metal station. Your Control Panel is an unchallenged tyranny — when you click the icons, you're taken to whatever graphically based administration tool you want.

Although the Control Panel itself can lead to some heavy-duty administration modules, you primarily use the icons to change your machine's appearance and functionality. Rather than jump directly into network configuration, peel into the following section, which tells you where you can go from the Control Panel and how to make your computer more accessible to your users.

 The items in the Control Panel itself are so user-friendly that they'll slip you crib notes on how to use them. For example, if you need additional help on any Control Panel item, click the appropriate book icon on the Contents tab that appears when you open Help from the Start button menu. Also, if you want to view a short description of each Control Panel item, click Details on the View pull-down menu in Control Panel.

Show Me What You've Got — Administrative Tools in the Control Panel

Feel like you're doing 360s trying to figure out which administrative tool you should use? One of the fastest ways to learn is via the Control Panel. Fortunately, the Control Panel is also the fastest way to get to the tool itself.

1. **Click the Start button to open the Control Panel.**

2. **Choose Settings⇨Control Panel.**

   The Control Panel appears, as shown in Figure 16-1.

3. **Double-click the Administrative Tools icon.**

   The icon is toward the top of the screen because the Control Panel is labeled alphabetically by default. Clicking Administrative Tools takes you to all the available administrative utilities.

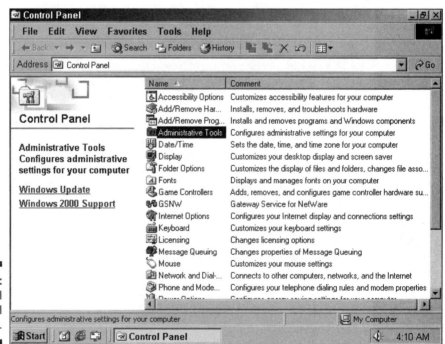

Figure 16-1:
The Control
Panel
screen.

This folder may not be accessible on a machine running Windows 2000 Professional or Server if you lack Administrator privileges.

The following sections give you a look under the Administrative Tools' hood. You might want to wear an old shirt as you read on.

Component Services

The Component Services utility — serviceable as it is — offers the most actual usefulness to two groups of users. What's more, the two groups of users that it helps are among the most technically inclined — and thus the hardest to satisfy. Trust me on this one.

- ✔ **Software developers.** A developer can use the Component Services utility to visually configure routine component and program behavior, such as security and participation in transactions. She can also use the CS utility to integrate components into COM+ programs.

- ✔ **System administrators.** Administrators can use this utility to deploy COM+ programs from a *graphical user interface* (GUI). It also helps them script automated administrative tasks, such as monitoring system tasks and performing backups.

Computer Management

You can use the Computer Management utility for a large number of administrative tasks, such as checking your disk quotas or sending backups to a tape machine, when you work with local or remote computers.

Keep in mind that in Windows 2000 terms, a *remote computer* doesn't necessarily refer to physical distance. Any computer that you administer or connect to and do not have physical contact with (for example, your keyboard isn't plugged into the back of the machine) is by definition a *remote machine*.

Data sources — Just say ODBC

Open Database Connectivity is a programming interface that enables programs to access data in database management systems. The catch is that those database management systems must use Structured Query Language (SQL) as a data access standard. Open Database Connectivity is also a real mouthful, so feel free to say ODBC.

Event Viewer

The Windows 2000 Event Viewer acts like a 24-hour recording device (sort of like those sneaky little cameras mounted on stop lights to catch those who run them), storing information about hardware and software problems. It also monitors Windows 2000 security events, which you can access and retrieve whenever you note a security problem. (Boogie on over to Chapter 21 for more information about that.)

When you click the Event Viewer, you can review and manage logs of several sorts:

- ✔ Application
- ✔ DNS Server
- ✔ Security
- ✔ System

Any of these can be viewed with a single click as long as you're permissioned for Administrative rights.

Performance Monitor

The Performance Monitor allows you to collect and view real-time data about memory, disk, processor, network, and other activity. The display method is a scrolling graph or histogram. A *scrolling graph* is a display that moves slowly from right to left in real time, with the computer plotting a line that marks the level of CPU usage. A *histogram* is a different form of graph — sort of a cross between a bar graph and a scrolling graph. (And no matter what other people tell you, it's not something you take when you have hay fever.)

Services

The Services icon is, appropriately, a set of intermeshing gears: These components help run your computer's innermost workings. The services utility manages services and sets recovery actions to take place if a service fails, an important function in case of a power outage or other critical system error.

4-x-4 — Control Panel Accessibility Options

The second of the two major Control Panel functions is providing increased accessibility for all users when controlling the computer's immediate environment. If you want to take your car out for a little drive in the mud, lock in the four-wheel drive and take 'er out. If you want to take your keyboard for a spin, use the Accessibility Options to customize the way your keyboard, monitor display, and mouse function. What's more, none of these components (such as the mouse) have to be made by Microsoft or by a Microsoft affiliate.

Many of these features are useful to people who have vision or hearing problems. I've also found that these options can be used to set up a machine to prevent eyestrain on a poor monitor or to create a more convenient way to access a command that takes multiple keys to type.

Follow these steps to set or edit these ease-of-use options:

1. **Click the Start button to open the Control Panel.**

2. **Choose Settings⇨Control Panel.**

3. **Double-click Accessibility Options. The screen is shown in Figure 16-2.**

   You can view the current setup by clicking the Settings button on each tab. Implement all-new settings for each component by selecting the check boxes by each Option panel.

You can access several options from the Accessibility Options screen:

✔ **StickyKeys** selects a single keystroke to perform a multiple-key operation, such as selecting Esc to do the work of Ctrl+Alt+Delete. Hallelujah! Your fingers are freed! Very useful for those of us with stubby fingers, carpal tunnel, or a recent case of frostbite.

✔ **FilterKeys** adjusts the keyboard response rate. For example, when I run into a Windows problem, I prefer the keyboard to ignore repeated keystrokes. That way I can bang my head against the keyboard with little or no (ouch) consequence.

✔ **ToggleKeys** enables certain keys to play tones when pressed, which can help visually impaired users confirm that a toggle is either on or off. (I'm still working out the second movement of Beethoven's Fifth in the key of Ctrl+C.)

✔ **MouseKeys** enables the keyboard to move the mouse pointer. This is pretty helpful if your mouse is malfunctioning and you're waiting to get a new one.

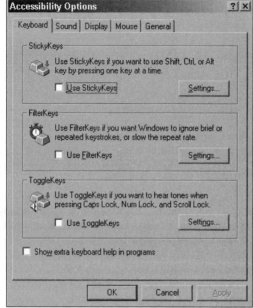

Figure 16-2:
The
Accessibility
Options
screen, with
tabs labeled
from
Keyboard to
General.

Where's Gandalf When You Need Him? The Accessibility Wizard

You can quickly and painlessly set up accessibility options via the Accessibility Wizard. The wizard quizzes you about your accessibility needs and automatically configures settings for you. If you're a more independent-minded sort, high-tail it past the wizard and go to the Accessibility Options to directly customize keyboard, display, and mouse functions.

You may get the most use out of the Accessibility Wizard by allowing it to guide you through the setup of an environment customized with tools designed to help you meet vision, hearing, or mobility needs. To start working with this wizard, complete the following:

1. **Click the Start button.**

2. **Choose Programs⇨Accessories⇨Accessibility⇨Accessibility Wizard.**

   The screen shown in Figure 16-3 appears.

3. **Follow the instructions that appear.**

Welcome to the Accessibility
Wizard

This wizard helps you configure Windows for your vision,
hearing, and mobility needs.

If you are using an input device other than a mouse,
instead of clicking, use the appropriate action to complete
commands or select items throughout the wizard.

To continue, click Next

< Back   Next >   Cancel

Figure 16-3:
The
Accessibility
Wizard's
grand
opening.

After the Accessibility Wizard has set up the tools that you need, those tools
can be accessed through the Control Panel's Accessibility menu.

Chapter 17

Windows 2000 Server TCP/IP Connectivity

● ●

In This Chapter

▶ Understanding the TCP/IP virtual circuit

▶ Installing TCP

▶ Configuring automatic addressing

▶ Configuring dynamic addressing

▶ Configuring static addressing

● ●

*T*he *Transmission Control Protocol/Internet Protocol (TCP/IP)* is not a single protocol, as some people think; it's an entire suite of standard protocols used in connecting computers and building networks. It's become the standard protocol suite in allowing computers to communicate with each other in the swiftest, most reliable manner known to date.

Now, if you hang out at any cocktail party (or pizza party, for that matter) with a high percentage of technical types milling about, you may hear a few TCP/IP buzzwords thrown around. If you don't duck in time, you may hear about Ethernet cards, Ethernet cabling, the virtual circuit and, of course, the client-server relationship. That's because all kinds of protocols exist for only one real reason: to allow two different computers to follow a pre-set sequence of orders to communicate properly with each other.

The Virtual Circuit World of TCP/IP

The TCP/IP networking protocol is the current standard used by PCs around the world. There are two main reasons for this. First, TCP/IP was developed as the first standardized set of computer protocols by ARPAnet (Advanced Research Projects Agency). ARPAnet needed standardized protocols for both compatibility and computer security, due to the fact that ARPA was primarily funded by military research projects.

The other reason is because TCP/IP's design and open system policy allows *any* kind of computer hardware to use it, from Compaq PCs to Sun boxes, CRAY 3000 supercomputers to Atari 2600s in the middle of a game of Space Invaders. While TCP/IP sacrifices some speed, it is the overall best product to use because of its flexibility and reliability.

The reliability of the TCP/IP system is built into the protocol's structure. When a TCP/IP packet of information is sent over the network, it signals its receiver to send back a packet that tells the sender, in essence, "Okay, I got it!" Until that okay comes back, the sender does not continue to forward TCP/IP packets.

That's why TCP/IP is called the *virtual circuit.* A real, physical circuit constructed out of batteries and wires must have a complete connection, or the circuit is broken and no power flows through. A virtual circuit connection works the same way, except that electrical current is replaced with packets of information.

The slight penalty in speed is usually a cheap enough price to pay for a guarantee that important data reaches its destination. Because of this, the vast majority of the communications that take place on a computer network — and almost 100 percent of Internet connections — happen thanks to TCP/IP.

Installing TCP/IP (If You Really Need To)

Windows 2000 puts TCP/IP on your machine as the default network protocol. If the TCP/IP default selection is overridden during setup for some strange, unknown reason, then you can use this section. Otherwise, you get a freebie from this section. Take the day off; you deserve it. (Wish it were that easy.)

To install TCP/IP (or for that matter of fact, any sort of network protocol), you have to go into the Network and Dial-up Connections directories.

You must log on as an administrator or a member of the Administrators group in order to complete any of the procedures listed in this chapter.

1. **Choose Start⇨Settings⇨Network and Dial-up Connections.**

2. **Right-click the network connection for which you want to install and enable TCP/IP, and then choose Properties.**

3. **On the Networking tab, look for TCP/IP in the list of installed components.**

   Although normally installed, TCP/IP may not be specifically installed or enabled on some newly created machines, as shown in Figure 17-1.

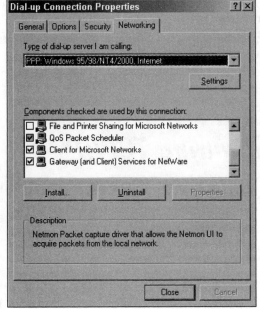

Figure 17-1:
The Networking tab shows that TCP/IP is neither installed nor enabled.

4. **If you don't see TCP/IP, then complete Steps 5 through 8.**

5. **Click the Install button.**

   A dialog box appears in which you can select the network component type.

   (Hint: You have a one-in-three chance in figuring which selection to make to install the TCP/IP protocol. See Figure 17-2 as an example.)

6. **Click Protocol⇨Add.**

Figure 17-2:
The component type correctly set to Protocol.

7. **In the Select Network Protocol dialog box, click Internet Protocol (TCP/IP) and then click OK.**

8. **Make sure that the check box is selected in the Properties dialog box. Click Close to accept this configuration.**

The check box has no name. It simply exists to the left of the TCP/IP setting. (hmm . . . that sounds Zen . . . .)

Methods of Configuring TCP/IP

You can configure your TCP/IP network setup in Windows 2000 by using any of the following three methods.

Automatic configuration

Windows 2000 provides automatic configuration of an IP address in the default, reserved range of 169.254.0.1 through 169.254.255.254, with a subnet mask of 255.255.0.0.

Alas, a DNS server has no automatic configuration. But don't despair; Chapter 18 shows you how to do it manually. What the heck — think of it as job security.

Dynamic configuration

By using DHCP, TCP/IP configuration happens dynamically and automatically when the computer starts up. By default, computers running Windows 2000 are DHCP clients.

DHCP stands for *Dynamic Host Configuration Protocol,* an advanced protocol designed to work with TCP/IP in a never-ending quest for truth, justice, and improved connections on large networks.

Manual configuration

If you're on a network with multiple segments, plan to connect to a very primitive ISP. (You really have to click the mastodon icon? Eww. . . .) Or if you don't have a DHCP server running, you can take up the ancient duty of network administrators: manually configuring the properties of the TCP/IP protocol. You can manually assign an IP address, subnet mask, default gateway, DNS server, and WINS server whenever you want.

Configuring TCP/IP for Automatic or Dynamic Addressing

Windows 2000 uses a feature called APIPA (Automatic Private IP Addressing) to automate Internet Protocol (IP) configuration of network connections. Windows 2000 determines an address in the Microsoft-reserved IP addressing range from 169.254.0.1 through 169.254.255.254. This address is used until a DHCP server is located. The subnet mask is set to 255.255.0.0.

Here's how to set up TCP/IP for automatic addressing:

1. **Choose Start⇨Settings⇨Network and Dial-up Connections.**

2. **Right-click the network connection that you want to configure, and then select Properties from the pop-up menu.**

3. **On the Networking tab, highlight Internet Protocol (TCP/IP) by clicking it.**

4. **Click the Properties button.**

5. **In the Internet Protocol (TCP/IP) Properties dialog box, click Obtain an IP Address Automatically, and then click OK. See Figure 17-3 as an example.**

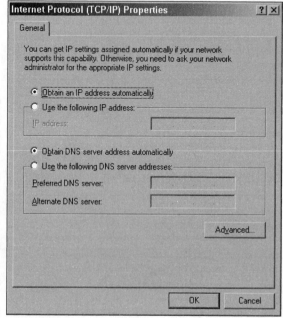

Figure 17-3:
The Internet Protocol (TCP/IP) Properties dialog box and the settings you can choose for obtaining IP addresses automatically.

Configuring TCP/IP for (Crackle, Crackle) Static Addressing

Setting up static TCP/IP addressing is essentially the same procedure as setting up other forms of the addressing system. You just click one button and type an IP address into the appropriate open field.

1. **Choose Start⇨Settings⇨Network and Dial-up Connections.**

2. **Right-click the network connection that you want to configure, and then select Properties from the pop-up menu.**

3. **On the Networking tab, highlight Internet Protocol (TCP/IP) by clicking it.**

4. **Click the Properties button.**

5. **In the Internet Protocol (TCP/IP) Properties dialog box, click Use the following IP address, and type in the IP address you want to use.**

   An example is presented in Figure 17-4.

6. **Click OK.**

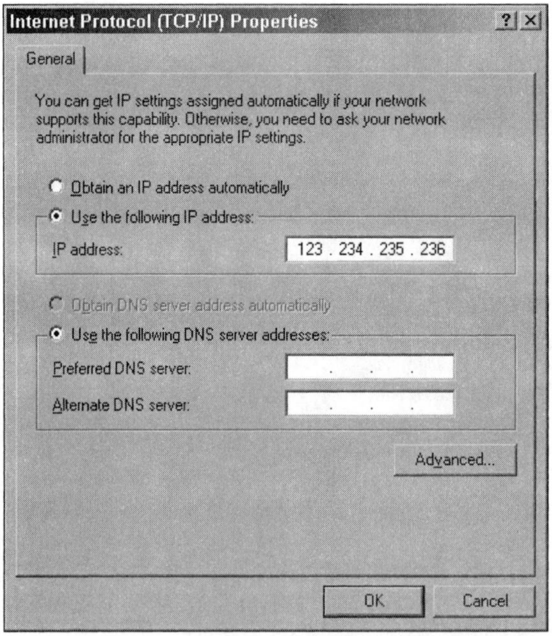

Figure 17-4:
Typing in the IP address in the Internet Protocol (TCP/IP) Properties dialog box.

When you click Use the Following IP Address, the IP address field is no longer shaded. Also by default, the DNS setting changes to Use the Following DNS Server Addresses and the fields there became unshaded. When a shaded field doffs its shades, you are ready to rock 'n roll.

Chapter 18

The Domain in Spain Stays Mainly on the Server

NS, the *Domain Name Server,* is a standard feature of the Internet and networking landscape today, but it's still what many technical types call a *black box* kind of program. Unfortunately, that doesn't mean it's well-nigh indestructible, like the black box on an airliner.

Instead, it means that DNS is by and large a mysterious utility, an untamed dark continent of technology. If DNS were part of a magic show, it would be at the part where the conjurer puts the white scarves into his hat and pulls out a flock of white doves.

Entire books have been dedicated to DNS, whole virgin rain forests felled to discuss it, and yes, had it not been for copyright problems someone would have made a miniseries on it by now. This chapter gives you a walking tour of the basics, plus a fast-and-dirty rundown on how to install a DNS server on a Windows 2000 machine.

The Delightfully Dark and Dense Descent of DNS

DNS servers are regular features on most network landscapes today, but it wasn't always such an enlightened age. On the earliest large networks — we're talking the early Internet here — address information was stored in a centrally administered file. The *NIC* or *Network Information Center* maintained the file, which had to be downloaded and installed by all participating sites.

As the network grew beyond a couple of offices inhabited by hard-core computer aficionados, this cumbersome scheme began to fall apart. The load on the servers that distributed the information grew out of control. Contributing to the problem was the fact that *all* names had to be registered with the NIC; part of the NICs mission in life was to ensure that early machine names weren't duplicated, which could cause some serious network malfunctions.

In the mid-1980s, Paul Mockapetris attempted to solve these problems by inventing DNS. To put it mildly, the system's been a smashing success. If you've ever used an obscure little device called the Internet, then you've had an interaction with a DNS server.

DNS is difficult but worth the struggle to master. One seasoned administrator had an appetizing take on how the system performs: "DNS is like chocolate. It's hard, it's dark, and it's very, very good."

Standing resolute in the face of DNS

DNS is at its most useful to you as a converter of machine names to IP addresses and vice versa. This DNS process is also known as *hostname resolution* — an association that the machine makes for us poor humans between a machine name, like `ftp.megastuff.net`, and the numeric code that a computer can make sense of, such as 123.45.67.89

DNS — the domain denizen of the Web

The simplest kind of domain is a collection of related Windows 2000 hosts (as chronicled in Chapter 3). DNS uses a more ambitious and flexible definition of a domain — which is why true Net surfers are more familiar with the most visible portion of DNS: a hierarchy of host names called the *domain name grouping*. It's where the whole idea of "dot.com" came from.

DNS groups online hosts by type of organization — for example, university, corporation, or branch of government. The largest such groupings are known as *top-level domains*, which you've seen if you've ever ventured within eyeshot of the World Wide Web. Some top-level domains you see frequently include these:

.com	*The* standard commercial domain name that everybody knows. It also apparently has magical powers: If you add this suffix to nearly anything (oh, say `Burnpilesofmoney.com`), people will start throwing piles of money at you in hopes that some will stick. (Lovely problem to have!)
.edu	Educational institutions such as universities, colleges, and vocational schools. Often these are treasure troves of intriguing and useful info — but keep an eye on the academic calendar if you surf these sites. Steer clear of them during midterms or finals week — everyone is on the Net researching term papers!
.gov	U.S. government institutions. Often slow — which leads me to believe these sites must be using Cold War-era equipment (or are run by the Postal Service).
.net	Gateways, administrative hosts, and ISPs (Internet Service Providers) on a given network. I *guess* the Internet counts as an "organization" of sorts . . . if you like organized chaos . . . .

Turning Your Machine into a Domain Name Server

Well, okay, this section *does* express a *little* bias: You can thank your lucky stars that you're administering a Windows 2000 system and not a Linux or UNIX network. A system without a GUI means more mucking around with weird files in hand-to-hand combat at the command prompt — together with the requisite confusion, panic, and assorted screams of despair from down the hall. (Gee. Sometimes progress is good.)

Windows 2000 comes with a lovely invention called the *DNS console,* located in the Administrative tools section. Its mission in life is to simplify the creation and maintenance of your DNS server files. The DNS console is your faithful vassal. Use it whenever possible. Of course, before you even get to that stage of the game, you should use the Windows Component wizard to ensure that you've got the appropriate DNS software set up for your system. How to do that? Stay tuned; it's coming up.

Alas, installing DNS software can be disruptive to the operation of your network. Among other things, you have to reboot at least once — and maybe more than once — before your machine graduates to DNS serverhood. Your best bet is to do the installation after hours. (Yes, it's a tough life as an administrator. But you can mambo on the boardroom table when you're done. No one will know . . . provided you didn't wear your golf shoes or combat boots . . . .)

Microsoft strongly recommends that you configure your computer to use a static IP address with your DNS server. For more information on how to do so, see Chapter 17.

Off to see the (Component) wizard

Okay. If you haven't yet enlisted the aid of the Windows Component wizard, be kind to yourself and go get acquainted. The following steps may not be a yellow brick road, but they'll get you there.

Before you start working with the Component wizard, write down the complete path to your Windows 2000 distribution files (normally that'll be to your distribution disk, sitting ready in your CD-ROM drive). You'll have to produce the complete path later on, to prove to the wizard that you've been paying attention.

1. **Click the Start button, point to Settings, and click Control Panel.**

2. **When the Control Panel opens, double-click the Add/Remove Programs icon.**

   It should reward you with a screen that resembles Figure 18-1.

Figure 18-1:
Adding or removing Windows components in the Add/Remove Programs administrative utility.

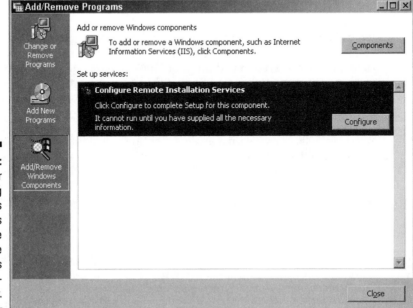

Don't get the Add/Remove programs icon mixed up with the Add/Remove *hardware* icon or you can end up well and truly confused. Or you may end up with your printer pretending to be your DNS server. Either way, it'll only end in tears.

3. **Next, click Add/Remove Windows Components. Click the Components button in the upper right to activate the Windows Component wizard.**

4. **Open the Windows Component wizard.**

5. **In Components, click Networking Services; when the screen shown in Figure 18-2 appears, click Details.**

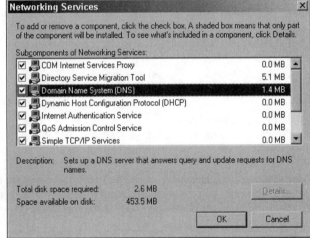

Figure 18-2: The Networking Services screen — selecting DNS to add to your system.

6. **In Subcomponents of Networking Services, select the Domain Name System (DNS) check box, click OK, and then click Next.**

7. **In Copy files from, type the full path to the Windows 2000 distribution files (you *did* write it down, right?), and then click OK.**

   The required files will be copied to your hard disk.

After all this drama, the server software will start up the next time you reboot — after which you should configure your machine as a new DNS server, as described in the next section.

Configuring a new DNS server

After you have the right software on the machine, you can easily configure the newly created DNS server to your specifications. Easily, that is, if you do the configuration from the DNS console.

To open the DNS console, perform the following mystic ritual:

1. **Click the Start button, point to Programs, point to Administrative Tools, and then click DNS.**

2. **If you're running a DNS server on a different machine, you can add and connect to this server by clicking its icon in the console. (Is that way cool or what?)**

3. **In the console tree, click the applicable DNS server.**

4. **On the Action menu, click Configure the Server.**

5. **Follow the instructions in the Configure DNS Server Wizard.**

When you finish configuring the server, you might need to enable dynamic updates for its zones or add resource records to its zones.

Starting and Stopping DNS Servers

Okay, you have a newly created and configured DNS server ready to rock your network. Congratulations! I suppose you want to get it started and running as soon as possible, yes? (Call it an inspired guess.)

When your user community gets used to seeing the DNS server on the network, you'll want to be just as prompt in shutting it down when it needs maintenance. (Such telltale urges mean you're mutating into even more of a Windows 2000 administrator. Might as well enjoy it.)

 Always be sure to stop a DNS server *manually* when you plan to reboot a machine. The specific Stop commands in the DNS software shut down the server processes more cleanly than the generic Shut Down command under the Windows 2000 Start button.

Fortunately, you can follow the same steps to start up or shut down the DNS server. And whaddaya know — here they come.

1. **Open DNS.**

2. **In the console tree, highlight the applicable DNS server by clicking it.**

3. **Click the Action menu; it displays the list of commands shown in Figure 18-3.**

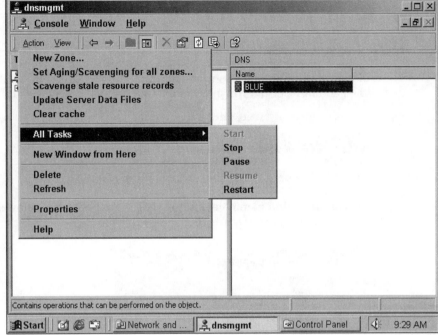

Figure 18-3:
The commands available to you from the Action menu.

4. **Point to All Tasks and then select one of the following commands from the submenu:**

   • **To start the service, click Start.**

   • **To stop the service, click Stop.**

   • **To interrupt the service, click Pause.**

   • **To stop and then automatically restart the service, click Restart.**

Note that because the DNS server on this machine is already running, the Start and Resume actions are grayed out and unavailable. Somebody must've figured that a server doesn't need them if it's running. (Gee. Ya think?)

You can also perform most of these tasks at a command prompt in a DOS shell window by typing the corresponding commands for Start, Stop, Pause, and Restart (and then pressing Enter, of course). Here they are, in that order:

```
net start dns
net stop dns
net pause dns
net continue dns
```

Adding or Removing a Server to the DNS Console

Adding or removing a DNS server entry in the DNS console is equally easy. When adding a server, you may want to open the DNS manager utility again.

Adding a server

Ready to add one? Go for it; follow these steps:

1. **On the Action menu, click Connect To Computer. You should get a screen similar to Figure 18-4.**

Figure 18-4:
The Select
Target
Computer
screen.

2. **From the Select Target Computer dialog box, select one of your two options:**

   • **This computer.** Use this setting if the server you want to connect to and manage is located on the same computer you are using to manage it.

   • **The following computer.** If the server you want to connect to and manage is a remote computer, type in its DNS computer name or its IP address.

3. **Select the Connect to the Specified Computer Now check box. Then click the OK button.**

Note that by default, the check mark appears next to Connect to the Specified Computer Now. Remove that check if you're still setting up the target computer.

Adios, muchachos

When you remove a server, go back to the DNS console window and follow these steps:

1. **In the console tree on the left pane, highlight the applicable DNS server by clicking it.**

2. **On the Action menu, click the Delete command.**

3. **When you're prompted to confirm that you want to delete this server from the list, click OK.**

   The server vanishes from the management screen and into oblivion.

Part V
Securing the Environment

The 5th Wave   By Rich Tennant

"We're not sure what it is. Rob cobbled it together from paper clips and stuff in the mail room, but MAN wait till you see how scalable it is."

In this part . . .

Welcome to the cloak-and-dagger part of the book. You can put away the Walther PPK-7 and the Aston Martin. Computer security is never quite that exotic or explosive. I keep as light and interesting a tone as I can (it sells better), but security is no laughing matter. Whether you run a system that is a part of a multimillion-dollar bank or a humble six-system computer lab, security is an indispensable part of what you need to master as a Windows administrator.

Chapter 19

Activating the Active Directory

. . . .

In This Chapter

▶ Getting hyper with Active Directory services

▶ Doing it again (replication of information)

▶ Declining the extra (automatic avoidance of superfluous replication)

▶ Pulling it all together (automatic synchronization of information)

▶ Creating a Domain Controller — and knowing when to do it

. . . .

I have to hand it to the Microsoft Corporation — through rain, sleet, snow, and blizzards of user criticism, they continue to come out with newer — and ever more useful — services. Active Directory is a perfect example. This chapter celebrates the delightful fact that much of Active Directory does exactly what it claims to do — handle things for you automatically, behind the scenes.

As *the* directory service for Windows 2000 Server, Active Directory organizes almost all the file and object information on your network into a logical, hierarchical structure of directories. Active Directory stores information about these objects on the network — and distributes this information — in a manner that makes it easy for administrators and users to find and use.

As with other major Windows 2000 features (such as DNS in Chapter 18), Active Directory could take up another whole book or miniseries — but we've got other fish to fry just now. You'll have a head start on the application if take a good look at what Active Directory does — and how you can use it to expand your network by creating Domain Controllers. That's what this chapter is for.

(In case you need to refresh your memory as to what a Domain Controller is, check back in Chapter 3. Go ahead — I'll wait for you.)

Active Directory Services — More Than Hype

Active Directory makes use of a new concept that Microsoft calls *multimaster replication*. In plain(er) English, it means that any Domain Controller on your Windows 2000 network can take care of additions or changes that modify the directory structure.

Such versatility creates a quicker update time overall, without a *trickle-down* factor (common to many UNIX systems based on NIS, the network operating system) that means the latest information takes nearly forever to get around.

Replication of information — major advantage

Active Directory uses multimaster replication to provide or enhance information availability, fault tolerance, load balancing, and performance benefits for the entire network. When users make a change to an object in Active Directory (say, changing their user password), they are updating a single copy of the directory. After directory information has been modified at one of your Domain Controllers, the changed information is sent out to all other Domain Controllers in the domain, so their directory information is current and synchronized with each other.

Another major advance is that Active Directory is intelligent enough to know how to only replicate (or distribute, depending on the way you look at it) only the changed directory information. Otherwise, if Active Directory kept updating the vast amounts of information it contained — all day — you would quickly have a slow, overloaded network that consisted of all updates and very little real work being done.

How replication works . . . how replication works . . .

Replication in the Windows 2000 Active Directory system works because each Domain Controller is intelligent enough to keep in sync automatically with its fellow controllers. The controllers keep track of how many changes they've made to their copies of the directory — and also how many changes they've received from their replication *partners*.

If they sense a discrepancy, the machines don't bother you. They hash it out between themselves like well-behaved siblings (yeah, right) and replicate the needed information. (See? Windows 2000 promotes the sort of "family values" that you can actually use on the job. Maybe it ought to run for office. . . .)

How Active Directory prevents unnecessary replication

Active Directory eschews superfluous replication (make that *prevents useless extra changes*) by tracking which attributes changed in the updated object. Active Directory software is also smart enough to know how many times the object's Originating Write property has been incremented.

A change that increments an Originating Write property indicates a change made by a client to an object. Had Active Directory made the change when replicating updated directory information, the increment would not be placed there, so the system knows that a replicable change has taken place. Otherwise, Windows 2000 wouldn't waste the TCP/IP packets to start shipping the change around the network. (Gad. That's a tad more savvy than some humans I've worked with.)

Originating Write is a sort of template that Active Directory uses to keep track of object changes (hence the *increment* marks).

Resolving conflicting changes

What if two different users try to change to the exact same object property — at the same time — in conflicting ways? But wait, it gets worse: What if they made these changes at two different Domain Controllers in the same domain — *before* replication of either change could happen?

To resolve this poser, the Domain Controller will accept the change with *the most recent timestamp* and discard the older change. This is a command decision made by Active Directory that *newer* equals *more current* — even if the difference is only significant in computer time (.0002 nanoseconds, which seems — from a computer's point of view — like a wait in a long bank teller line.)

Ticklish situations, such as a conflict between sets of changes, really make the case for setting up your systems with accurate system times! (Besides conflict resolution, it also performs such useful functions as telling you when it's time to break for coffee, a four-martini lunch, or the door if you're gonna beat rush hour.)

Child domains

You can create a new child domain when you want to create a domain that shares a contiguous namespace with one or more domains. For consistency's sake (and for some sound technical reasons), the name of the new domain must contain the full name of the original parent domain.

Example: Your logging company has a parent domain of `forest.com`. You can logically create a hierarchical structure by calling the child domain something like `woodpulp.forest.com`, `toothpick.forest.com`, or `dee.forest.com`.

When to Create a New Domain Controller

Adding a new controller either creates a domain — or adds an additional Domain Controller to an existing domain. (That's because the act of creating the Domain Controller also creates a domain for it to control. Windows 2000 won't let anybody have a domain without a Domain Controller — and vice versa — so there.) So what you've got here is either an organizational shift or an expansion of your administrative privileges. (Ah, the sweet smell of power. Being an administrator is good.)

It's a good time to create a Domain Controller whenever:

- You create the first domain in your network.

- You need to improve network availability and reliability.

- You just *feel like it,* for obscure administrative reasons of your own.

Installing a Domain Controller

When you decide to go ahead with creating a Domain Controller, keep in mind that it can't be installed on a computer running Windows Professional. Windows 2000 Server is snobbish about its cousin version; a machine running Windows 2000 Professional doesn't get to be a Domain Controller (nyah-nyah). As if to rub it in, neither the Configure Your Server menu option nor the `dcpromo` commands (which you need for installation) are not available on a Windows Professional computer. (Hmmph. Well, I *never.*)

You can open the Active Directory Installation Wizard, click Start, click Run, and then type **dcpromo** to start the process. Alternatively, you can use the following method:

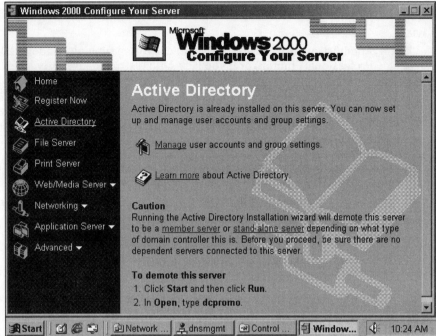

Figure 19-1:
The screen
for
Configure
Your Server.

1. **Click the Start button, point to Programs, point to Administrative Tools, and then click Configure Your Server.**

   As if by magic, the Configure Your Server screen opens, looking remarkably like Figure 19-1.

2. **Select Active Directory, and click Start to start the Active Directory Installation Wizard.**

   Note that if you have Active Directory already properly running on your Domain Controller, you won't be automatically taken to the Wizard screen. Instead, you'll be offered more information on working with your Active Directory, including tips and extensive Help files.

3. **Follow the instructions in the Active Directory Installation Wizard.**

Managing Remote Servers

As Administrator, you can manage a server remotely from any computer that is running Windows 2000 Server. You can access the built-in set of Administration Tools from the Start button menus (or from the Control Panel).

For a detailed review of the available managing tools, take a spin through Chapter 16.

Administration Tools aren't available if you're running Windows 2000 Professional (hmph!) or if you lack Administrative-level privileges.

To manage a remote server, you need the Administration Tools — and they should be ready to use. If haven't done so already, you can install Windows 2000 Administration Tools on a local computer by completing the following steps:

1. **Insert your Windows 2000 CD-ROM in the CD-ROM drive of the computer you want to perform the install on.**

2. **Next, click the desktop icon of the CD-ROM and open the I386 folder in CD-ROM's list of directories.**

3. **Double-click the file Adminpak.msi.**

4. **Follow the instructions that appear in the Windows 2000 Administration Tools Setup Wizard.**

   Obligingly, the izard installs the Administration Tools in their correct locations on your machine.

5. **After Windows 2000 Administration Tools is installed, you can access the server administrative tools by clicking Start, pointing to Programs, and then pointing to Administrative Tools.**

You can then set up Windows 2000 Administration Tools in Active Directory. After you do this, you can use the Add/Remove Programs in the Control Panel on the remote computer to install what you need, when you need it, from a remote location (though I wouldn't try it via satellite if you're on vacation in Zanzibar).

Chapter 20

Halt, Who Goes There?

. . . .

In This Chapter

▶ Foiling hackers and crackers

▶ Redefining what makes a good password

▶ Protecting and changing passwords

▶ Resetting passwords

▶ Putting your computer in standby mode

▶ Putting your computer in hibernation mode

. . . .

The first and best defense for your security needs is a series of good user and root passwords. Having secure passwords that are hard to *guess* or *crack* (unlike your user name, nickname, spouse's name, or birthday) is important for both you and your users.

Windows 2000 has, in essence, a *two-tiered* password system that acts as a double layer of security for your network and you. But don't rely on this system alone to defend your network. As you discover in this chapter, using a password that prevents a cracker from having easy access to your system is critical to your system's security.

Creating the Mighty Password

The trouble with *good* passwords is that what defines a *good* or a *bad* password is completely different to the user than to the administrator. For example, one of my users refused to change his password, which was his first name. "It's an excellent password," he explained, "because I can always remember it."

Arguing with logic like that is difficult because he was right, at least from his point of view. But as an administrator, your top priority is to keep the system secure, even if that means being bothered by users because they can't remember their passwords.

Hackers are not crackers

To many people, a *hacker* is the same thing as a *cracker*. In reality, the two are very different. The term *hacker* describes anyone who likes to program, tinker, or just bang on a computer keyboard with his or her fingers, toes, or forehead — hence the terms, *computer hack* (someone who likes to fool with machines) and *hacking* (programming or fiddling around).

The *cracker* is a subspecies of the hacker. *Cracker* is a term used to describe those few, unscrupulous hackers who like to *crack* security and break into systems. A hacker won't try to crack into your system's security, but a cracker certainly will *hack* in.

On the other hand, demanding that people use random, meaningless strings of numbers and/or letters is equally useless. Any user who knows how to change a password (and most eventually figure it out) will change the string to something else out of sheer frustration. So, where does one draw the dividing line?

Good computer security includes using passwords for your network login and your computer's Administrator account that aren't easy to break. This becomes increasingly important because the software programs and computers designed to crack your system's passwords are more powerful than ever today. Network passwords that once took weeks to break now can be broken in hours (or even minutes) with the latest password-cracking systems. And you can bet on one constant fact: Cracking systems are getting better all the time.

A *dictionary-based* cracking program gives you insight into how a strong, strong 'n' mighty password can be constructed. The first thing a *dictionary-based* cracking program does is run your password against every word in its database. The program then runs all variations of words in combination with numbers — your password is *attitude* but spelled *attit00de* — which is why using character strings with no connection to *real-world* words and phrases is a good idea.

Building the power of the password

To create a good, strong password, start with Microsoft's guidelines, which recommend that your password

  ✔ Be at least seven characters long

  ✔ Contain at least one character from each of these three character groups:

• Letters (upper- and lowercase)	A, B, C, . . .; a, b, c, . . .
• Numerals	0, 1, 2, 3, 4, 5, 6 . . .
• Symbols	~ ! @ # $ % ^ & * + . . .

Symbols are keyboard characters that aren't defined as letters or numerals.

✔ Be significantly different from previous passwords each time a new password is created

✔ Be other than a common word or name

✔ Be a name other than your name or user name

Besides the dictionary approach, password-cracking software also uses *intelligent-guessing* techniques, automatically trying every possible combination of characters. Given enough time, an automated method with a powerful computing source can crack almost any password that you can think up, even if it's completely random. That's why systems that need high levels of security use durable passwords as a delay tactic. If cracking a password takes on average four months, then changing passwords every three months foils the cracker.

According to Microsoft, a password on Windows 2000 can hold up to 127 characters (although typing such a password is a pain in the neck). Windows 95 and Windows 98, however, only support passwords of up to 14 characters. A longer password is automatically truncated on these machines. So, don't use passwords longer than 14 characters if you plan to use Windows 2000 on a network that also has computers using Windows 95 and 98. Otherwise, you may not be able to log in to your network from those computers.

In cyberspace, no one can hear you scream

No one best password exists. However, a *worst* one does! Without further ado, I give you the worst password of all:

Horrifying wasn't it? Yes, I know — you didn't see anything. That's the point. For convenience's sake, some administrators actually allow a user account (usually a system-maintenance account) to log on without a password! *Never, ever let this happen.* Even a novice user can press the Enter key by accident and discover your *big secret.*

Protecting your passwords

You may have the best lock on your front door that money can buy, but does that really do you any good if you leave your door unlocked when you go to work? Or does it do you any good if you lock your front door but leave the key on the doormat? Strangely enough, otherwise-sensible people (for Windows administrators, anyway) who would never leave their front doors so vulnerable are amazingly cavalier about the way they treat their sensitive network-security passwords.

Here are some tips about what *not* to do with your passwords:

- ✔ Don't use your network login password for any other purpose where it can be seen.
- ✔ Don't use the same password on different networks that you administrate.
- ✔ Don't leave your password anywhere on your desk.
- ✔ Don't leave your password on a piece of paper taped to the wall. (Yes, I've *seen* this happen.)
- ✔ Never write down your password, in general.

Here are some ideas on what you *should* do with passwords:

- ✔ Do use different passwords for your network logon and for the Administrator account on your computer.
- ✔ Do change your network password every 60 to 90 days.
- ✔ Do change your password immediately if you think it's been compromised.
- ✔ If you *must* write down the password, do leave it in a locked drawer, safe, or at your home.
- ✔ Do remember that for every additional person who has your password, the chances triple that someone will discover the password.

Some dialog boxes, such as one for a telephone-modem connection, give you the option to save your password. Don't select the save option, however, or someone can easily *pull* your password from the computer memory. Yes, going without that extra convenience is a pain, but that's why only the strong can survive as Windows-system administrators.

Changing passwords

Unless specifically barred from doing so, you or any of the users on the network can change passwords in Windows 2000 by pressing the Ctrl+Alt+ Delete keys and then selecting Change Password from the six option buttons available.

To restart or not restart, that is the question

Contrary to what you may think, the *three-fingered nerve pinch* (Ctrl+Alt+Delete) to the computer doesn't shut the computer down. Although on older operating systems this *pinch* did shut down the computer, that doesn't hold true for Windows 2000. Rather, you get a wider list of options, depending on what you want to do.

Keep in mind that even though you're not shutting down *per se*, once you get your options, your computer is almost frozen; you won't be able to do anything else with your computer until you choose an option.

If you're changing passwords for a user, you can open Computer Management to complete the task. Click the Start button, select Settings, and then click Control Panel. Double-click Administrative Tools, and then double-click Computer Management. In the console tree, in Local Users and Groups, click Users. Select the user account you want to change by highlighting it with a single mouse click. Finally, click Action, and then select Set Password. Type the password you want to use.

On Domain Controllers, you must make the change in the Active Directory. Although you still can change your own password with the *three-fingered salute,* you can't use the Computer Management utility for changing passwords on user accounts.

Resetting passwords

With only a few exceptions, Windows 2000 passwords are set to expire. The administrator's password, however, never expires, and by default, neither do any of the administrative accounts or the *guest* account. Whenever you schedule recurring tasks that run indefinitely, be aware of the expiration dates on your passwords.

Resetting a password takes place in the Active Directory. Click the Start button, select Programs, and then select Administrative Tools. Select Active Directory Users and Computers and then follow these steps:

1. **Click Users in the Active Directory screen's console tree (located in the left pane).**

2. **Right-click the user (in the right details pane) whose password you want to reset.**

3. **Select Reset Password from the pop-up menu, as shown in Figure 20-1.**

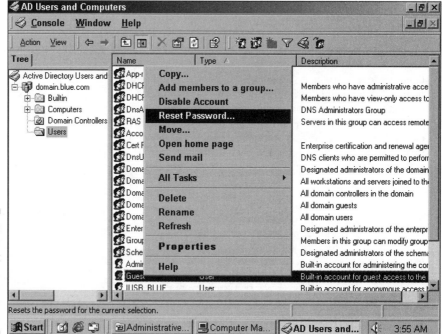

Figure 20-1:
Selecting
Reset
Password
from the
pop-up
menu.

4. **Type and then confirm the password.**

You can also click the user account you want to change, choose Action on the pull-down menu and then select Reset Password (see Figure 20-2).

Password Protection with Computer Standby and Hibernation

No matter what some administrators may tell you, you don't have to put your computer in a cave for the winter. By configuring your computer to go into standby or hibernation mode, you're improving your basic level of system security. If you leave your machine to answer a call for help, this feature prevents your machine from staying *open* and unprotected for a long time — which can prevent someone from wreaking havoc on your system.

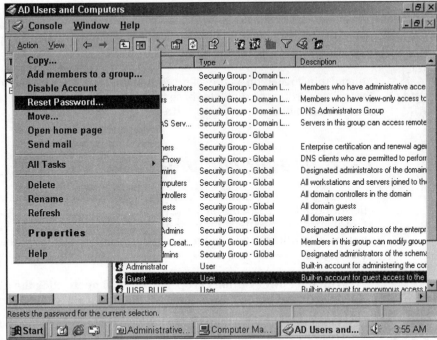

Standing by . . .

When the computer enters standby mode, the screen saver turns on and effectively *locks* your computer with your password. You will have to re-enter your password to get back on the system. Keep in mind that if your system is in standby, information in your computer's memory isn't saved on your hard disk. If a power interruption occurs, information in memory is lost.

To put your computer on standby, you must be using a computer that's set up by the manufacturer to support the standby option. About 90 percent of the computers made in the last five years or so have this option — if you don't have the standby option, however, there's no way to install it. You'll be able to adjust any power management option that your computer's hardware configuration supports by using the Power Options in the Control Panel.

Hibernation

Your computer hibernates after being idle for a period that's specified in the system parameter System hibernates, which is described in detail later in this chapter. When a computer enters hibernation mode, everything in computer memory is saved on your hard disk. Afterward, your computer goes through a shutdown procedure and then switches off.

After you turn the computer back on, all programs and documents that were open when you turned the computer off are restored on the desktop. Keep in mind that, as with standby, you must have a computer that's set up by the manufacturer to support the hibernation option.

You must be logged on as the all-powerful administrator or be a member of the Admins group to complete these procedures. Being a member of the user-account peasantry doesn't help matters here.

Putting your computer into standby

To set up a standby scheme, click the Start button and select Settings, then click Control Panel. Double-click the Power Options icon, which is appropriately shaped like a battery. (Rumor has it that the next version's Power Options icon will be a pink bunny with sunglasses and a bass drum, but then you never know with Microsoft.) Complete the task by doing the following:

1. **With the Power Options Properties screen open, click the down-arrow (to the right of the Power Schemes field) and select a power scheme.**

   I suggest you stick with the default, Always On, as shown in Figure 20-3. The time settings for the power scheme are Turn Off Monitor and Turn Off Hard Disks.

2. **To turn off your monitor before your computer goes on standby, select a time in Turn Off Monitor.**

3. **To turn off your hard disk before your computer goes on standby, select a time in Turn Off Hard Disks.**

4. **Click OK to accept your settings.**

Putting your computer into hibernation

If you want to put your computer into hibernation, you can do so with the Power Options located in your Control Panel. Open the Power Options by clicking the Power Options icon in the Control Panel and then do the following:

1. **In the Power Options Properties screen, click the Hibernate tab.**

2. **Select the Enable Hibernate Support check box and then choose Apply.**

3. **Click the APM tab, choose Enable Advanced Power Management Support, and then choose Apply to ensure your changes are made.**

4. **Select the Power Schemes tab.**

   Be sure to select a time for the system to go into hibernation.

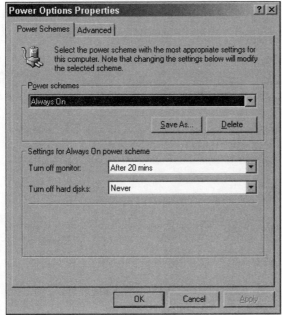

Figure 20-3:
The Power
Options
Properties
window.

5. **Click the OK button to accept your selections.**

If the Hibernate tab is unavailable, your computer doesn't support this feature.

Chapter 21

Security in the New Millennium

● ●

In This Chapter

▶ Applying new security features

▶ Using default security settings

▶ Controlling access

▶ Implementing the Active Directory

▶ Viewing the Security Log

▶ Starting programs under another account

● ●

*I*f you're like too many administrators, you may be thinking, "Security? I don't need it. No cracker is going to waste all that time looking at my data."

You may be right. But do you want to risk being wrong? A basic understanding of how Windows 2000 security works can be a real boon to your administration skills.

Good security prevents crackers from stealing or damaging sensitive data or applications. Even if this isn't important to you, a good security system protects specific resources in the environment from inept access by users.

Properly utilized security prevents unauthorized users from reading the company personnel files or erasing mission-critical information. If you tailor your security setup to meet your needs, no matter how small, you create an environment that is easier to manage and maintain.

Eureka! Innovations in Windows 2000 Security

While not completely different from the original NT security setup, Windows 2000 has major differences.

✔ The Administrator account controls membership for four groups:

  • Admins

  • Backup Operators

  • Power Users

  • Users

✔ An overarching group — the *Authenticated Users* group — has the widest membership and is controlled by the Windows 2000 operating system or domain.

It's much like the catch-all *Everyone* group under NT but it also has some important differences:

  • It doesn't contain the Guest accounts.

  • The Authenticated Users group is not used to assign permissions.

  • By default, any Authenticated User is a member of the Users group.

When a Windows 2000 Professional or Server computer joins a domain, domain administrators are added to the local Admins group and Domain Users are added to the local Users group.

Windows 2000 Power Users have all the capabilities of a Windows NT 4.0 User. This helps NT 4.0 backward compatibility.

The user system on Windows NT 4.0 divided everyone into two key groups: Admins and Users. The catchall group *Everyone* had a membership roll controlled by the operating system or domain. User membership is more like an army than a rabble; it's controlled by the Administrator account.

Default User Security Settings

The default security settings for Windows 2000 can be described by summarizing the permissions granted to either Admins, Power Users, Users, or Backup Operators.

✔ Each type of user has a role to play on the Windows system.

✔ The permissions, if you don't meddle with them too much, allow users to operate as they should in your environment.

Admins

The Administrator account and the members of the Admins group are the blessed ones: They have the power to access all the tools, utilities, and processes supported by the operating system. By default, few (if any) restrictions fetter administrative access to any Registry or file-system object.

Any restrictions would be pretty laughable anyway: Administrators have the power to grant themselves any rights that Windows 2000 hasn't already given them by default.

If you're from the UNIX or Linux world, you know of this kind of power as the *root account.*

Exert administrative permissions to regulate the following tasks:

- ✔ Backing up and restoring the system
- ✔ Configuring operating system rules for file systems and passwords
- ✔ Installing the operating system and components
- ✔ Installing hardware drivers and system services
- ✔ Installing Service Packs
- ✔ Managing security and auditing logs
- ✔ Repairing and upgrading the operating system
- ✔ Taking ownership of files

Users

Your average Joe (or Josephine) user accounts have full control over all of their own data files and their own part of the Registry (this is the HKEY_CURRENT_USER parameter that lurks in Chapter 15). The default security settings prevent members of this group from compromising the integrity of the operating system and installed programs.

- ✔ Users can't modify remote Registry settings or program files.
- ✔ A regular user account can shut down a workstation, not a server.
- ✔ User account permissions can't install programs that can be run by other users. (This prevents lost productivity via networked Quake/DOOM sessions and Trojan Horse programs.)

What breed of horse is a Trojan, anyway?

If you haven't browsed your copy of *The Iliad* lately, the Trojan horse was a wooden war machine that the Greeks left as a "tribute" for their enemies to take into their stronghold. After the Trojans brought the giant tchotchke inside, their agents swarmed out of the seemingly innocuous object and took the city from the inside.

Trojan horses (in the technical sense) do the same thing. They're programs that are designed to look peaceful so you place them on your hard drive. Once there, they can spread virus programs or otherwise damage your system. Some even self-delete themselves so you never know what hit you (in the literal sense).

Regular user accounts aren't able to use the majority of programs written for previous versions of Windows. This is primarily because previous versions of Windows (such as 95 and 98) didn't support file system or Registry security.

Power Users (yep, it's capitalized)

Power Users fall somewhere between the administrative users and the everyday User accounts. Power Users have permission to complete any system task except tasks reserved for the Admins group, such as installing new programs and accessing the Control Panel.

Power Users can perform all kinds of, well, powerful feats:

- ✔ Create and manage local user accounts and groups
- ✔ Customize system-wide resources
- ✔ Install programs that don't modify operating system files or install system services
- ✔ Run legacy applications in addition to Windows 2000-certified applications
- ✔ Stop and start system services that aren't started by default.

Even Power Users have a limit on their powers:

- ✔ They can't add themselves to the Admins group. (Otherwise, there really wouldn't be much distinction between the two groups.)
- ✔ They can't convince the media that the new millennium doesn't *actually* begin until the year 2001. (But who can?)

Backup operators

As you may guess, members of the Backup Operators group do not have bee-hive hairdos and names like Ronette, Shaunette, and Lanette. They are, however, empowered to back up and restore files on the computer. What you may not know is that they can do this *regardless* of any permissions that protect those files.

The Backup Operators permissions that allow them to back up and restore files also make it possible for Backup Operators to use their permissions for other purposes, such as reading another user's files! Once backed up and restored to a different location, an Operator from this group can (at the least) read, if not edit, valuable or private information.

The Windows 2000 Security Model Strikes a Pose

Windows 2000 security revolves around users, networks, and objects. As a model, whatever it might lack in glitz it makes up for in practicality:

- ✔ *Authentication* controls users and networks
- ✔ *Access control* protects objects.

User authentication

User *authentication* gives users the ability to log onto a system and access resources across the network that may be very remote from the user's physical location. There are two types of system authentication: *interactive login* and *network authentication*.

Interactive login

The interactive login confirms the user's identification against a user's local computer or Active Directory account.

- ✔ Locally, the identification is compared to the local computer's stored database, also known as the Security Account Manager (SAM). If you can truthfully say that SAM knows you, you're on your way in.
- ✔ With a domain account, a user logs in to the network with a password that is stored in Active Directory.

If a password is used to log on to a domain account, Windows 2000 uses Kerberos V5 security software for authentication.

Network authentication

Network authentication confirms the user's identification for (surprise, surprise) your network services.

- ✔ Users with a *local account* must provide credentials (such as a user name and password) every time they access a network resource.

- ✔ Network authentication is invisible to users on a *domain account.*

  A user using the domain account saves time and helps avoid carpal tunnel syndrome from too much typing (at any rate, we can hope).

Object-based access control

Windows 2000 allows administrators to control network resources (known as *objects* in Windows-speak) on the network. Access control — say-so over who uses what — is based on administrator-assigned security descriptors linked to objects stored in Active Directory.

A *security descriptor* lists users and groups that have access to an object. By managing properties on objects, administrators can set permissions, assign ownership, and monitor user access.

Examples of *objects* include

- ✔ Shared files
- ✔ Networked printers
- ✔ Network services, such as File Transfer

Access control and the Active Directory

The Active Directory provides protected storage for user account and group information. It does this by utilizing access control on objects and user account credentials.

Active Directory stores both user credentials and access control information. Users who log in to the network can obtain both authentication and authorization to access system resources from the Active Directory. And how.

Viewing the Security Log

Suppose that as Administrator, you keep getting a nagging little voice in the back of your head that tells you somebody's not exactly playing fair. If you have a security alert, or suspect that a Power User has skulked up to

Administrator level, you can check the Windows 2000 security log. Among other useful capabilities, the Security log tells you whether anyone has tried to crack the Administrator account password — or whether there's a Trojan horse program sitting like a little atomic bomb on your hard drive (hey, that's always good to know). To view the log, do the following:

1. **Open Computer Management.**

2. **In the console tree on the left-hand pane, click Event Viewer, as shown in Figure 21-1.**

3. **Double-click Security Log.**

4. **In the right-hand details pane, examine the list of events for anything out of the ordinary.**

It's even truer of computers than it is of real life: The devil's in the details. Wanna configure your Security Log's devil to raise a little less Cain? Take a look at these steps:

1. **Right-click the Security Log.**

2. **Select Properties from the pop-up menu.**

    The resulting window should be similar to Figure 21-2.

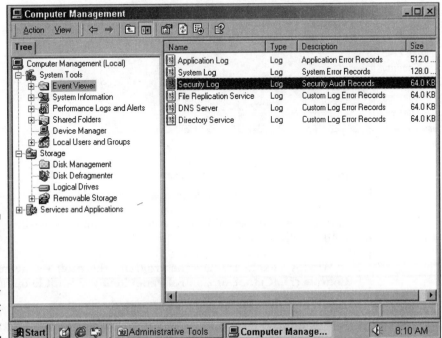

Figure 21-1:
Select the Security Log from the Computer Management window.

Most commonly, you want to expand or decrease your Security Log size. This can be done by clicking the arrows to the right of the Maximum Log Size field (near the center of the window).

By default, your Maximum log size is 512K, which shouldn't eat into your disk space by much at all.

Because the log writes over itself on a busy day — and you may have many *questionable* messages on a large system — it's usually best to expand the log size. If you really want to know what's going on, *never reduce the log size.*

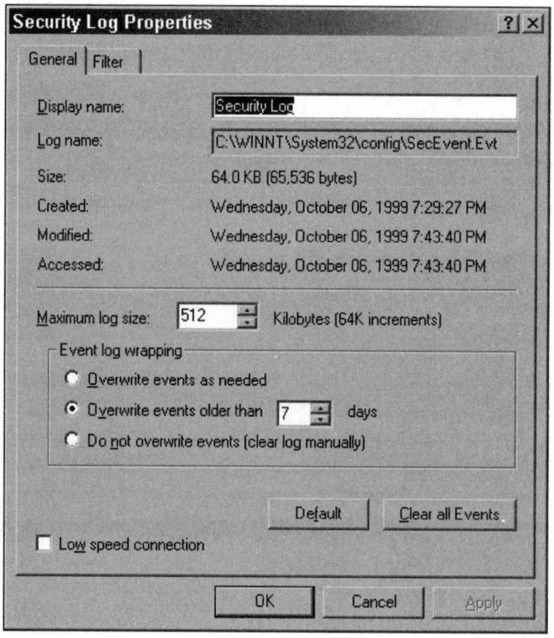

Figure 21-2:
The Security
Log
Properties
screen.

> **Security Log Properties**   ? ×
>
> General | Filter |
>
> Display name: [Security Log]
> Log name: C:\WINNT\System32\config\SecEvent.Evt
> Size: 64.0 KB (65,536 bytes)
> Created: Wednesday, October 06, 1999 7:29:27 PM
> Modified: Wednesday, October 06, 1999 7:43:40 PM
> Accessed: Wednesday, October 06, 1999 7:43:40 PM
>
> Maximum log size: [512] Kilobytes (64K increments)
>
> Event log wrapping
> ○ Overwrite events as needed
> ● Overwrite events older than [7] days
> ○ Do not overwrite events (clear log manually)
>
>   Default   Clear all Events
> ☐ Low speed connection
>
>   OK   Cancel   Apply

Starting a program as another user

To spare you the time of logging out of a system and back in as someone else to run a program, you can use the *Run As* command. This allows you to stay logged in as a regular user or Power User while running a sensitive program as the Administrative account.

1. **In Windows Explorer, click the program, Microsoft Management Console (MMC) tool, or Control Panel item you want to open.**

2. **Hold down the Shift key and right-click the program.**

3. **Select "Run as" from the pop-up menu, as shown in Figure 21-3.**

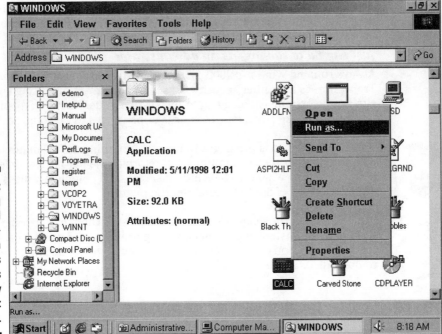

Figure 21-3:
Pressing
Shift and
right-
clicking a
program's
icon gives
you a new
option:
Run as.

4. **From the Run as Other User screen, click next to the second option (Run program as the following user:) and get ready to type.**

5. **Type the user name, password, and domain of the Administrator account you want to use, as shown in Figure 21-4.**

6. **Click the OK button to save your changes (imagine if politics were that easy).**

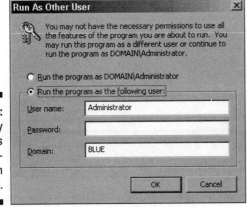

Figure 21-4:
Identify
yourself as
an adminis-
trator to run
a program.

Windows 2000 launches Windows Explorer, the Printers folder, and desktop items indirectly. These items can't be started with the Run as command.

Just say no to running as an administrator

Always running Windows 2000 as an administrator opens the system to Trojan horses and other security risks. The simple act of visiting an Internet site can be extremely damaging to the system. A destructive Trojan horse program can take advantage of your user privileges to do some nasty stuff.

An administrator has privileges to do, well, anything. A Trojan horse program unleashed under these conditions can reformat the hard drive, delete all your files, cause gray whales to beach themselves, and completely mess up the entire economy of South Dakota. Get the picture?

Add yourself to the *Power Users* group. You're still able to perform routine tasks, such as installing programs, adding printers, and using most of the Control Panel. You can log back in as the Administrator account if you need to upgrade or repair the operating system.

Chapter 22

Not This File, Soldier

• •

• •

*N*TFS stands for the *Network File System*. It's the style, or (in tech-speak) *flavor,* of file system that Windows 2000 and NT 4.0 use by default to store and organize data. This file system is crucial in Windows 2000. Without NTFS, you lose most of the new Windows 2000 file management features.

Microsoft tries very hard to keep full *backward compatibility* with most of their software (documents on Excel 95 still work with Excel 98, et cetera). Given the choice between compromising for backward compatibility or forging ahead to a brave new operating system, Microsoft chose to go ahead with NTFS in Windows 2000, and darn the consequences.

As far as security is concerned, NTFS-based permissioning allows you greater control over permissioning and sharing objects than ever before. All *objects* on the file system (such as text files, program files, hard drives, printers) can be permissioned and shared out with greater *granularity* of control. (For an explanation of granularity, backtrack to Chapter 9.) It's truly a brave new world for Microsoft, so it's worth your time and effort to understand it.

Establishing Permissions

It's a given: To set up permissions for files and folders under Windows 2000, you must use drives formatted to use NTFS. You set the file permissions by viewing the security properties of files, printers, and Active Directory objects.

When setting up permissions, you can specify the level of access for users as well as user groups. You have several different levels of permissions you can assign users to files, from the ability to simply read, or *access,* files, to the ability to edit files or execute and stop programs.

The reverse is also true:

✔ You can deny a given user or group the ability to edit the file, but allow them to read it.

✔ You can prevent editing while allowing execution.

✔ You can allow a user or group to *edit* a file but not allow *access* to it — which, when you think about it, doesn't make much sense.

You can set similar permissions on a piece of hardware. For example, you can set permissions on a shared printer so certain users can configure the printer and other users only can print on it.

Editing Permissions

To change permissions on a file or a folder, you must

✔ Own the file, or

✔ Be the Administrator account, or

✔ Be a member of the Administrative group, or

✔ Be granted permission by the file owner

Groups or users granted Full Control of a folder can delete files and sub-folders within that folder *regardless* of the permissions protecting the files and subfolders. This is why you should use the Full Control setting sparingly. It's like a limited form of the Administrator's privileges. Only localized harm can come from it, but it's best to avoid any problems of this sort.

Treat the granting of Full Control privileges like hot-pepper sauce — a little goes a long way.

To view file permissions, do the following:

1. **Open Windows Explorer.**

2. **Locate the file or folder for which you want to set permissions.**

3. **Right-click the file or folder, then select Properties from the pop-up menu.**

4. **Click the Security tab on the Properties window. See Figure 21-1 for an example.**

   The current permissions allocated to this file are displayed. In the fol-lowing example, if you want to view the permissions for the Administrators or SYSTEM, you must click in the Name box in the upper half of the Properties screen to select them.

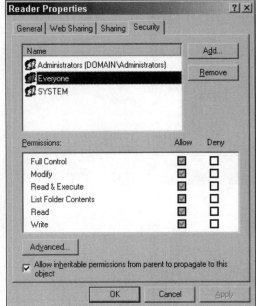

Figure 22-1:
The
permissions
for each
account are
displayed on
the Security
tab.

To edit or add accounts to permission, perform the following tasks:

1. **View the file permissions, as described in the preceding steps.**

2. **Click the Allow or Deny check boxes for each permission you want to allow or deny.**

To set up permissions for a new group or user, follow these steps:

1. **Click the Add button.**

   The Select Users, Computers, or Groups screen appears.

2. **Type the name of the group or user you want to give permission, using the format** domainname\name.

   If you find the name you want in the list inside the upper field, click it once to select it. See Figure 22-2 as an example.

3. **Click OK to close the dialog box.**

To remove a group or user from the permissions list, select the user you want to remove (the name appears conveniently on the Security screen) and click the Remove button.

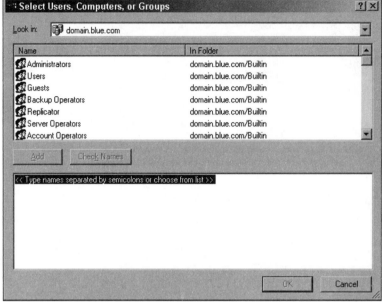

Advanced permissioning

If you want to edit specific permissions on files or folders, you can do so in Windows 2000. You easily can allow or deny permissions, such as Traversing Folders or Reading Extended Attributes. The following steps show how:

1. **Open the Windows Explorer, right-click the file you want to re-permission, and select Properties⇨Security.**

2. **Click Advanced on the Security table.**

    The Access control screen appears (shown for your amusement in Figure 22-3), where you can add, remove, or edit user permissions in the same manner as in the regular security tab.

Denial isn't just a river in Egypt

Remember that a denial, on any level, is final. For example, if you permission users so they can't access a file, then they absolutely, positively can't access it — even if other members of their group members can access the file.

It's an important distinction. For privacy purposes, the security system on Windows 2000 is conservative — if there's a conflict of permissions, the user is denied access.

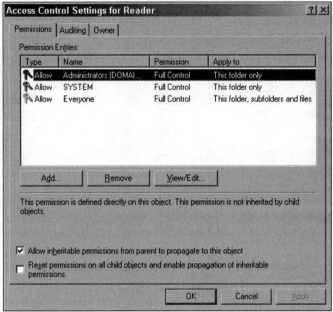

Figure 22-3:
Clicking the
Advanced
button takes
you to the
Access
Control
Settings for
Reader
screen.

3. **Click the View/Edit button at the bottom of the Permissions Entries field to edit permissions.**

4. **Set special permissions for a new group or user by selecting the Allow or Deny check boxes, as seen in Figure 22-4.**

5. **If you want to apply these permissions to other files and folders**

   • Click the arrow to the right of the Apply onto field.

   • Select the application scope you want. (Anything from This Folder Only to This Folder, Subfolders, and Files. Sorry: The Known Universe isn't an option.)

   • Click OK.

6. **If you want to allow subfolders and files within the tree to inherit these permissions, click the Allow Inheritable Permissions from Parent to Propagate This Object check box.**

Inheritance

Inherited permissions apply to a file because the permissions have been set as a higher level than the specific file or folder. In the base of a file, you (or someone else) may have changed the folder permissions to be different. A folder may be a subfolder of another folder that's permissioned differently.

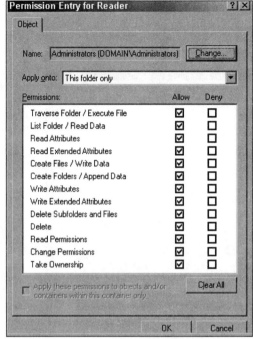

Figure 22-4:
Add or
remove
specialized
permissions
in the
Permission
Entry
screen.

When you don't want files or subfolders to inherit permissions, you can *cheat* these file-system objects out of their expected inheritance:

1. **Right-click the file or subfolder.**
2. **Click Properties.**
3. **Click the Security tab.**
4. **Deselect the Allow Inheritable Permissions from Parent to Propagate to This Object check box.**

An administrator can tell whether a file or folder has inherited permissions. Hey, that's almost as good as being Santa Claus.

✔ If the check boxes appear shaded, it's a case of inheritance.

✔ Clear white check boxes indicate that this is a self-made file.

File server permissions

By and large, you want to set up certain folders a specific way on your file server. This depends on

> ✔ The function of the folder
>
> ✔ How useful it is for the folder (and the files that inherit its permissions) to be able to read or edit files

Applications folders

Applications folders store the vast majority of the programs that come with a default installation of Windows 2000 Professional or Server. They're also created in default locations by programs when you install them off of floppy disks and CD-ROMs.

In these folders, make all executable programs read-only to all users. This prevents users from damaging the fragile code of the programs. It also prevents the spread of computer viruses.

If none of your programs write initialization files in their own folders, set all the folders containing programs to read-only.

Home folders

Each user account, when created, has its own *home folder* to store and edit files that the user creates or imports. Due to the limited scope of these folders, you can safely give users Full Control over their own folders.

Public folders

Public folders store data that you want to make available to the maximum number of people. It's appropriate for you to give all users Change permissions in these folders.

Change permissions are safer and more appropriate than Full Control, because Full Control also allows users to set permissions for the public folder and take ownership of it. Because it is a hassle (to say the least) if a user with a misguided lust for power takes ownership of the folder and denies it to others, it's best to head that idea off at the pass.

Sharing hard drives

All drives on your computer, such as drive C or D, automatically are shared on Windows 2000. They are shared with the syntax `<drive letter$>` (such as `<C$>` or `<D$>`). A networked user can view all folders and files on a shared drive.

These drives don't have the special drive-and-hand icon that indicates sharing in the My Computer or Windows Explorer windows. They also are hidden when users connect to your computer remotely. (The sound principle here is *out of sight, out of mind.*)

To help keep your shared drives secure, create a difficult password for the Administrator account. You may also want to rename the Administrator account using the Local Users and Groups snap-in.

To *temporarily* stop sharing a drive, right-click it and select Sharing from the pop-up menu. Click Do not share this folder. It's off the market! However, keep in mind that Windows 2000 shares the drive again once the computer is restarted.

Sharing printers

Sharing a printer, as with any shared device, allows it to be seen and used by the Windows network. You should share as many devices as you can to maximize utility of your networked assets.

Avoid sharing only where you have a *mobile* unit (such as the portable printers that some laptops can use).

If you're using Windows 2000 Server, any printer you add is shared by default.

With Windows 2000 Professional, printers *aren't* shared by default, but you can choose to make them shared. Here's how:

1. **Click the Start button and choose Settings⇨Printers.**

2. **Right-click the printer you want to share and choose Sharing from the pop-up menu.**

   The Sharing tab appears.

3. **Click Shared As and type a name for the shared printer.**

   The Sharing tab is shown in Figure 22-5. I think the tab has his father's eyes.

4. **Click OK.**

5. **If you share a printer with users who use an operating system that isn't as cool as Windows 2000, follow these steps:**

   • Click the Additional Drivers button in the Properties window.

   • Select the environment and operating system for the other computer(s), as shown in Figure 22-6.

   • Click OK to install the drivers.

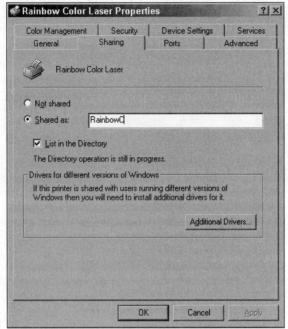

Figure 22-5:
The Sharing
tab: a chip
off the old
dialog box.

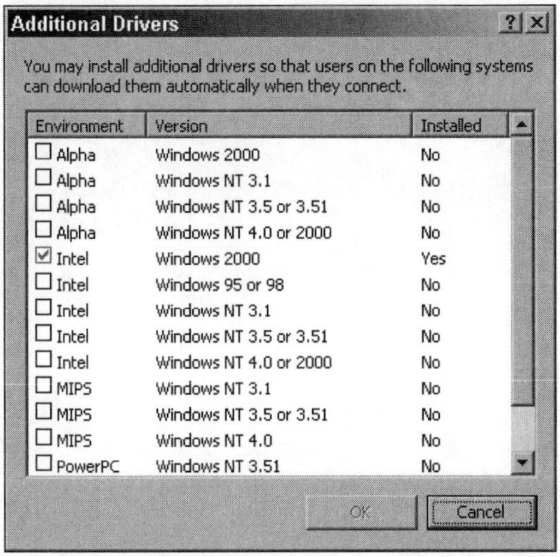

Figure 22-6:
Select
additional
drivers
for other
operating
systems.

6. **As you find yourself back in the Properties window, click OK once more to exit and to apply your settings.**

Part VI
Troubleshooting

The 5th Wave   By Rich Tennant

Maintenance is chagrined to find out the squeak in Clark's disk drive is really a whistle in Clark's nose.

In this part . . .

1 know that it's hard to believe, but you may actually run into trouble when you use Windows 2000. I don't mean trouble along the lines of fonts that make you squint to read them, or a disk label color that is completely, totally out of fashion. I mean big, major league trouble like a disk expiring on you, right before your annual salary review. (Murphy's Catch-22 is that chaos has to work overtime to keep everything else from working.)

Take advantage of the guidance in this part so you can save time later to catch up on your last game of *Shoot-Em-Up, Quake,* or *Doom.* (Did I say *Doom?* I meant to say *Latest Network Techniques.* Yeah, that's the ticket.)

Chapter 23

Nobody Knows the Troubles I've Shot

*B*efore you read this chapter, you may remember that Microsoft says their new paradigm is *Zero Administration*. If Windows 2000 is so easy and trouble-free, why have a chapter on shooting whatever trouble crops up?

Difficult as it is for me to defend Bill Gates (he has many more well-paid people to do that), I have to argue for understanding. *Every* system has flaws and bugs. That includes the latest and greatest edition of Windows. Take Zero Administration as a goal as just that, a goal that probably will be reached, but not in your lifetime (at least your time as a Windows administrator). This chapter delivers general troubleshooting techniques, plus fixes for common problem spots in Windows 2000.

No matter the problem, there's always a possibility that you may need to reboot your machine. To counter most of the problems that result from the reboot fix, keep frequent backups!

Troubleshooting in Windows 2000

Before you even start clicking at random around the desktop in a *something's gotta work* frenzy, take a deep breath.

Relax.

Microsoft has gifted you with a truly new benefit for Windows 2000.

Based on the same idea of the *wizard* setup programs, Microsoft has created several programs that guide you through a troubleshooting checklist. These are called (in a truly creative spasm) *troubleshooters.* While hardly an encyclopedia of all the things that can go wrong, this is a major boon for a new administrator.

Microsoft has created troubleshooting programs for

- Client Services for NetWare
- Display (your monitor setup)
- Hardware (all peripherals)
- Internet connections (ISOP)
- Modem settings
- MS-DOS programs
- Multimedia & Games (Need to know how to beat Solitaire? This is the place!)
- Networking in TCP/IP
- Printing
- Remote access
- Sound (beeps, boings, and squawks only)
- System setup
- Windows 3.*x* programs

Starting a troubleshooter

The best way to start a troubleshooter is through the Windows 2000 Help command from the Start menu. This summons the entire list of troubleshooters for you to start.

The complete list is helpful because certain problems can overlap between subjects (an external speaker problem can fall under Sounds or Multimedia). So . . .

1. **Click the Start button and point to Help.**

2. **Click the Index tab.**

   The Index is *type-sensitive* and jumps to the right subject as you type your keyword into the field at the top.

3. **Type the word** troubleshooters.

Behold the several subcategories under troubleshooters.

4. **Click basic guidelines for the list of all troubleshooter programs.**

The troubleshooter programs appear in the right-hand pane with hyper-links, as shown in Figure 23-1.

5. **Click a hyperlink to start a troubleshooter process.**

Working with a troubleshooter

To use a troubleshooting program, follow the steps that appear on the screen.

Two tips can make a troubleshooting program more productive:

✔ Resize the Help window where you're running the troubleshooter and move the window to the right side of your screen. This lets you open programs and windows where you can actually do the work that the troubleshooter instructs you to do. As an example of how to do this, see Figure 23-2.

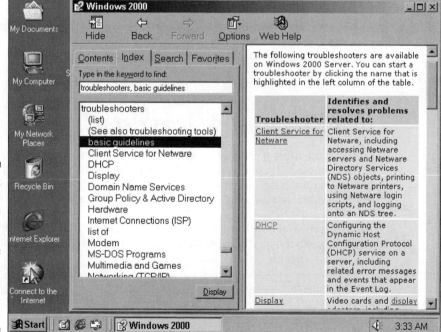

Figure 23-1:
The
Windows
2000 Help
screen and
the list of
trouble-
shooters in
the right-
hand pane.

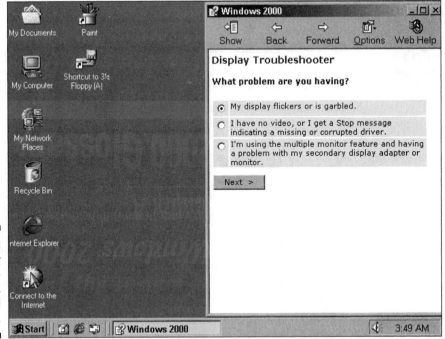

Figure 23-2:
The Display
Trouble-
shooter,
resized
and hidden.

✔ Follow the troubleshooter steps as close to verbatim as you can. If you don't, you're missing the point about working within a troubleshooter program. If you want to try different solutions, do it outside of the troubleshooter.

Help! The system won't start!

Probably the most frustrating problem with any operating system is when it fails to boot up. Of course, a fix for this is to reinstall the operating system, but this is time consuming. Also, it may be the worst thing to do if you haven't performed a recent backup. You can lose important data.

There are several possible problems with startup. If you rule out the supremely obvious (you know where the power switch is, you're sure that you have a working wall socket), it can be

✔ Corrupt or damaged Windows 2000 Registry

✔ Corrupt or damaged system files

✔ Corrupt or damaged partition boot sector

✔ Failing hard drive

Don't play Blind Man's Bluff

If you need to close the troubleshooter window or, if you're unlucky enough that you need to restart the computer, you may run into trouble with the troubleshooter if you only have one monitor available! That's because, unless you're one of the rare folks who keep a bank of monitors handy, you lose your place in the troubleshooter when the computer shuts down.

To get around this, print the current troubleshooter step by clicking the Options button on the Help toolbar and selecting Print. Make sure to double-click all headings within the step you are printing so that all the subprocedures are open and thus printed out.

Let the print job get to the printer *before* you shut the computer down.

In the case of the failing hard drive, you should be tipped off to the problem (as with most hardware problems) by the sound. As low-tech as it sounds, a bad disk drive or failing disk head often can be identified by a high-pitched whine or a clicking noise like a stapler. If you hear anything like these noises, try to access the drive and save as much data as you can before yanking it from the system.

If you have really critical data on the drive, you can do a search on the Internet (from a different machine, of course) to find firms that specialize in prying data from corrupt, failed, smashed, or pureed hard drives. This will cost you, but if you have the budget and the company feels it's critical enough, you can try it.

For the remainder of the problems, a problem with software can be repaired with other software. You're on your way to computer wellness when you repair your system with the Emergency Repair Disk (ERD).

Mr. Sulu, set phasers to fluff!

A client asked me, "If I spill cola or water on a keyboard or hard drive, can I fix it by using a hair dryer to evaporate the liquid inside the machine?"

Sadly, this does not work, nor does it make your server more stylish and sexually appealing to other servers. Spilling liquids into a machine disrupts the delicate contacts and circuits that allow it to function. The fluid acts as a

conductor, allowing electricity to pass from one section of the machine to areas which can be garbled or erased with exposure.

Your only solution, in all honesty, is prevention. If you must have your 32-ounce Slurpfest Supreme while working on your machine, place it where a spill does the least damage. A keyboard's a lot cheaper than a motherboard.

What, you don't have an Emergency Repair Disk? Skip over to Appendix D. Do it now. I'll wait here until you come back.

The repair process itself is simple:

1. **Start your computer from the Windows 2000 Setup disks or the CD.**

2. **Choose the repair option during setup.**

3. **Choose the type of repair you need.**

   • *Fast Repair* is the easiest. With Fast Repair, the repair process automatically solves problems related to the Registry, system files, the partition boot sector on your boot volume, and your startup environment.

   The Fast Repair option only repairs a Registry file if the file is missing or corrupted.

   • *Manual Repair* option requires user action. You can choose to repair system files, partition boot-sector problems, and startup-environment problems. Registry problems aren't corrected.

   Only experienced administrators or users with administrative privileges should use the Manual Repair option.

4. **Click the OK button to begin the repair process. If you selected Fast Repair, the whole process is automatic. If you selected Manual Repair, you may be asked to click buttons that ask which options you want to choose as the computer works through the repair process a step at a time.**

   Use the ERD that you created, and the original Windows 2000 installation CD, by inserting them into the proper drives on your machine. (You'll likely receive a prompt to do so, in any case.) Missing or corrupt files are copied and replaced with fresh files either from the Windows 2000 CD or the `systemroot\repair` directory.

5. **Restart your computer.**

   If the repair process is successful, you should have your system working again!

Troubleshooting the Active Directory

As part of the Windows 2000 operating system, the Active Directory is almost bulletproof. It's a very stable component of the Windows 2000 system, but it has an Achilles heel (that isn't related to its actual coding).

Because the Active Directory operates almost purely on a networked level, it's seriously vulnerable to *network disruption*.

In fact, any of the following problems that you encounter in Active Directory are really network problems:

- ✔ The infrastructure master isn't available.
- ✔ The primary Domain Controller emulator isn't available.
- ✔ The schema master isn't available.
- ✔ You can't add or remove a domain.

To resolve the problem in any of these situations, you must troubleshoot the network, not the Windows software. Network troubleshooting involves everything from checking the connections of your cables to tracking down who can use the network skillfully — and who can't.

Although the vast majority of Active Directory problems are network connectivity woes or slowdowns, some other potential failures should be looked at more closely:

Incorrect (or malfunctioning) name registration and name resolution

Although the network should be checked, this can be caused by a NetBIOS or DNS problem.

Try running the Netdiag /debug utility on the server that is experiencing the problem. This is a command-line tool that evaluates the NetBIOS and DNS services.

Users aren't allowed to log on to a Domain Controller

To allow one or more users to log on locally to your domain controller, enable the policy from *only* the Default Domain Controllers Policy.

Networking and dial-up troubleshooting

Some of the most common problems in this area are simple hardware mismatches (or mismanagement). Often, two common problems bedevil modems:

- ✔ The modem refuses to work with a new Windows 2000 machine.

  Sometimes the modem is simply incompatible with the Windows 2000 operating system. Unfortunately, while this is easy to diagnose, it's next to impossible to cure with that modem. Because modems are going for the price of McDonald's Happy Meals these days (well, almost), just go out and buy a different modem.

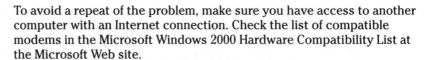

To avoid a repeat of the problem, make sure you have access to another computer with an Internet connection. Check the list of compatible modems in the Microsoft Windows 2000 Hardware Compatibility List at the Microsoft Web site.

✔ The modem isn't connected properly, although it shows as part of the connected peripheral hardware.

Verify that the modem is connected properly to the correct port on your computer. If you're not sure, switch ports until you get a response.

✔ Of course, if the modem is external, verify that the power is on.

But wait! There's more!

User account or remote access permission denied

Go to the User Management utility and confirm that you, in fact, have these permissions. Sometimes, when you're setting up accounts, you may forget to apply the changes you've made to the accounts. Discarded changes do you as much good as paper you've pushed through the office shredder.

Can't dial out of your building with your modem network connection

This is another deceptive problem. A typical office building is on its own little telephonic circuit. You have to dial 9, or whatever, before you can call out from a building, *even with a modem connection!*

You may also run into this problem when traveling. If you plug your laptop into the phone line, expect problems connecting from the hotel. Make sure to ask the hotel management about the appropriate dial procedures.

Some offices and hotels have moved to *digital* lines. If you have an older modem, don't connect it to these lines — you can damage your machine. Newer modems have a built-in shutoff *shunt* that prevents damage, but you still aren't able to connect.

Your hotel telephone line doesn't accommodate your modem speed

Simple solution: Call the hotel manager to request a *direct line*.

Staying someplace Internet-challenged, like Bubba's Bunk House/Pool Hall/Oil Change Emporium? You may need to select a lower bits-per-second (bps) rate on your modem.

The hotel line is digital

Find an analog phone line. Otherwise, you need a modem that can handle digital lines.

I keep getting kicked off

The quality of your telephone line is insufficient. This has nothing to do with Windows 2000 or your computer!

Your best bet is to contact your telephone company and have them check your line. On a fiber-optic network, so many fibers can be broken that the quality of your line drops below par.

Users at home can't reach the Internet through your network

Most likely, the TCP/IP settings aren't correct on their computers. Check their TCP/IP settings in Network Connection to make sure they match what you've set up.

Call waiting breaks my connection!

There is only one solution: Disable call waiting. (Yes, being an administrator is tough, rather like being a brain surgeon. But at least you don't get icky stuff on your hands.)

The disk is off-line or missing

Problems relating to disks usually are physical in nature. You have to keep your ear tuned more than your eyes for problems of that sort. If you don't hear an odd whine or buzz from the drive, consider checking the troubleshooter program for your disk, or refer to the following information.

Assuming that nobody's come in during the night and swiped the whole disk (don't laugh, it happens), the disk may be corrupted, shut off, or disconnected.

DNS clients and servers

DNS is tricky to troubleshoot. You may end up having to visit the Microsoft site to research your particular problem. The following problems are the most common.

Client receives Name not found error message

If the DNS client computer does not have a valid IP configuration for the network, it can get this message. Immediately check to see that TCP/IP configuration settings for the client computer are correct.

To verify a client IP configuration, use the ipconfig command in the Command Prompt window.

Client can't contact its servers

First, make sure the client and servers are configured for each other.

If the client and server are configured for each other, ping the preferred DNS server by its IP address to verify whether a client has basic TCP/IP access to the DNS server. To do this, type **ping** and the DNS server address in the Command Prompt window, then press Enter. If you get a response back, you're connected.

If the DNS server isn't running or responding to queries, try pinging from another machine (on a different network subnet, if you can manage it). If this doesn't work, work on that DNS server or notify those who can — you have a serious network problem if the DNS server dies.

The DNS server isn't responding to queries

Confirm that the DNS server processes have started on this computer, especially if you've just rebooted it. Use the nslookup command to test whether the server can respond to DNS clients.

Common printing problems

Most problems of printers are in the physical world or answered in the Troubleshooter program. Most of the physical problems are real heavy-duty skull-busters:

- ✔ How do I get a ream of paper into that printer?
- ✔ How do I shake that toner cartridge before I stick it into the machine?
- ✔ Which hand do I sacrifice to get to that jammed printout?

Before you run for the handyman or the troubleshooter program, consider the answers to some of the following questions

The printer doesn't print

(And I checked the power cord and switch, so that's not it!)

There are a lot of possible solutions. Depending on the situation, try the following tech-ninja moves:

- ✔ Try printing a page from the Notepad application. This verifies that the printer driver is correct — the problem lies with the user's application, not the printer. If you can't print from Notepad, the problem lies with the printer driver

✔ Check the available disk space on the system drive — and the amount allocated to the print spool! If you run out of room to spool the job, larger jobs may fail when smaller jobs don't (which causes no end of perplexed users).

✔ Verify basic network connectivity. Can you *see* the server in your Print Manager?

✔ Check user rights, protocols, and share names if only one person can't get a document to print.

Print jobs for non-English type are slow

Most likely, multiple languages are installed on the client computer but not on your print server. To add these languages to the Windows 2000 print server, search for these language fonts and drivers on the Microsoft Web site.

Documents won't print or delete

Your print spooler probably is stalled. Manually stop and restart the Print Spooler service.

A printer driver I need isn't listed

The printer is either too *old* or too *new* to be included in the latest set of printer drivers for Windows 2000. For the latest printer drivers

✔ Check out Microsoft printing support at the Microsoft Web site.

✔ Go to the Web site of the company that made your printer.

Most likely, the printer driver is marked by an text hyperlink. When you click the link, you can download the driver to your machine. Agree to this generous offer and then let the Internet connection do its thing.

The printer's driver is corrupted or incorrect

Reinstall the correct printer driver on the computer.

Chapter 24

An Ounce of Prevention

●●●

In This Chapter

▶ Making a list

▶ Checking it twice

▶ Finding out what's been naughty or nice

▶ Downloading support tools

▶ Installing Resource Kits

▶ Automating protection tasks

●●●

*H*urricanes. Tornadoes. Earthquakes. Tidal waves.

None of these disasters can compare with your system going down when you're a Windows 2000 administrator. Don't believe me? Well, maybe you won't have to. Windows 2000 is more than a major advance in the Microsoft world for flexibility and new features. It's also out to set a new benchmark in networked operating system stability.

Preliminary indications are that Windows 2000 Server and Windows 2000 Professional Editions are more stable than Windows NT 4.0 — and a lot more stable than Windows 95 or (heaven help you) Windows 3.1 or Windows for Workgroups. Time will tell whether Windows 2000 is the defiant answer of the Seattle crowd to the legions of UNIX and Linux wonks around the globe.

This chapter operates under an important assumption: *If you whack it hard enough, you'll break it.* (That never seemed to be enough to protect my cast-iron Tonka trucks, but that's beside the point.)

Your Disaster-Preparedness Checklist

When cost isn't an issue, several steps can move you to maximum preparedness.

Of course, not everyone has the national budget of IBM to make systems bulletproof. When money is a large (or massive) problem, discount the suggestions that fall outside your price range.

✔ Connect your server to an emergency generator to avoid blackouts.

✔ Use redundant disks to recover data in case of mechanical failure.

✔ Install a backup system (preferably automated) to save data at regular intervals on tape or disk.

✔ Create a Backup schedule. Follow it religiously.

✔ Create and store a set of System Boot Disks. (See Appendix C.)

✔ Create and store a set of Emergency Repair Disks. (See Appendix D.)

✔ Store your installation CD-ROM in a safe, accessible location.

✔ Configure your system to protect itself and restart when the system stops unexpectedly because of a software malfunction or a power outage.

Not sure how to do this? Continue reading!

What Windows 2000 does when it hangs

A feature that causes UNIX and NetWare administrators to drool in envy is the luxury of giving your Windows 2000 system *standing orders* that tell it what to do in case the system freezes, dies, or otherwise ends its activities unexpectedly. So long as you are recognized as an Administrator or a member of the Admins group on the computer, you have a unique and useful tool at your command.

To issue your standard operating procedures when the system runs smack into disaster, do the following:

1. **Open Computer Management by clicking the Start button and pointing to Settings.**

2. **Select Control Panel and then double-click Administrative Tools.**

3. **Double-click Computer Management.**

   You can view or change system properties on a remote computer or a local computer.

4. **Right-click Computer Management (Local), then select Properties from the pop-up menu.**

   See Figure 24-1 as an example.

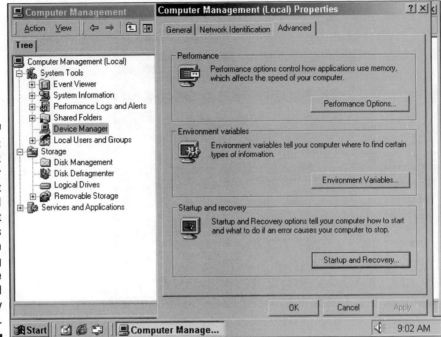

Figure 24-1:
Right-click
Computer
Management
(Local) and
select
Properties
to begin
setting
up the
Startup and
Recovery
Options.

5. **On the Advanced tab of the menu, click Startup and Recovery.**

6. **Under Startup and Recovery, select the actions Windows 2000 should perform when an error occurs.**

   See Figure 24-2 as an example of the listed options.

   Only rarely should you need to change selected default settings such as these:

   • Write an event to the system log

   • Send an administrative alert

   • Write debugging information

   • Automatically reboot

You should only deselect the log or stop the recording of debugging info if you are critically short on space. Otherwise, you need those capabilities to determine what went wrong with your system. Also, you might deselect the automatic reboot if you're sure the problem is a failing piece of hardware. Then the machine can stay powered down so you can open it safely, remove a failed hard drive or floppy disk drive, and never feel the bite of the electric snake.

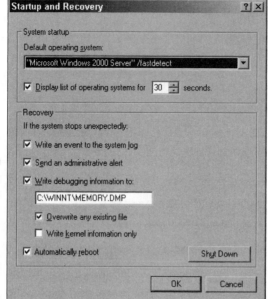

Figure 24-2:
The options
available
to you
under the
Startup and
Recovery
window.

When you select the option(s) labeled Write an Event to the System Log or
Send an Administrative Alert, then you have more information to help you
track the cause of the problem. (After you bring your system back to life,
that is.)

On the Windows 2000 Server, this action occurs by default every time a Stop
error occurs. On Windows 2000 Professional, you must manually set this
option. On Windows 2000 Professional, Write an Event to the System Log is
an option that you must set manually.

A remote chance . . .

Although a real need to do so is rare, you may
want to access a remote computer. For example, if this computer is a file or mail server, you
may want to connect to it as soon as possible to
re-establish file and e-mail links for your users.
To access a remote computer, use these steps:

1. **Right-click Computer Management (Local).**

2. **Click Connect to another computer.**

3. **Select the computer you want to connect
   from the list.**

Remote shutdowns

One of the joys of administering Windows 2000 over a network is that you can impose your wishes on a machine even when it's not within arm's reach. In the bad old days of token-ring connectors and tape drives, you couldn't administer a computer that you couldn't hit with a swing of your mouse from your desk.

Times have changed indeed. Even when users are on the machine you need to change, you can upstage their work to do a forced change — or, in this case, a forced shutdown of the system. Ah, the feeling of power. (Almost balances the responsibility, doesn't it?)

Exercising power from afar . . .

To complete a remote shutdown, carefully follow these steps:

1. **Open Computer Management by clicking the Start button and pointing to Settings.**

2. **Select Control Panel, then double-click Administrative Tools.**

3. **Right-click Computer Management (Local).**

4. **Click Connect to another computer from the pop-up menu.**

   The Select Computer dialog box appears.

5. **Under Name, choose the computer that you want to restart or shut down. Then click OK.**

   You can also type the name instead.

6. **In the console tree, right-click Computer Management (of the Remote computer name), then click Properties from the pop-up menu.**

7. **Select the Advanced tab, then click the Startup and Recovery button.**

8. **Click the Shut Down button.**

   This action opens the Shut Down dialog box, as shown in Figure 24-3.

9. **Under Action, select the actions you want to perform on the remote computer.**

10. **Under Force Apps Closed, select when you want to force applications to close when you shut down or restart the computer.**

    As a general rule, this is a good idea when you expect problems. Otherwise, avoid it. Forcing programs to close avoids the remote computer *hanging,* but it may damage it when a program hasn't been shut down cleanly.

11. **Click OK to apply your changes.**

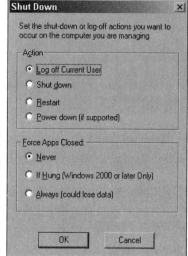

Figure 24-3:
The Shut Down dialog box and the many options you can choose.

You must be recognized as an administrator or a member of the Admins group on both your computer *and* the computer you are managing to perform a remote shutdown.

The limits of power

As a rule, you should stick with the default shutdown settings — which log off a user at Shut Down and never force applications to close, even when the system is hung. The default settings aim to accomplish two goals:

✔ Logging off the user limits the stress of shutting down and restarting by limiting the number of times the system has to do it.

✔ Not forcing a hung program to close allows it to exit without corruption or loss of data.

About the only time you should change the settings is when you're dealing with a server

machine that is absolutely triple-platinum *key-key-key* to your system. In that case, when a Shut Down command is received, the machine should either be restarted or powered off, and all applications that are hung should be forced to close. This is because servers are never powered down except in an emergency, so it should be brought down at all costs, no matter what programs are hung, so you can reboot it or start the repair work immediately.

Help files, lists, and Resource Kits

Of course, you should keep up with the latest news from Microsoft about Windows 2000. This is important when Microsoft comes out with a bug patch or a Service Pack that can enhance your existing system or reduce down time of any sort. Remember that you can download drivers, patches, and the latest Help files from the Windows Update Web site.

Hardware Compatibility List

The Windows 2000 Hardware Compatibility List is a list of computers, system components, and peripherals that work with Windows 2000 Server. Whenever you plan to add a new video card, tape drive, or printer to your network, this should be your first stop before you ever get to the cashier's line at your local electronics store.

To view this list, go to one of the sub-divisions on the Microsoft Web site at `www.microsoft.com/hcl/default.asp`.

Windows 2000 Resource Kits

Microsoft Windows 2000 Resource Kits provide updated, detailed support for system administrators and webmasters. They are the official source of technical information about the Windows 2000 operating system. Because of their usefulness, they're like Christmas whenever Microsoft releases them (at least to the technical folks that run the network).

Windows 2000 Resource Kits normally include one or more of the following:

- Printed Windows 2000 Resource Kit books
- Online Windows 2000 Resource Kit books (Microsoft considers a book on a CD-ROM *online*. Go figure.)
- A CD-ROM whose contents can be installed on a computer running Windows 2000
- Documentation on other technical subject matter pertinent to Windows 2000 administrators

Windows 2000 Support Tools

If you kept your Windows 2000 installation CD-ROM set (as you should have, for restoration purposes if nothing else), here's a treat. The Windows 2000 CD-ROM set contains some of the Resource Kit material, including the *online version* of the Microsoft Windows 2000 Server Deployment Planning Guide.

Online resources

To view the online documents Open Deployment Planning Guide and Open Windows 2000 Support Tools Help, you must install the Windows 2000 Support Tools from the Windows 2000 CD. To do this, click the Start button, point to Programs, point to Windows 2000 Support Tools, and click Deployment Planning Guide.

To open the Windows 2000 Support Tools Help after it is installed, click the Start button and point to Programs. Point to Windows 2000 Support Tools, then click Tools Help.

Task Scheduler

One of the best ways to ensure that you have a measure of safety should disaster strike is to utilize the *Task Scheduler* utility in Windows 2000. You can use Task Scheduler to schedule commands, programs, or scripts to run at specific times.

This protects you two ways:

- ✔ It prevents you from forgetting to run programs or processes that keep your system from crashing.
- ✔ It notifies you when a task doesn't complete, alerting you to a potential problem that is building up on your system before the whole world stops.

To open the Task Scheduler, follow these steps:

1. **Click the Start button and point to Settings.**
2. **Click Control Panel, then double-click the Scheduled Tasks icon.**

   The Scheduled Task Directory opens.

Scheduling tasks

After you open the Task Scheduler (really its *directory*), simply click the Add Scheduled Task icon to begin the process.

Make sure that your system's date and time are accurate! Task Scheduler relies on this information to run scheduled tasks, so if you're off on the time, you may be lucky to get your task run in 2499 A.D. To double-check or change your system time, double-click your clock on the lower right of your screen, on the computer taskbar.

To schedule your new task:

1. **Open Task Scheduler.**

2. **Double-click Add Scheduled Task.**

3. **Follow the instructions in the Scheduled Task wizard, as shown in Figure 24-4.**

Viewing scheduled tasks on a remote computer

Of course, because you're taking advantage of the beauty of networking, you don't need to remain on one computer to use the Task Scheduler. To see what tasks are scheduled for a remote computer, do the following:

1. **On the desktop, double-click My Network Places.**

2. **Search for a remote computer by double-clicking Entire Network.**

   You don't have to search for it when you know the name or the location already.

3. **Double-click the remote computer where you want to view scheduled tasks to select it.**

4. **Double-click Scheduled Tasks.**

   You're viewing what is scheduled to run.

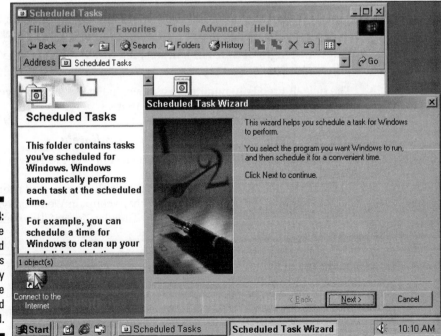

Figure 24-4:
The
Scheduled
Tasks
Directory
and the
Scheduled
Task wizard.

According to Microsoft, You can edit tasks on remote computers, but only if they are running operating systems dating from Windows 95 or later.

You can view scheduled tasks on a remote computer that is running Windows only when you have administrator rights (or belong to the administrator group) for the remote computer.

Running tasks during idle time

Idle (eye-dull): A computer that is turned on, while there is no mouse or keyboard activity.

Unlike a standard definition, computer *idleness* is a bit more flexible. After all, you're the person who can specify how many minutes a computer has to be inactive. The computer tries to find this period to run the scheduled task. You can also specify that any task should be stopped when the computer is in use by checking the box next to Stop the task when the computer ceases to be idle.

1. **Open Task Scheduler.**

   The Task Schedule window opens and the tasks currently scheduled on your computer are displayed in the right pane.

2. **Right-click the task that you want to run when the computer is idle. Select Properties from the pop-up menu.**

   The Properties window opens.

3. **Choose the Settings tab. Under the Idle Time field, select the Only Start the Task When the Computer Has Been Idle for at Least check box.**

4. **Enter the length of time (in minutes) for which the computer must be idle before the task runs.**

   The default time is 10 minutes (as shown in Figure 24-5), but you can set it to wait for up to 999 minutes of inactivity.

Running and stopping scheduled tasks immediately

It's very easy to run or stop a task that you've set up in the Task Scheduler.

You may want to do this when you can't wait for the automated sequence to kick in. For example, if you perform a weekly backup on Wednesday, but there's going to be a big system change on Tuesday, for safety's sake you should run the backup task immediately.

To run the backup, follow these steps:

1. **Open Task Scheduler.**

   The Task Scheduler window appears and the tasks are listed in the right pane.

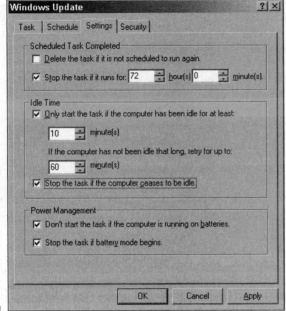

Figure 24-5:
The default idle time is 10 minutes; the Retry for idle time default is 60 minutes.

2. **Right-click the task that you want to start.**

3. **Click Run.**

When a task should have run but didn't, click View Log from the Advanced menu to examine the task log.

When the task is malfunctioning or hogging system resources at a peak use time, you can stop the task by clicking End Scheduled Task on the File menu.

When the scheduled task is started and then stopped, End Task doesn't stop all other programs that the scheduled task may have started. To restart a stopped task, right-click the task, then select the Run command from the pop-up menu again.

When you stop a scheduled task that is currently running, you may have a delay (up to three minutes) before the task shuts down.

Pausing the Task Scheduler

The Pause Task Scheduler command is useful when you don't want scheduled tasks to run when other processes demand heavy CPU usage. This would include, for example, a late-night networked game of *DOOM* that you and your friends have been planning all week.

Tasks that are scheduled to run while Task Scheduler is paused aren't run until their next scheduled time. When you pause a job that runs once a day, you've delayed the job for 24 hours. Pause a task that runs once a week? It won't run for a total of 14 days since the last time it ran!

To resume the schedules for all tasks, click Continue Task Scheduler on the Advanced menu:

1. **Open the Task Scheduler.**
2. **On the Advanced menu, click Pause Task Scheduler.**

Viewing the task log

The default log file for Task Scheduler, `SchedLog.txt`, is stored in the `\Winnt` folder. It's set to grow no larger in size than 32 kilobytes, but you should consider resetting it.

When the log file reaches its maximum size, it automatically starts recording new information at the beginning of the log file. Because there's nowhere unused for the extra data, the log writes over old log file information. When the log file grows larger than its maximum, you can lose valuable information on a deep-rooted problem.

To set the log file size, here's the drill:

1. **On the desktop, double-click My Network Places.**
2. **Search for a remote computer by double-clicking Entire Network.**

   You don't have to search for it when you know the name or the location already.

3. **Double-click the remote computer where you want to view scheduled tasks to select it.**
4. **Double-click Scheduled Tasks to open the Task Scheduler utility.**
5. **On the Advanced menu, click View Log.**

Receiving the missed task notification

It's in your interest to know whether your system actually performs the tasks it should. To make sure you're notified of this, be sure to turn on the Notification option in the Task Scheduler.

Always, always, always turn on this notification. A check mark next to Notify Me of Missed Tasks indicates that the service is on.

To switch the notification on, give it the ol' one-two:

1. **Open the Task Scheduler utility.**

2. **On the Advanced menu, click the Notify Me of Missed Tasks check box.**

   See Figure 24-6 for an example of how this looks.

Removing scheduled tasks

Removing a scheduled task only removes the task from the schedule. The program file that the task runs isn't removed from the hard disk.

Here's how to remove the task:

1. **Open Task Scheduler.**

2. **Right-click the task that you want to remove.**

3. **Click Delete.**

You can also remove a scheduled task by selecting it and then pressing the Delete key.

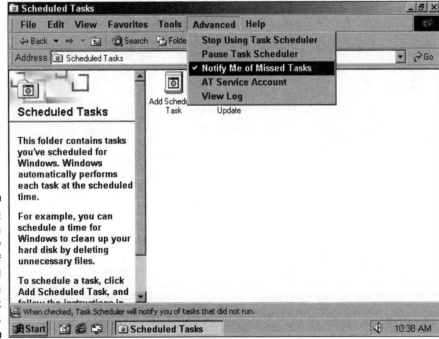

Figure 24-6:
When you select Notify Me of Missed Tasks, a check mark appears.

Part VII
The Part of Tens

In this part . . .

Veteran *For Dummies* readers know that the Part of Tens is all about giving you especially valuable information in condensed form. If you're new to the *For Dummies* fold or you happen to be an avid listomaniac like me, you're in for a treat.

Chapter 25

Ten Tips for Other Operating Systems

*W*hen you're in charge of a network of machines that are set up with 100-percent-pure Windows 2000, you can count your blessings and sleep with an untroubled mind. For the rest of us mortals, upgrading a network — or inheriting one — means more stress and toil. Everything from file-system setup to printer drivers must be checked with the electronic equivalent of a fine-toothed comb.

The reason for this is the nature of a *multi-platform network* (a network with multiple operating systems). Your network can run as many as five major operating systems for the Intel-compatible PC. And that's not counting the revival of the Macintosh OS.

While Windows 2000 has been made as backward-compatible as can be reasonably expected, transitions rarely are seamless. However, you can try to be a sport (and role model) about the whole business — think of it as extra incentive to move your user community to Windows 2000 as soon as possible.

One More Trip to the Words Well

Tired of all the new words you've seen? Normal people can't quite make out what you're saying? But this is the last time, I promise. For now.

When you have to discuss a network or machine that runs more than one operating system, don't swap words like *mixed* and *dual boot*. They're completely different concepts.

Dual-boot systems

A dual-boot system has nothing to do with the network at large. Instead, a *dual-boot* machine is a single computer that can run more than one operating system. You can configure almost any PC to be dual-boot (for example, to run either Windows 2000 or Windows 95).

With enough patience and disk space, you can make a system *triple-boot*. Or *quadruple-boot*. But that's more than a little silly, unless you collect antique operating systems.

Mixed networks

A *mixed network* describes the vast majority of systems out in the real world today. A mixed network *is any network of machines that run different operating systems.* For example, a network comprised of 20 machines running Windows 2000 and one machine running Windows NT 4.0 is technically a *mixed* system.

Your world may be complicated by more even distributions of multiple operating systems. On top of that, there may not even by a physical analogy (such as all the marketing people in the Quonset hut using iMac computers), so you may be faced with special hardware and cabling requirements all over your building.

Hinged networks

In a *hinged network*, most computers run one operating system. But the central computer, the server that most networking operations *hinge* on, is a different operating system!

An example of this is a network of a dozen Windows 2000 machines with a UNIX e-mail server. Hinged networks don't pose worse problems than mixed ones, but you should take pains to understand and document the operating system that runs on your main server.

Remember or Suffer

Most of these items mentioned aren't just to *do* but only ones that you have to *remember,* so that you don't configure a system in such a way that it complains.

Installing other multiple operating systems

Setting up a dual-boot system that contains Windows 2000 depends entirely on whether you want to use it with Windows 95 or Windows 98.

✔ Install Windows 2000 *last* on a machine where you plan to run Windows 95 and Windows 2000.

✔ The installation of Windows 95 overwrites important files needed for starting Windows 2000. It turns your dual-boot system back into a single-boot one.

✔ When setting up a dual-boot system using Windows 98 and Windows 2000, it isn't necessary to install the operating systems in a specific order. Windows 98 doesn't overwrite the files that Windows 2000 needs to start up properly.

According to Microsoft, a machine that runs both Windows 2000 and Windows 95 must format the primary partition with the FAT file system. This disables most Windows 2000 file security features.

File-system compatibility with multiple operating systems

NTFS normally is the recommended file system because it supports important features, including Active Directory and domain-based security. However, the version of NTFS in Windows 2000 Server has new features in addition to those in Windows NT Server — which means you have a potential compatibility problem.

Files that use any new Windows 2000 security features only work properly when the computer is started with Windows 2000 Server. To run a computer with both Windows NT and Windows 2000, you must run Windows NT Version 4.0 with Service Pack 4 or later.

Even the latest Windows NT Service Pack doesn't provide access to files using the new features in NTFS.

If you set up a computer with Windows NT 3.51 on a FAT partition and Windows 2000 Server on an NTFS partition, you're bound to run into trouble. When that computer starts with Windows NT 3.51, your entire NTFS partition isn't *visible*, let alone accessible.

Platform compatibility

Windows 2000 supports Dfs shared folders on the following platforms:

Operating System	Dfs Client	Dfs Root
MS-DOS	No	No
Windows 3.1	No	No
Windows for Workgroups	No	No
Windows 95	Yes (may require client for Dfs 4.*x*)	No
Windows 98	Yes (may require client for Dfs 4.*x*)	No
Windows NT 4.0	Yes (with Service Pack 3 or later)	Yes (with Service Pack 3 or later)

Compressing with Windows 95, 98, and Windows 2000

On dual-boot machines that run Windows 2000 with Windows 95 or Windows 98

✔ Compressed DriveSpace or DoubleSpace volumes aren't available when your machine is running.

✔ It's not necessary to uncompress DriveSpace or DoubleSpace volumes on Windows 2000 that you plan to access only with Windows 95 or Windows 98.

Group policy on Windows versions

Remember these rules for group policy on the different *networked* Microsoft operating systems.

Windows 2000

Computers running Windows 2000 Server can be member servers of either Active Directory or domain controllers. Group Policy is fully supported. On machines running Windows 2000 Professional, client computers also are supported.

Windows NT 4.0

Windows NT 4.0 doesn't use the Active Directory utility (regardless of which service packs you've installed), so it doesn't use Group Policy objects. Group Policy doesn't apply to these machines.

Windows NT 3.51, Windows for Workgroups, MS-DOS

In Windows NT 3.51, Windows for Workgroups, and MS-DOS, Group Policy doesn't apply.

Integrating Novell NetWare

Windows 2000 Server provides services that enable the computers that run Windows 2000 to work with Novell NetWare networks and servers. Some of these services are included in Windows 2000 Server. Others are on Windows 2000 Professional. Still more are available as separate products, which you can find on the Microsoft site. For one example, visit the site's information on the following product:

NWLink IPX/SPX/NetBIOS Compatible Transport Protocol (NWLink)

This product is included with both Windows 2000 Server and Windows 2000 Professional. NWLink supports connectivity between computers running Windows 2000 and computers running NetWare and compatible systems.

Using the NetWare Gateway Service

The NetWare Gateway service enables a computer running Windows 2000 Server to connect to computers running NetWare 3.*x* or 4.*x* server software. This product is included with Windows 2000 Server. Documentation on this product can be found in NetWare 4.*x* installation guides and on the Microsoft Web site.

You can use Gateway Service for NetWare to set up easier, faster connections to machines running NetWare. Creating connections enables computers running only Microsoft client software to access NetWare resources more easily.

Choosing the OS for a dual-boot system

A dual-boot machine allows you to choose between operating systems when you start the computer. During restarts, a display appears for a specified number of seconds, allowing you to select between the two operating systems. The default setting normally is either 5 or 20 seconds, depending on your setup.

You must place the Windows 2000 operating system in a *separate partition* on the computer when you plan to run it with another operating system. This ensures that Windows 2000 doesn't overwrite crucial files used by the other operating system.

Connecting printers to clients running other Windows versions

When connecting a printer to a Windows NT 4.0, 95, or 98 client, you must install the print drivers for these clients on your Windows 2000 print server. The print driver downloads to the client via the network connection without the need for the original compact disc or floppy-disk set.

1. **Open Printers by clicking the Start button, pointing to Settings, then clicking Printers.**

2. **Double-click the Add Printer icon, then click Next.**

3. **Select Network printer, then click Next.**

4. **Click the printer in Shared Printers.**

5. **Follow the instructions in the Printer Wizard to finish connecting to the printer.**

   After you complete these procedures, if you haven't already installed the printer driver, the driver downloads automatically. The icon for that printer appears in your Printers folder.

When the download can't take place, it's probably because you're using an off-brand, extremely old, or specialized printer (such as an engineering plotter). If that's the case, either install the driver manually on the server or download the driver from the printer company's Web site.

Chapter 26

Ten Rest Stops on the Information Highway

- -

In This Chapter

▶ Using search engines

▶ Researching the Microsoft sites

▶ Employing ISPs

▶ Trolling newsgroups

- -

*B*elieve it or not, the Internet is actually useful for more than ordering a Puff Daddy compact disc or downloading pictures of movie stars. (Not that there's anything wrong with these activities, of course.) This chapter doesn't cover how to set up your Internet connection, how to search for sites, or how to use the Bookmark function on your Web browser.

Instead, this chapter shows just what a valuable resource the Internet is for finding the information you need to run your network and solve vexing questions on administrative needs. You need know what kind of information you can tap into and why you need it.

Oh, Dot-Com All Ye Faithful . . .

Heard this before? *Never before in history have so many people known so little about so much.*

This statement is tailor-made for our Internet-ready world of the 1990s and beyond into the third millennium. With the World Wide Web, the problem isn't that you can find information. Instead, you find too much information on barely-related topics.

More than ever, it's a matter of *asking the right question.* Otherwise, you may end up spending days wading through the sea of information that comes pouring through your monitor screen. The techniques, sites, and groups recommended in this chapter give you some ideas about where and how to ask the right question.

The Internet isn't known for the stability of its addresses. Take the links with a large tablespoon of salt. What's here today may be gone tomorrow.

Gentlemen, start your search engines

Search engines are Web sites that connect you to an online database of stored information markers. You input the terms you want to search for in the search field, click the Search button (both clearly displayed), and get a truckload of Web-site addresses (URLs), documents, or links that can at least provide you with a decent lead.

URL stands for *Uniform Resource Locator,* which is the bit of information used by your system to locate and display a given Web site. Although *URL* (pronounced *earl*) is fun to say, I still prefer the more functional designation, *Web address.*

Depending on which search engine you use, you get different results. Unlike what many believe, search engines differ dramatically in the coverage and returns that they display back to you. This is because of their special search techniques. Some search engines count the number of times your search term comes up in a given document, some focus on terms that start sentences, and others perform a *Boolean* (logical) search. (It's handy when you're looking for Booleans. They taste like chicken.)

Some of the more popular search engines are www.altavista.com, www.looksmart.com, and www.yahoo.com.

In all of these cases, just make sure that you search for the most *specific* terms that you can. For example, you may have a question about setting up Windows 2000 printer drivers. Search for that: *Windows 2000 printer driver installation.* Simply searching for *printer drivers* or (heaven help you) *Windows 2000* will deliver you an avalanche of stuff.

On the other hand, the almost-inconceivable can happen: You get no *hits* from your query. If so, start peeling back the layers of specificity until you start getting some leads. For example, you may search for *Windows 2000 printer driver installation Hewlett-Packard Ramjet Inkmeister Model 667.*

No response?

Start by reducing the layers of detail to make a match more likely. Cut out the model number. When that doesn't work, get rid of the model's name. When that isn't helping matters, get rid of the brand name. Do whatever it takes to start building your lead.

The search engine www.excite.com is useful in finding to Web documents for your use. However, Excite.com also has a unique tool that helps you where other engines fail: a *News post* search.

The News search button has migrated a couple times in each revision of the engine. Normally, you can find it towards the bottom of the site, labeled News. Click here to go to the news search engine. From there, use this engine just as you would the regular one.

When you would prefer to search through the newsgroups yourself or you just want to better understand what they are, continue reading in this chapter. You learn which ones you ought to visit.

A second site is recommended by other *For Dummies* authors, such as Ed Tittel, Mary Madden, and Earl Follis. For what they term the Ultimate Web Search Tool, check out www.metacrawler.com.

The Microsoft Web server

As you may guess, the all-time best spot to answer basic questions on Windows 2000 is the Microsoft site itself, www.microsoft.com. Just like a search engine Web site, your main task isn't to find what you're looking for, but to separate the information you actually need from the stuff you don't need.

This problem is especially difficult because Windows 2000 is the *flagship* piece of software around which the Microsoft world will be built for the next line of software models. Therefore, Microsoft has oodles and oodles (I hope you enjoy my technical terms) of documents and resources to sift.

To help you make your way through this cornucopia, the Microsoft site comes equipped with its own search engine. Your best bet is to be as specific as possible. Unless your question is extremely obscure, a Microsoft staff member has probably written a product paper on it.

This site is the best for answering *mainstream questions*. These are questions about general networking or setup questions. When you must find out how to network your Windows 2000 with your Nintendo Game Boy, you're best off visiting a newsgroup, Web search engine, or the local house of worship.

Licensing information

When you're in growth mode, then you're going to bump into the limits of either the number of CAL licenses or the license mode that you've chosen.

To further determine what you need for the full suite of Microsoft BackOffice products, visit www.microsoft.com/backoffice.

Like the main Microsoft site, you're best off using the built-in search engine on this site to locate the information you want. Among the most valuable information here is the latest update about how Microsoft BackOffice products work in Per Server versus Per Seat mode (which affects how you structure your license server system).

FTP resources — enormous, anonymous, and free

Many Microsoft files are large enough to require a special server dedicated to downloading onto user's computers. These files normally fall into two groups:

- ✔ Small applications (applets) to enhance your system or correct small software bugs
- ✔ Fully formatted documents with graphics and hypertext links to direct you back to the main Microsoft sites

To get to this resource, open your Web browser and surf your way across the Net to ftp.microsoft.com.

This is a *big* site. There is tons of interesting material. Try to stick to what you came to find.

To check what is inside the gift you're downloading, always click the README.TXT file. This is a text file, usually made in WordPad, that gives you a synopsis of the underlying files and the subjects they cover. Don't surf the ftp site without it!

Some excellent subdirectories to check out underneath the vast caverns of the Microsoft FTP server include

/download	An excellent directory of fun stuff to take home on your hard drive
/peropsys/GEN_INFO/KB	The Microsoft Knowledge Base

/Win_News	News articles, how-to information, and the archives of Windows mailing lists

The mail's in the check(box)

Because Windows 2000 is heir to the Windows NT 4.0 legacy, you should also consider subscribing to the NT mailing list run by Beverly Hills Software. Over two-thirds of Windows 2000 Server installations are estimated to be running Windows NT through 2000 and on, you may find it's a good resource to administer a mixed network of machines.

To get on the mailing list, point your Web browser to `www.bhs.com/ microsoft.winntnews` or send an e-mail to `Winntnews-admin@microsoft. bhs.com` with *subscribe winntnews* in the first line of your message.

To CompuServe and protect

CompuServe and America Online are full-service Internet service providers. Being the full-service and full-fare organizations, they offer a lot more than simple Internet access accounts and a Web browser interface to get started. They run *forums* where users can meet and discuss questions and issues on various interests.

CompuServe is making the most headway. Not only are their forums known for slightly better technical content (as opposed to the *chat rooms* that focus on the latest doings of Britney Spears and Arnold Schwarzenegger), they're pushing to be included on all new computers.

USENET newsgroups

Newsgroups are postings on a specific subject from people located around the world who share an interest in that subject. At last count, there were more than 25,000 groups on various topics, trading the latest information on their professions, studies, and hobbies.

Windows 2000 groups are in their infancy. The newsgroups to watch are `comp.os.mis.windows.nt`, `microsoft.public.windowsnt`, and `msnews.microsoft.com`.

You may need to sign up with the Microsoft Internet service to access `msnews.microsoft.com`.

Dead trees as an information system

Impossibly *retro* people want to hold your information in the palm of your hand. (Bless you. Writers like to go on making a living, too.)

Several Web sites cater to your love of buying books with the information you need. Two catchall sites are www.amazon.com and www.barnesandnoble.com.

The pricing, service, and selection are similar. Amazon.com has a better search engine and has more information about the book.

Search Amazon.com under my name, Michael Bellomo. You see under the works that I've published a raft of information (from user reviews to Interviews with the Author — and here he blushes modestly). These connections allow you to research the available material for your topic quickly and efficiently. Just watch that postage meter when you're calculating your savings.

Chapter 27

Almost Ten Statements Windows Administrators Shouldn't Make

● ●

In This Chapter

▶ Staying in diagnostic mode

▶ Knowing what you own

▶ Documenting your system

▶ Maintaining your dignity

● ●

This sounds like a lighthearted chapter, and it is. But the lessons here are as serious as the rest of the book. Heed, and *never* say…

I Don't Have a Clue

Ambiguity is the stock-in-trade of a Windows administrator, simply for survival. However, you never should simply give up on a problem.

Always use your sense of logic.

✔ **Check your facts.**

Never operate under an assumption. When someone tells you that Server X is down because Server Y is *acting funny,* never assume that Server Y is even connected to the problem because of proximity to the event.

When event A and disaster B happen at the same time, it doesn't mean that A *caused* B.

✔ **Determine the symptoms and separate them from the problem.**

Symptoms are direct, repeated events that signal you to a problem. Something operating *funny* isn't a symptom.

Symptoms also are not problems. *Slow network response time every peak period* isn't a problem. It's a symptom of a problem.

✔ List what you've tried.

Don't just throw ideas at a problem and hope the solution becomes apparent. Even a failed attempt can alter the situation, complicating your solution.

✔ List the results — and look for a pattern.

Did one try lead to a *partial* resolution? If so, you may have passed a signpost marking the direction of the root cause. Don't pass up these vital clues.

✔ What is new or different on the system?

No matter how small, look for a new software installation or a server configuration.

You may be the first victim of a new bug! (After all, *somebody* has to be first.)

✔ Check the history.

If you inherited this system, check your predecessor's notes. It's now your turn at bat. See whether you can't get an edge.

✔ Suspect everyone.

Never take the word of anyone who says, "I didn't do anything important." The term *important* is a value judgment, not an objective standard. To most folks, if they didn't crash the system, they didn't do anything wrong. This isn't a court of law — presume guilt (technically speaking) until innocence is proved.

This standard applies to you, too!

✔ Accept the improbable.

A wise administrator gave me a somewhat mangled version of what the great Sherlock Holmes said:

"After you have discarded the impossible, then the improbable — no matter *how* improbable — is the answer."

I Don't Know How That's Connected

Just as printing isn't *beneath* the job of an administrator, neither are the wiring, cabling, and even power-cutoff switches in your computer lab. Always make it a personal point to know where every switch and plug is located on your system.

I Don't Know How That Affects the Network

Be aware of your network architecture. When you inherit a network from administrators who didn't keep much documentation, take action. Demand network diagrams from them before they leave. It's amazing what decisions people make because they're short three feet of Ethernet cabling.

Let the Users Sort It Out

This is your benevolent dictatorship, known as a user community. Letting it descend into a town meeting or, worse, *anarchy* isn't a smart idea. Always take decisive steps to prevent or resolve the following situations for your loyal (?) users:

- ✔ User Account naming schemes
- ✔ CPU hogs
- ✔ Disk hogs
- ✔ Printer hogs

If you're a literary sort, avoid reading treatises on democratic rule by Rousseau. Stick to Machiavelli's *The Prince* to help you learn how to administer your user community. Books by Friedrich Nietzsche are even better, but may get you into trouble with upper management.

It's Just an Error Message

Let me ask you: If you were driving through the desert and saw a warning light come up, would you stop the car, pull out a set of pliers, and rip the light out of your dashboard so you can go on driving in peace? I don't think so. But that's how many administrators operate!

The error-message list for Windows 2000 is still being compiled as of this writing, but it will be available from Microsoft later in 2000. Get this list when you can.

Volume 4 of the Windows NT Resource Kit devotes more than 700 pages to list the error messages you may see. Unless Microsoft needs to clear forests to expand its facilities, this is for a good reason. Pay attention when you get a warning message.

I Keep It in My Head

I don't care whether you were a star student of the Mega-Memory course. Under conditions of stress, people can't recall every twist of a sophisticated network.

Document everything.

In ink.

And make it legible!

Cut the Budget — No One Will Notice

Running a computer lab isn't a fixed expense. If your accounting department doesn't understand that, you're best off finding another position.

Even assuming zero growth in your lab, you're like a car that burns gas, not a house that increases in value over time. A car moving at five miles per hour still burns fuel — just burning it more slowly.

Even when you don't plan to buy new machines on a regular basis, you should allocate money for more RAM cards. Software always increases in power, and its demands for CPU cycles is always on an upward curve. You can avoid the expense of major upgrades by keeping your machines on the power curve with more RAM.

One of the most insidious processes that can take place is when you have a growing network and you don't increase the number of licenses available. The problem quickly reaches a crisis point after users realize that there isn't a reasonable chance to get back on a server at the peak times. To stop this, they simply stay on all the time and not log out, effectively removing a whole license slot from your pool.

Avoid situations like these at all costs. See to it that your IT budget suffers no reversals without a fight.

Come tax time, flag the accounting department about donating your older machines to local schools and charities. Not only do you help your community, you're able to wheedle a few extra dollars from this tax-break *windfall* you've been planning on all year.

Upgrade the System — Everyone Will Notice

One of the biggest myths in the computer world is that people are impressed with you when you accelerate the network. Well, that just doesn't happen.

As a rule, you're never going to be given enough money to double or triple the network speed. Most of the time, you eliminate a bottleneck, increasing the data transmission rate by five or maybe ten percent. Studies show that users may notice a ten-percent increase, but not less.

When you start making noise about a five-percent increase, everyone will simply pay more attention to network speed — and complain if it drops. When you announce a ten-percent speed increase, it is eaten up in a few days as people take advantage of the speed, making people complain that your *mucking around* has slowed the system!

Upgrade the network . But don't expect your own float in the Rose Bowl parade after you do it.

What a Cool Crash!

This makes you sound irresponsible. Fun, but irresponsible.

Part VIII
Appendixes

The 5th Wave   By Rich Tennant

"I'm sure there will be a good job market when I graduate. I created a virus that will go off that year."

In this part . . .

Check these pages for handy resources to simplify your life. There's a swell glossary, a nifty summary of licensing requirements, and system-saving instructions for making recovery disks.

Appendix A

Windows 2000 Glossary

Access Control List
Database of permissions assigned to resources, users allowed access, and access attempts.

Active Directory
Windows 2000 utility to locate, track, and make changes to objects on a Windows network.

Active Directory Service Interface (ADSI)
Utility to allow applications to communicate with the Active Directory.

Active Server Pages
Scripts executed on the Windows 2000 server before they're passed on to the user as HTML (Hypertext Markup Language) pages.

BOOTP Bootstrap Protocol (Bootstrap Protocol)
Protocol that allocates IP information to clients upon completion of the machine startup.

bridge
A piece of hardware that links two or more networks and is able to perform some of the more intelligent functions of routing communications to the right locations.

Central Processing Unit (CPU)
The part of the computer that performs the calculations and computations that are the *raison d'être* of a computer. (If it isn't the monitor, keyboard, or the mouse, it's probably the Central Processing Unit.)

clustering
Combining multiple systems to act as a single unit, usually for redundancy.

CPU throttling
Kernel-level capability that limits the number of CPU cycles used by a process, keeping this one process from hogging the system.

Distributed file system (Dfs)

A file-system mode that allows Windows 2000 Server file shares to be stored over multiple servers (or a server cluster) for backup and security.

DHCP (Dynamic Host Configuration Protocol)

A component protocol of the TCP/IP family. Used by Windows 2000 to assign clients an IP address and other IP information to communicate with the Internet.

disk quota

An amount of disk space set aside for a specific user account's storage. Under this system, a user can't store more data than is allowed under the quota.

DNS (Domain Name System)

A directory or database object that converts domain names into IP addresses that your networked computers can understand.

EFS (Encrypting File System)

A security feature that allows data encryption on the NTFS disk. This prevents bypassing the operating system to retrieve the information.

FAT (File Allocation Table)

A file system that provides backward compatibility with Windows 95, Windows NT, and even MS-DOS.

FAT32 (File Allocation Table-32)

A file system that provides backward compatibility with Windows 95, Windows NT, and MS-DOS. FAT32 manages larger hard drives than does the standard FAT file system.

FTP (File Transfer Protocol)

Process for transferring large amounts of data between machines or networks.

hub

Hardware that connects network subnets. Hubs aren't as powerful as bridges and routers.

IIS (Internet Information Services)

Microsoft's newest Web server.

IntelliMirror

Products that store data on both client and server.

IPX/SPX (Internetwork Packet Exchange/Sequences Packet Exchange)

Protocols that provide TCP/IP-like functionality in NetWare.

Internet Protocol Address

The quartet of numbers to state a machine's organization and location. An example of such an address is 166.100.20.4.

Kerberos

Security system that is supported by Windows 2000.

kernel

Software that has absolute priority to access hardware for any task.

LAN (Local Area Network)

The standard network setup for small companies.

Microsoft Management Console (MMC)

A utility allowing you to configure the suite of administrative tools for Windows 2000.

NetBIOS

The standard Windows network communications protocol.

NTFS (Network File System)

The preferred file system for Windows NT and Windows 2000.

Plug and Play

Automatic detection and configuration hardware plugged into a system.

pop-up menu

A menu of options that pops up on-screen (normally when an object is right-clicked).

pull-down menu

A menu of options that pulls down, like a window shade, on-screen.

RAID (Redundant Array of Inexpensive Disks)

A system that allows multiple disks to back up data automatically.

Remote Storage

Windows 2000 process that performs hierarchical storage tasks.

repeater

Booster that amplifies network-packet communication on a long line. Rare, but useful in a large Ethernet network.

router

An intelligent bridge for sending transmissions from one network to another.

subtree

A level of the Active Directory domain located below the main directory tree.

TCP/IP (Transmission Control Protocol/Internet Protocol)

The standard Internet communications protocol suite.

Token Ring

An outdated network system that prevents network collisions by providing an electronic token for machines to pass around as they turns communicating.

user account

A set of data that includes a home directory, a user name, and a password that allows a user to connect to a network system.

WAN (Wide-Area Network)

A larger network area that usually includes public communication lines, such as telephone lines or the Internet.

Windows Internet Name Service (WINS)

A component of Windows 2000 Server that provides NetBIOS name resolution and allows client systems to locate network servers for communication.

Windows Terminal Services

Service that allows multiple graphical sessions to be created and utilized on a single Windows 2000 server.

Appendix B

Windows 2000 Licensing

Just as a valid driver's license allows you to legally drive a car, an access permit allows you the legal right to connect to a server machine running Windows 2000 Server software. This access permit is called a *client access license,* or *CAL* for short. Whereas you need a CAL for most of what you do on a Windows 2000 network, there are a few types of services that you can use without licenses. These include

- Telnet (a low-level connection between machines)
- FTP (File Transfer Protocol) to move files between networked machines
- A Web application that provides Hypertext Transfer Protocol sharing of Hypertext Markup Language (HTML) files
- Anonymous access to a Windows 2000 Server with Microsoft Internet Information Services
- Authenticated access to a Windows 2000 Server with Microsoft Internet Information Services

Policy Coverage

Microsoft gives you a choice between two license modes to run your network. These modes are called *Per Server* and *Per Seat.* To use Windows 2000, you must choose one method and abide by its rules as you grow and expand your network accordingly. This choice of modes is called the *Microsoft BackOffice licensing model.*

Microsoft BackOffice is the entire suite of Microsoft products built for maximum networking ability with Windows NT 4.0 and Windows 2000.

Each license mode provides you with sets of functions for specific network environments. This allows you to purchase the number of licenses you need for running your organization.

A license for fishing is no good for deer hunting

Keep in mind that client licenses, though they are the only kind complex enough to demand an appendix to the book, aren't the only licenses you need with Windows 2000. You still need the license required to install and run Windows 2000 Server.

Depending on your network, you may well need another license to install and run the Windows 2000 operating system on each client computer. However, these licenses don't need more coverage than simply to remind you that they exist. Instructions on how to use your license codes for installation always come with your original installation disk set and your Windows 2000 CD-ROM.

✔ You can select one mode for your entire organization or different modes for different sites in your organization.

✔ You can't run both modes at the same time on the same network or sub-network in your company.

Connections made by administrators are counted as part of the total number of connections. Even when the number of legally licensed connections has reached the upper limit of your license purchase, administrators can still connect. This is a necessary safeguard to allow administrators to continue to manage the server in an emergency — even when the server is under heavy use or the problem centers on refusing to free up network connections.

Per Seat licensing

To run in Per Seat licensing mode, you must purchase a client access license (CAL) for *each* computer that accesses a Windows 2000 server on the network. After a license is allocated for a client computer, the computer can access that product on any server. A user can log in to the server without more client access licenses.

When both modes are available for a product, Per Seat mode is usually the best choice when you plan to run on *more than one Windows 2000 server* on your network. The Per Server mode is cheaper for *single-server networks* and when the server is reserved *for special uses,* such as an office database or for a specific company department.

The Per Seat licensing mode tends to be more common than the Per Server licensing mode.

When you run in Per Seat mode, you must purchase a client access license (CAL) for each client computer. It doesn't matter whether it uses a Microsoft client operating system or a different client operating system supported by the Windows 2000 Server operating system. A valid Per Seat CAL guarantees access to a server configured in the Per Seat mode but doesn't promise access to a server running in the Per Server mode.

Each connection uses up one of the slots in the pool of licenses available from the Windows 2000 Server running in Per Server mode. The License Logging service assigns and tracks client access licenses by user account name. This fulfills the legal requirement that one client access license covers each client computer only when every user has exactly *one* computer.

Because of this limit, the client can connect only when it doesn't cause the total number of connections to exceed the limit of the server. After the limit is reached on a server, it doesn't allow more connections. Clients trying to connect to the server display an error message.

A client access license isn't included when you acquire Windows 98, Windows 2000 Professional, or any other Windows operating system. You have to purchase the license(s) separately, in addition to the operating system software.

Per Server licensing

Under Per Server licensing, client access licenses for a server product are allocated to a *server* running the product, not the *clients*. It's the number of CALs allocated to the server that determines the number of user network connections that can be made into the server at the same time.

The number of *connections to the server* is what determines the number of CALs being used at a given time — not connections to specific share points or printers. When you log on with the same account to two different workstations and connect to the same server from both, you've just taken up two license spots.

As with the Per Seat license mode, a client can connect only when it doesn't cause the total number of connections to exceed the limit of the server. After the limit is reached on a server, it doesn't allow more connections. Clients trying to connect in this mode to the Windows 2000 server receive an error message.

Licensing Different Server Products

Depending on which Microsoft BackOffice server product is on your system, you must deal with different licensing requirements for client connections. Most Microsoft BackOffice server products require client access licenses (CALs).

About half the Microsoft BackOffice products that use CALs allow you to run in either Per Server or Per Seat mode. On the other hand, many products require the Per Seat licensing scheme.

You don't have to sacrifice your mode choices because of the products you choose to install. You won't have to use the same licensing mode for all Microsoft BackOffice products on your network. It simply depends on how you use a given product on your network (and on the modes allowed for the specific product). Usually the software can be licensed in either Per Server or Per Seat.

To find the most current licensing information for a server product, check the product's documentation. Microsoft also posts current licensing information for all Microsoft BackOffice products on its Web site.

For the latest-breaking information and news on licensing BackOffice products, see `www.microsoft.com/backoffice`.

Administering and Tracking Your Licenses

As a busy administrator, you're upgrading your network, adding to your domains, or fighting fires. It's highly unlikely that you have the time to manually track licenses within domains. Administering licenses in this manner is like chopping wood with a silver spoon — ineffective, time-consuming, and expensive.

Luckily for you, Windows 2000 provides two utilities that automate license tracking. These utilities allow you to view license data and manage licensing for Microsoft products.

Licensing in the Control Panel

You can use the Licensing utility from the Control Panel to manage your network's licensing requirements for Microsoft BackOffice software. Use the utility locally on the computer you are managing to add client access licenses, remove these licenses, or change the licensing scheme from Per Server mode to Per Seat mode.

1. **Click the Start button.**

2. **Click Control Panel.**

3. **Double-click the Licensing icon in the Control Panel window.**

   The Choose Licensing Mode window appears. Despite the name of the window, you can actually do a lot more configuration that just changing modes. (Modes are changed by clicking the Per Server or Per Seat buttons in the panel.) See Figure B-1 for an example.

   By clicking the arrow to the right of the Product window, you can select a different server product from a drop-down list and configure the license modes appropriately.

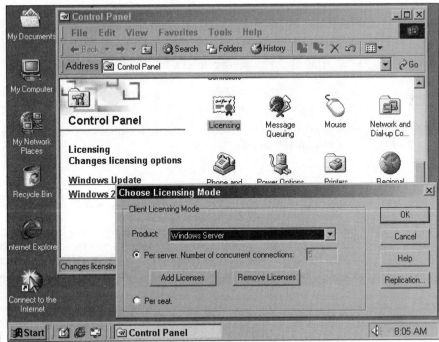

Figure B-1:
The Choose
Licensing
Mode
window.

Licensing in the Administrative Tools

You can also use the Licensing utility found in the Administrative Tools for license administration. Only the utility found here is designed to help you manage licensing for an enterprise environment. With this utility, you can administer site licenses in a central license database on the site license server.

Client Access Licenses

A client access license (CAL) allows a client computer to access a computer running a Microsoft BackOffice server product.

Client access licenses are distinct pieces of software, separate from the operating system software you use to connect to the Windows 2000 server itself.

Licensing is based on the number of client connections to computers running Windows 2000 Server. Every client computer must have a client access license to access the server for the following network services:

- ✔ Sharing files
- ✔ Disk storage
- ✔ Sharing and managing printers
- ✔ Macintosh connectivity
- ✔ NetWare connectivity
- ✔ Accessing the server from a remote location through a communication link

Adding Per Seat client access licenses

As users access the product anywhere in the site, they begin filling the allocated number of license slots. After the pool of available licenses is depleted, no further users may connect. When you are having chronic difficulty with server license overload, you should add more licenses in the following manner:

1. **Click the Start button.**

2. **Point to Settings and then click Control Panel.**

3. **Double-click Administrative Tools.**

4. **Double-click Licensing.**

5. **On the License menu, click New License.**

6. **Click the server product you want to manage.**

7. **In the Quantity field, type the number of licenses purchased.**

8. **In the Comment field, type a note to identify the purchase.**

Deleting Per Seat client access licenses

1. **Click the Start button.**

2. **Point to Settings. and then click Control Panel.**

3. **Double-click Administrative Tools.**

4. **Double-click Licensing.**

5. **On the Products Views tab, click the product from which you want to delete licenses.**

6. **On the License menu, click Delete.**

7. **In the field Number of Licenses to remove, type the number of licenses to be deleted.**

8. **Click the Remove button.**

9. **To close the dialog box, click the Close button.**

Server Licenses

Server licenses allow you to run a server product on a specific Windows 2000 Server machine. A server license is required for each server product. Unlike a CAL, server licenses don't give you the right to connect to the server from a client computer.

By default, a server license is included with your software package when you purchase a Microsoft BackOffice server product.

Adding Per Server client access licenses

1. **Click the Start button.**

2. **Point to Settings, then click Control Panel.**

3. Double-click Administrative Tools.

4. Double-click Licensing.

5. On the Server Browser tab, expand Enterprise. Enter the domain name, then the name of the server you want to configure.

6. Right-click the product name, and then click Properties from the pop-up menu.

7. Click Add Licenses.

8. In the Quantity field, type the number of licenses to add.

9. After you read the information in Per Server Licensing, select the check box to agree to be bound by the license agreements for this product, and then click OK.

If you don't agree to the license agreements, your new setting isn't accepted.

Deleting Per Server client access licenses

1. Click the Start button.

2. Point to Settings, and then click Control Panel.

3. Double-click the Administrative Tools icon.

4. Double-click Licensing.

5. On the Server Browser tab, expand Enterprise. Enter the domain name, then the name of the server you want to configure.

6. Right-click the product name, then select Properties from the resulting pop-up menu.

7. Click the Remove Licenses button.

8. In the Number of licenses to remove field, type the number of licenses you want to remove.

9. Click the Remove button, then click Yes to confirm your license change.

10. Click Cancel to close the dialog box.

11. Click OK to save the changes.

Appendix C

Windows 2000 Boot Disks

• •

*O*ne recurring nightmare that has young, innocent Windows 2000 administrators tossing and turning in their sleep is: What happens when a key machine goes on unpaid administrative leave (that is, crashes) and refuses to boot up again from the CD-ROM? The answer is a *boot disk*.

If for any reason your CD-ROM or CD-ROM drive isn't recognized by the damaged installation, you can boot your Windows 2000 machine from a set of boot disks so that you can get Windows 2000 back into running shape (or salvage as much data as you can before the machine sinks into cybernetic oblivion).

The typical Windows 2000 installation kit that Microsoft sends you should have a couple of sets of boot disks. But you can't count on finding these disks. So make some new copies now, before the new Senior VP of Information Systems finds that everything crashed that morning.

Captain, my stress sensors detect management heading this way!

Don't forget, before you try to start a computer from a CD-ROM or a floppy disk set, you should always first try to start in the computer's *safe mode*.

1. **Beg, borrow, or steal four 3.5-inch, 1.44MB floppy disks. (Reformat old AOL disks if you must.)**

2. **Format the disks (when needed) on a Windows 2000 machine.**

3. **Select Quick Format if the disk is already formatted but has inconsequential data on it.**

4. **Insert one of the disks into the floppy disk drive on a computer running any version of Windows or MS-DOS.**

5. **Insert the Windows 2000 compact disc (CD) into the CD-ROM drive.**

6. **Click the Start button and then click Run.**

7. **In the Open box, type this:**

   <CD-ROM drive>:\bootdisk\makeboot a:

   On most systems, the CD-ROM drive is d:. a: is your floppy drive, where the boot-up information is copied.

8. **Click OK.**

9. **Follow the screen prompt that follows, as shown in Figure C-1.**

After you successfully start your machine from your boot disks, you can then use the Emergency Repair Disk to try to get your machine up and running again.

If you created a boot disk from the Windows 2000 Professional CD-ROM, you can't use it to boot up Windows 2000 Server. No amount of hacking, pleading, or prayer allows you to boot up a Windows 2000 Professional machine with a boot disk made from a 2000 Server CD-ROM.

Don't just label your boot disk something generic like Boot Disk. Make sure to identify whether it's a boot disk for 2000 Professional or Server!

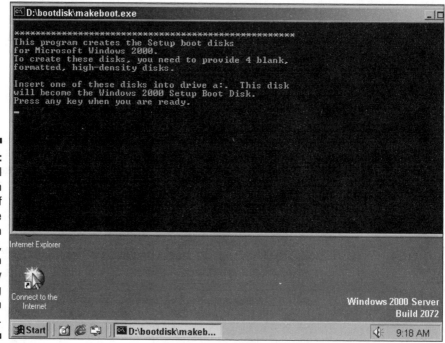

Figure C-1:
The initial screen prompt. If you have a floppy in the drive, you're on your way to creating a system boot disk.

Appendix D

Windows 2000 Emergency Repair Disks

. . . .

*Y*ou can use your Windows 2000 Emergency Repair Disk (ERD) to fix problems that prevent you from starting your computer. Of course, you won't get very far unless you're able to boot your machine. You may need to use the system boot disk to get to the stage where you can even pop the Repair Disk into the drive and have it read. (For more information on the system boot disk, see Appendix C.)

Always be sure that you have an ERD that hasn't been used as a coaster for a hot coffee mug. While you can't repair everything that can go wrong with your machine from this disk, it covers a lot of extensive repair work:

- ✔ Basic system files repair
- ✔ Patching the partition boot sector
- ✔ Mending the startup environment

The Emergency Repair Disk doesn't back up data or programs. It isn't a replacement for regularly backing up your system.

The repair process on the ERD doesn't help you with Registry issues. To replace lost Registry files, use the Recovery Console, which is covered in Chapter 11.

The emergency repair process has the potential to wreak havoc on your system. It's a power that only you, the administrator, should be able to call upon.

Creating the Disk

To create your Emergency Repair Disk, open your black bag and follow these steps:

1. **Beg, borrow, or steal a 3.5-inch, 1.44MB floppy disk.**

2. **Format the disk (if needed) on a Windows 2000 machine.**

3. **Select Quick Format if the disk is already formatted but has useless data on it, such as the latest Beanie Babies catalog or your brother's recipe for Chili with Crushed Oreos.**

4. **Insert the formatted disk into the floppy disk drive on a computer running Windows 2000.**

5. **Click the Start button, point to Programs, point to Accessories, point to System Tools, and then click Backup.**

6. **On the Welcome tab, click Emergency Repair Disk.**

7. **Follow the instructions on the Emergency Repair Diskette Screen, as shown in Figure D-1.**

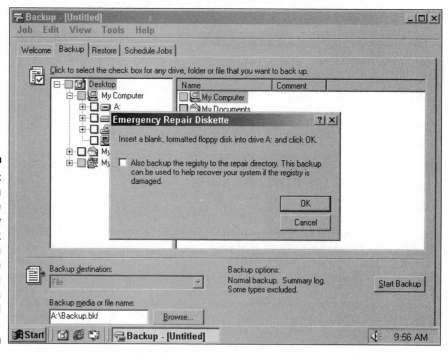

Figure D-1:
After you click the Emergency Repair Disk button on the Backup tab, you're taken to this instructional window.

Using Your ERD

One afternoon it happens: A machine goes down, hard. What do you do next? Well, for openers, these steps:

1. **Insert the Windows 2000 Setup CD and bring up the system.**

2. **If the CD-ROM drive is dead or the CD-ROM is missing, insert the first of the four floppy disks you created as system boot disks in the appropriate drive.**

3. **Restart the computer. If you're using the four floppies formatted as system boot disks, respond to the prompts that request each floppy disk in turn.**

4. **When the Setup process starts, select the Repair/Recover option by pressing the letter R on your keyboard.**

5. **When prompted, insert your Windows 2000 Setup CD-ROM in the machine's CD-ROM drive. If there is a problem with the CD-ROM drive, if it's not a hardware issue, it should be online now.**

6. **When prompted, select the emergency repair process by pressing the R key again.**

7. **When prompted, choose between the following:**

   - **(M) Manual Repair:** With this option, you can choose to repair your system files, partition-boot-sector problems, or startup-environment problems.

   Unless you're experienced with the Windows 2000 system, you should avoid this option, as you can miss an area that needs to be repaired. Unless you're feeling really lucky, only advanced administrators should consider this option.

   - **(F) Fast Repair:** The Fast-Repair option automatically tries to repair system files, the partition boot sector, and your startup environment. Unless you're concerned about saving some system setting, select this option.

8. **Follow the instructions on the screen.**

9. **When you're prompted, insert your Emergency Repair Disk in the appropriate disk drive.**

   During the repair process, missing or corrupted files are replaced with files from the Windows 2000 CD-ROM. If these files aren't available, the program may grab the files from the systemroot\Repair folder on your system partition.

10. **You're notified if the repair is successful. You're prompted at that point to click Finish to complete the job and restart the computer.**

Index

• *W* •

Notes

Notes

Notes